MAYAN COOKING
Recipes from the
Sun Kingdoms of Mexico

❄   ❄   ❄

MAYAN COOKING
Recipes from the
Sun Kingdoms of Mexico

Cherry Hamman

HIPPOCRENE BOOKS
New York

Acknowledgments

Over the last two decades, numerous people helped me in compiling this book. To everyone who offered so many kindnesses I give a heartfelt thank you. There are several people whom I would like to mention in particular for making this study a reality.

My beloved parents, Tiger and Taco Hamman invited me to visit them in Belize and whetted my appetite for all things Maya. Brenda Menendez de Peraza and her son, Rommel Menendez, offered their home and restaurant kitchens for my apprenticeship in Mayan cuisine. Their home became my home whenever I visited Merida. Chefs Julio, Juan, and Fernando at La Carreta and San Valentin were an integral part of my learning process. Javier Luna, the restaurant manager, offered many prized recipes and technical information.

The late Dr. Antonio Cabrera and his wife, Melba Menendez, were my mentors in both Mayan culture and cuisine. Their family jeep often escorted me to the edge of the jungle where the path to Acabchen began.

Sidney Hollander, my former husband, shared many adventures, including an authentic Mayan wedding atop the Temple of the Seven Dolls in Dzibilchaltun. Dr. Bill Helfrich, a dear friend and inspired teacher, provided weeks of patient manuscript reading.

None of my research and recipes would have extended beyond the confines of tattered field-worn notebooks without the encouragement and enthusiastic support of Elizabeth Backman, my agent who believed in the value of this book from its inception. Carol Chitnis, my wonderful editor at Hippocrene, has provided guidance throughout the publication process with tremendous help, understanding, and unending patience. To both of these literary professionals I give a special thank you.

The inhabitants of Acabchen, who adopted me as one of their own, are truly the focus of this book. To my extended Mayan family I am deeply indebted and truly grateful.

For information, address:
HIPPOCRENE BOOKS, INC.
171 Madison Avenue
New York, NY 10016

Library of Congress Cataloging-in-Publication Data

Hamman, Cherry.
      Mayan cooking: recipes from the sun kingdoms of Mexico / Cherry Hamman.
         p.   cm.
      Includes index.
      ISBN 0-7818-0580-5
      1. Maya cookery. 2. Cookery—Mexico—Yucatán (State) I. Title.
    TX716.M4H35   1997
    641.59'2974152—dc21   97-41256
                                                      CIP

Printed in the United States of America.
Cover photograph by Brian Leatart, originally published in BON APPÉTIT magazine. BON APPÉTIT is a registered trademark of Advance Magazine Publishers Inc., published through its division, the Condé Nast Publications, Inc. Copyright © 1984 by The Condé Nast Publications Inc. Reprinted with permission.

Contents

This book is dedicated to
Brenda Peraza de Menendez and the people of Acabchen,
a village that opened its hearts and hearths to "La Gringa"

The cross marking the entrance to Acabchen

REFLECTIONS

$\mathcal{T}$here is a magnetic ambience about the land: miles and miles of sandy beaches, clear turquoise waters and blue-green lagoons give way to a sweeping tapestry of gentle jungle green. Dusty sage, subtle olive and apple jade trace the boundaries of well-tended fields. The jungle throbs with mystery—lost cities, buried treasure and strange mythical creatures. This is the land of the Mayab—a magical place for me.

Seen from the air, the majesty of this vast peninsula makes a profound and lasting impression. As I look down from my window seat, my thoughts leap back over the years. This particular journey is a very special and poignant one for me, for it marks yet another anniversary in my Yucatecan affair. It is spring again, very much like that spring some fifteen years ago when I first fell in love with this country and its people.

I have returned at the most colorful time of the year, with shimmering *lluvia de oro*, flaming poincianas and crimson *tulipanes* gracing the countryside. The air is pungent with the smell of smoke, as campesinos burn their fields to ready the milpas for new crops. It is the season for planting, rebirth and rejuvenation.

That first sojourn was an introduction, a "sip and savour tour" that allowed me a tiny taste of this wondrous land. The first "sip" led to a passion for more: I hungered for a remote village, a place far removed from the pressures of urban life. I hoped to discover the distant past while researching the immediate present. That hope became a dream, even an obsession, which I resolved to pursue with relentless vigor. I became an anthropologist, went to live among the Maya in the village of Acabchen, recorded what I could about their vanishing way of life, and unraveled some of the mysteries of the ancient Mayan diet.

Acabchen, which became the focus of my anthropological research, proved to be an ideal "study site." It was not then and still is not a typical Yucatecan village, primarily because of its remoteness and its separation from a market economy. The inhabitants had not yet been exposed to the modern "conveniences" of urban communities; all of

7

the men spoke only a few words of Spanish, the women only their native Maya. All in all, this sleepy little enclave radiated the aura of yesteryear; it was a place still enshrouded with the mists of an ancient time.

This tiny, colorful hamlet became my adopted village, or to be more accurate, I became the adopted gringa of these gracious people, for the village really adopted me. Their trust for this prying, gawking foreigner from an alien culture did not come easily; it took years of patience and perseverance on my part as well as theirs.

Perhaps it was my original eagerness and naivete that persuaded Don Luis, the *comisario*, or mayor, to allow me to conduct dietary research among his villagers. Luis was especially concerned that a gringa accustomed to city foods might have trouble adjusting to the local diet. Nevertheless, I was invited to stay and study for as long as I wished. Amelia Cime, a young woman from Chan Kom, volunteered to accompany me as an informant and translator. The schoolhouse, vacant for the summer, was offered as a place of residence, and arrangements were made for my July 7, 1981, arrival.

The first few weeks in Acabchen I took turns spending time with each of the householders. I would spend the day taking part in their daily routine, helping with the chores, gathering food, and preparing meals. Each of the families had built a home within close promixity to the plaza, a grass and wildflower expanse that surrounds the well and serves as a center for the community.

My new home, the schoolhouse, was ingeniously designed and luxuriously spacious. Constructed, like the other houses of Acabchen, of sturdy *palos*, vines, and thatch, it was cool and shady. With grassy cathedral ceilings, there was no need for a fan. The breezes circulated freely through the tightly laced poles. It was a system of natural air-conditioning unsurpassed by any modern invention. Upkeep was minimal, for packed earthen floors need only a light sweeping.

My typical day began when the roosters crowed, usually around 3:30 in the morning. Corn that had been cooked and set aside to soak throughout the night was ground with the hand grinder and the lengthy process of making tortillas began. The woman of the household prepared breads for her husband and any older boys who leave at daybreak for the milpa. She continued to *tortillar* for herself and the children only after the menfolk and any guests had been fed.

Breakfast usually consists of a hot bowl of coffee or *chocosaká*, a thick corn porridge flavored with liquid chili. Either beverage is accompanied by tortillas, plenty of ground dried chili, and a bowl of thick black beans. If eggs are plentiful, a fried egg *torta* or "scrambled omelette" marries well with the toasty tortillas and creamy beans. After the family is finished with breakfast, the animals have their turn. They eat, of course, the same thing that people do ... corn. Pigs and chickens adore corn in any form, but even the cats, dogs, and parrots are given their portion of freshly ground *masa* or a few hand-patted tortillas.

After all hunger pangs have been satiated, the women and children ready their house to offer a greeting as the sun god ushers in another day. One-room homes must be space efficient. Hammocks must be knotted and looped over rafters to get them up and out of the way. Should a guest arrive, the hammock is ceremoniously lowered to provide appropriate seating. The next chore is to wield a palm frond broom to sweep the earthen floor clean of breakfast remnants and windblown debris.

Once the residence is tidied, it's time for a trek to the village plaza to *jalar agua* (haul water) from the well. This daily ritual can be compared to the neighborhood coffee klatch. Laughter, gossip, and chatter ring from the plaza as womenfolk indulge themselves in a sisterly social gathering. The Maya are frugal in their use of water, but are fastidiously clean in all of their personal habits and lavish their kitchen gardens with exceptional care. A typical small family will need about 25 pails of water each day to fulfill their requirements for cooking, drinking, washing, bathing and gardening.

Fetching water is hard work and since I didn't want anyone to spread the word that the gringa was a weakling, I tried not to pant, gasp, and groan excessively. It was bad enough that all of the women and even the children broke into uncontrollable giggles at my first attempts to fill a bucket. One of the ladies returned to her house and came back with two special buckets for me to use. They were munchkin-sized and belonged to her five-year old daughter. We all had a good laugh, but my dignity made me determined to use a grownup bucket. Luckily, my first-aid kit contained plenty of bandaids, for my hands became a mass of cuts and blisters.

Located about fifty feet from the well is the sacred *cenote* or sinkhole, which serves as a companion to the well. Settlers had to locate near these *cenotes* or utilize ingenious methods to harness the underground water supply because Yucatan's vast northern limestone plain has no surface rivers or lakes. Rainwater sinks easily into the porous earth and flows into the river below. This subterranean water source is tapped into by natural caves and *cenotes*, as well as the man-made wells that date from post-Conquest times.

Neither the *cenote* nor the well are ordinary, for both house a *yuntzil*, a capricious little spirit that sometimes whistles and screams at night. Women must not venture too close to the sacred *cenote*, for the *yuntzil* patrols it with a vengeance. Because the *yuntzil* does not like women to come near the well after dark, every household must have its supply of water collected before the sun goes down. As dusk approaches, the *yuntzil* becomes offended and crotchety with imprudent trespassers. He may cause such interlopers to develop a headache or more serious illness that cannot be cured. I learned early on to give the well and cenote wide berth during the twilight and evening hours.

After the daily water supply has been collected, the next chore might be chopping wood, gardening, or doing the laundry. Clothes washing is done on a *batea*, a rectangular basin about five feet long, sometimes made of wood, but more recently, of ceramic composition. Each end has a ledge that rests on a support, one end propped higher that the other so that the *batea* can slope. Washing takes place at the more elevated end while the sudsy/dirty water collects at the bottom. It is customary to ladle several gourds or *jícaras* of water into the *batea* and add a bit of detergent. Each ladleful is particularly precious since it must be mined like a diamond from the bowels of the earth and schlepped all the way from the plaza. Maya women sometimes add the ashes from their hearth fire and swear that it gives everything a good cleaning. This "pre-Columbian Clorox" never became my favorite laundry booster, for the water just kept getting grayer and dirtier and the clothes became even grittier.

After the midmorning chores, it's time to begin preparations for the main meal of the day. If the menu calls for a simple bean soup, some crushed chilies and a *jícara* of hot tortillas, this task will not take more than a couple of hours. When sufficient time and an abundant *milpa* permit, culinary procedures can take up a significant part of the day. Maya women and children share the responsibilities and tasks. Men do not generally lend a hand in culinary chores unless they are preparing breads for a religious ceremony. When the midday meal has been consumed, it is a time for relaxation, talking, and visiting.

An open door, one carefully propped ajar, is an invitation for visitors to stop by and chat for awhile. As a closed door can be indicative of the desire for privacy, no one would dream of entering without a greeting. Houses have no locks, only a rope lashed between the door and an adjoining wall. Sometimes a pole is angled against the door to barricade the entrance against the intrusion of unwelcome livestock. The accepted procedure for neighborly strolling is to approach a house and call out, *"Días,"* if it is morning, *"Tardes,"* if it is afternoon, and *"Noches,"* if it is evening. After someone responds with the same greeting, an invitation is extended to enter. Guests are always offered a foldup chair or a hammock. Family members pull up a small bench called a *k'anche*, carved from a hollowed out log.

As the late afternoon hours are often allotted to the beautiful embroidery that the Maya do with care and precision, I often found them taking part in a sewing bee while enjoying the warmth of the sun. Some of the women would be concentrating on lovely hand embroidery, while others turned their attention to the intricate needlework executed by machine. Every home has its own treadle sewing machine for turning out the flowered *huipiles* (dresses) and *justanes* (petticoats) that are the pride of every Maya maid and matron.

The menfolk come home from the milpa around 3:00 in the afternoon, sometimes laden with the daily harvest and a small animal for the evening meal. They are hungry, having subsisted only on sips of *posole* throughout the morning and afternoon. *Posole*, a ball of coarsely-ground corn, is mixed with water to form a thin gruel. It serves as both food and beverage for the men as they tend their fields. Any returning males might feast upon a pot of freshly harvested vegetables, some roasted game, or leftovers.

Later, if anyone is still hungry, it might be time for a light supper. More often than not, I was still too stuffed from my midday indulgences to want more than a cup of coffee. This late meal often consists of a small bowl of leftovers or a stack of crackers, for the cook's chores are usually completed as the sun begins its descent in the sky.

The autumn of each day is a time for relaxing, communing and enjoying the company of spouse, child and neighbor. It is time to gather round the hearthfire, laugh, tell stories, and share the day's activities.

The hearthfire is kept aglow to heat water for a hot bath. Back home, I have always taken a warm shower for granted, a 20 minute interlude with plenty of steaming water, foaming suds and scented oils. Strange

11

as it may seem, I never had a bath as luxurious as my jungle baths in Acabchen. It may be that the hard physical labor endured during the day renders something especially soul-satisfying in the bathing ritual.

My bathroom was a corner of the hut temporarily curtained from sight. A single candle glowed softly in its holder. A steaming bucket, clean towel, shoes and a bar of soap were positioned nearby. I sat on a *k'anche* and ladled water from the bucket with a *jícara*. I found it wise to start with the head and a shampoo, then end up with the feet. The feet must be last, for they get really grimy, resting in the accumulated sludge as bathing progresses. The final step was to plunge them into the last bit of water in the pail, dry them carefully and place each foot in a shoe. At this point it was essential to head for dry ground immediately, for the bathwater made a mudslide in a matter of minutes. What a luxurious feeling as the dust of the earth and the cares of my soul vaporized, transported by a gentle breeze into the velvety blackness of night.

The daily regimen in Acabchen can be a difficult one, with demanding physical labor. Though life is often hard and survival a constant challenge, I am drawn to the simplicity, the rewards of a life pared down to essentials. There is no rush, no hurry, no deadline to meet. One's goals are delineated by the demands of the milpa, the agricultural cycle and the forest gods. When to burn the fields, when to sow the seeds and when to expect the rains for the harvest—these are the crucial issues, the vital questions. All of the needs for a family of five can be met with less than 60 days of work tending the fields. The rest of the year a man is free to work or play as he pleases, to enjoy whatever blessings he may encounter. It is a life in which one lives gently with the earth, mindfully taking only what is needed, and giving thanks to the wondrous spirits that generously bestow the grace of the universe.

Around 9:00 each evening it was time to lower my hammock from the rafters. The air was cool, the hour was still and my weary bones were only too glad to call it a day. Candles glowed throughout the night on each family's altar, an offering to the Maya gods, Catholic saints, and one's departed ancestors. As I nestled into my hammock, a euphoria began to grow. Nesting turkeys tucked eggs to wing in a soft earthen hollow close to my feet. The evening's slumber was a delicious one because it was a sleep well earned. I blew out my candle and felt a connectedness to all that sustained me, the earth, the sky, and the underground waters that run swift and deep.

August 1998

Several years have passed since I first penned these reflections. Many changes have taken place during that time. My dad, my wonderful Tiger, who first introduced me to the Maya world, is no longer with me. His death brought a great sadness into my life. Several friends from Mérida, Fernando Huertas, "Guacho" Muñoz, and Dr. Antonio Cabrera have also passed on. In Mérida, the restaurants, La Carreta and San Valentin, are no longer in existence.

There have been some profound changes in Acabchen over the last 17 years. As an adopted resident of the village, I have celebrated and witnessed a profusion of births and rites of passage. Maria and Teresita, the two little girls who were my constant companions and helpers have grown up, married, and moved to another village. Don Victor and Isabella now live in the town of Chan Kom. I have also mourned some deaths. I will always miss my dear friend Rosita, wife of the *xmen*, Don Casellano. Don Pablo, husband of Alberta, succumbed to a lingering illness. I considered them my family and think of them often.

Other changes have been wrought by some of the younger generation in Acabchen who chose to abandon village life for the lure and luxury of the larger town or city. Fortunately there will always be romantics like me, who dream of abandoning city life for the lure of the village. It can be a hard, rather precarious existence, but it is a reality that feeds and nourishes the hunger in my soul.

The Author's home in Acabchen.

INTRODUCTION

$\mathcal{M}$exico is a land of vibrant contrasts, a blend of ancient and modern that cradles within its mountains, valleys, coasts and plains a wonderful legacy of ancient civilizations, each quite varied from the others in genetic background and history. Noble families once reigned supreme over zealously guarded territorial kingdoms. Despite any obvious diversity in ancestry, there is ample evidence of common threads that formed the warp and woof of their collective tapestries. These prehistoric Mexican peoples paid homage to Father Sun, Mother Moon, and a colorful pantheon of lesser deities. All shared the same calendar, an interlocking sacred/solar cycle more accurate than our own, an ingenious system of measuring the relentless march of days, months, and years into the vastness of eternity. Festal celebrations also bore strikingly similar rituals, but common themes were orchestrated with individual flair.

The Yucatec Maya, while sharing in that common heritage, developed a way of life distinctly their own. Their home spans the modern Mexican states of Yucatan, Campeche, and Quintana Roo, and the northern regions of Belize and Guatemala. The region that they inhabited was initially a jungle garden, with forests lush with fresh fruit, honey bees, deer, peccary, monkeys, and an incredible variety of birds. Salt beds in the shallow coastal waters provided an economic base that allowed the Maya to thrive with a seafaring trade. The seas were a haven for fish, lobster, mollusks, and conch, commodities that could be bartered or sold for the grains, fruits, vegetables and game that flourished in the interior provinces.

While no one is quite sure when the first inhabitants settled in the Yucatan Peninsula, we do know that approximately 2,000 years ago, the Maya made their appearance rather suddenly, constructing massive ceremonial centers with the distinctive corbeled arch so typical of their monumental architecture. This was the Classic or Early Period, when glyphs, calendars, and building construction were given great importance. Beautiful stuccoed walls adorned the civic and ceremonial centers. These golden years emphasized the influence and prestige of the artist and sky-gazing priest. It was a time of regionalism, although trade was active with such sites as Teotihuácan and other outside influences can be detected in the archaeological remains and language.

At the end of the Early Period, isolationism became the political policy and there was a gradual evolution to the Florescent Era (650—900 A.D.) This was a time of cultural flowering that appears to have been contained within the Northern Yucatan Plains. The collapse that occurred within the southern Maya region (Belize, Guatemala, and Honduras) did not occur in the north. Focus was directed away from the religious priest as homage shifted to the secular ruler. Architectural achievements were impressive, with the beautiful stucco walls of the Early Period giving way to carved stone veneers, each block carefully cut in a manner that was intended to be more decorative than functional or structural.

Later centuries bore witness to repeated invasions of foreign intruders, some thought to have come from Tulá in the highlands of central Mexico. These newcomers have never been identified with certainty, but they established a new capital at the Maya site of Uuc-yab-nal and renamed it *Chichén Itzá*. It is believed that a noble family called the *Itzá* ruled at *Chichén Itzá* from the tenth to the twelfth centuries. For two hundred years a triumvirate successfully ruled the peninsula, with *Mayapan*, *Chichén Itzá*, and *Uxmal* sharing the reigns of power. These invaders from the west retained their ascendency for several centuries and left their distinctive mark upon the architecture, language, and culinary traditions of the Maya.

Following the "Trojan War of Yucatan" with its brutal sacking of *Chichén Itzá*, the *Itzá* abandoned their city and fled to the safety of Lake Peten in Guatemala. This was a period of power struggles, for gone were the days when a single ruling power controlled Yucatan. Incessant warfare and shifting alliances became the new political pattern. There were attempts to create a renaissance modeled upon the magnificence of earlier periods, but the golden age of the ancient Maya was never again to be recaptured.

It was upon this fragmented scene that the Spaniards entered the picture. Francisco de Montejo had been awarded permission to conquer Yucatan and Cozumel, but two attempts to subdue the Maya ended in failure. By the mid-sixteenth century, Spaniards found their position more secure, but problems with small groups of irrascible Maya continued well into the nineteenth century. The *War of the Castes*, a civil war characterized by much bloodshed, is evidence of the strong animosity many Maya felt against the foreign intruder.

The Maya have endured the onslaught of countless invaders over the centuries and have successfully preserved the heart of their culture. Foreign art, religion, and language have imparted only a thin veneer to the world of the Maya peoples living in remote rural villages.

The Maya, like their neighbors in regions with radically different climates and topography, relied then as now on the basic native American staples of corn, beans, squash and chili. Yet the culinary creations of the rural Maya are quite different from those of the other peoples and regions of Mexico, for each native population incorporated in their dishes distinctive bouquets of garden vegetables, fruits of the forest, aromatic herbs and exotic spices. A varied cornicopia, unique cooking practices and boundless creativity resulted in the exciting diversity inherent in the cuisines of Old Mexico.

Traditional Mexican recipes and culinary methods have as much validity today as they did for a native populace many centuries ago. Techniques such as roasting, toasting, and grinding were developed to release essential oils from each culinary ingredient, an inspiration causing individual flavors to dance. Health conscious/budget minded cooks appreciate menus with a heavy emphasis on fruits, vegetables, grains, and little meat. A typical daily menu in the countryside is usually vegetarian. Those wonderful recipes featuring meats such as turkey, beef, pork, and venison are encountered on special occasions, perhaps on a weekly or monthly basis—celebration foods fit for heavenly gods, earthly kings, and even us, the lowly mortal.

As village dwellers have more to do each day than tend to their bubbling pots, it is not surprising that ingenuity, even in antiquity, was called upon for "packaged mixes," and "convenience foods." The resulting array of exciting menus developed by these creative people stands worlds apart from the typical dishes commonly associated with Mexican food. Such traditional recipes are often cooked in one pot, for the Maya woman has only one stewpot supported by a three-stone hearth. All foods are either dropped into the stewpot or tucked within the smoking ashes of burning embers. It is a most efficient setup, for there is only one pan to wash, one table to clean, and no counters to dirty.

There is another bonus reaped by traditional woman. Without refrigeration, any food appears again and again on the menu until every last morsel is eaten. A pot of beans, vegetable/meat stew, or special tamales will be the main feature at every meal for at least a day or two, a time-saving pattern when there is no objection to indulging in leftovers. Luckily for those who require some variation, most of these recipes freeze beautifully.

Corn is unequivocally the mainstay of a traditional Maya diet, often serving as bread, beverage, entree, and dessert. Many dishes start out with *masa*, a mixture of finely ground corn meal. Most women use a metal hand grinder, a wonderful tool that has released women from the drudgery of a grinding stone. Larger villages have access to an even greater labor-saving process with their mechanized *molinerias*. Women stand patiently in line during the morning hours to have their softened corn ground by a miraculous machine. An early drive through the village countryside reveals women of all ages, immaculately dressed in sparkling white, elaborately embroidered *huipiles*, with unwieldy containers of golden corn perfectly poised atop their heads. It is a mission of grace and dexterity, for even the tiniest young miss executes her daily journey without mishap, in spite of rocky inclines, slippery paths, and neighborhood dogs underfoot.

I once tried my hand at grinding corn on the *metate* and ended up with blisters, aching arms and lumpy *masa*. My *metate* now rests on permanent living-room display, a picturesque receptacle for winter squash and Indian corn, a loving monument to the brawn and fortitude of the rural Mexican woman. I respectfully salute her, but must confess to having inherited a more delicate nature that gives thanks for the benefits of modern machinery.

There are certain local ingredients and distinctive techniques that give Maya cuisine its special flair. Undoubtedly, the most exotic and typical seasoning comes from the fruit of the tropical *achiote* (Bixa orellana), a tiny brick-red seed used throughout antiquity as beverage, food coloring, spice, and even money. Maya priests considered it one of the most sacred of all offerings, using it to paint their bodies, robes, and ceremonial ceramics.

Yucatecans are reknowned for their illustrious *recados*, zesty seasoning pastes that may be thought of as "the curries of Mexico." There are several different recados, redolent in such fragrant condiments as achiote, black pepper, cinnamon, allspice, and cloves. The first recados show evidence of dating back to early ceremonial centers, but were unquestionably later enriched after the Spanish conquest when shiploads of herbs and spices found their way to the New World from the Indies. Recados are used to marinate all varieties of meats and to flavor sauces, vegetables, soups and stews. Ingredients that go into the recados are enriched by toasting, a culinary technique that enhances and concentrates each flavor essence.

The exciting foods prepared in this region are hearty, flavorful, and certainly lacking the "fire" often mistakenly associated with Mexican food. Undeniably, there are hot sauces to be found, but these *salsas* are most often served on the side in the Yucatan and spooned onto individual portions as desired. Although Yucatecan food is not considered hot, *Xnipek* (Nose of the Dog), a salsa appearing on every table at almost every meal, contains the *jabanero*, perhaps one of the world's fiercest chilies.

Maya recipes bear a bit of history that can foster a greater appreciation for the ingenious ways in which these Native Americans chose to deal with the challenge of circumstance and environment. Each creation is surely perfection in Maya art, as much a treasure of their glorious heritage as the ruins of Chichén and Uxmal.

Hopefully, some will find hidden within these pages the importance of a message dispatched from civilizations long past, an introduction to a pattern of living that establishes firm bonds with the earth and strives to maintain the fragile balance between nature and man. Such has been the philosophy of the Mesoamerican Indians and stands as a legacy to future generations who choose to follow the tread of their footsteps.

THE MAYA KITCHEN

Equipment and Basic Techniques

A typical Maya kitchen might win an award for efficiency. It is compact, with no wasted space and everything is within easy reach. As one might imagine, the focal point of the entire household is the hearth.

The hearth is known as the *koben*. It is composed of three large stones that can easily be moved. When the stones are spread apart, they form a sturdy base for the griddle or *comal* that is used for toasting tortillas, *pimes*, and other thin breads. Moved more closely together, the stones make a firm support for a large stewpot or *cazuela*. On occasion, some wires are twisted and secured so that a pot may be suspended over the hearthfire, without actually touching the hearth stones.

An additional hearth is sometimes constructed beyond the confines of the house. It is a temporary one and is usually disassembled after only one day. The extra "stove" might be needed for two reasons. Most sacred rituals require that a new hearth be prepared to simmer a stew for the gods; an everyday hearth will not suffice for ceremonial occasions. Burning chilies for a recado also necessitates plans for an additional cooking fire. The acrid smoke is so hard on eyes and lungs that cooking within the housewalls is out of the question. If daily meal preparations require another hearth, a Maya woman will simply borrow one from her neighbor and offer some of the food in exchange.

Utensils for the Maya kitchen are quite basic. The most important is the circular *xamach* or *comal* that serves as a griddle for making tortillas. It is carefully cleaned with cornhusks after each use and positioned so that it leans against a wall near the fire to dry. Two or three pots of varying size serve as kettles or stockpots.

The main furniture is a *banqueta*, a low circular table that serves as a kitchen counter and eating area. The *banqueta* provides an ideal surface for making tortillas, cutting onions, chopping leaves and herbs or making tamales. The surface is small, usually only about two feet in diameter, but a tiny "kitchen counter" also means that there is less surface to clean. Some *banquetas* are carved with a little circular extension at the side for holding a stack of freshly made tortillas. Any ingredients that will be assembled on the *banqueta* for cooking are arranged on the floor in a *lec* (large gourd), *luch* (small gourd), or bucket.

A low hollow *k'anche*, a small bench carved from a single piece of wood, is the usual form of seating. It is light, comfortable and portable, easily moved from one section of the house to another. When not in use, it is propped up against a wall. Three or four people can easily arrange their benches around the *banqueta* to prepare a meal or consume one. Most Maya houses have a small table and some folding chairs that are easily set up for company, but the *banqueta* and *kanche* are more comfortable for family use. If guests stay for a meal, the table is always covered with a painstakingly embroidered white cloth.

No disposal is needed in a Maya kitchen, for nothing goes to waste. Any food scraps are reserved for the animals to eat. Tin cans serve as flower pots and glass bottles can be cleaned and refilled. Paper, cardboard, or other dispensible materials provide fuel for the fire. A precious plastic bag is recycled and used again and again for wrapping food, plugging bottles, or making tortillas. Sturdy leaves were at one time utilized for patting out tortillas, but nature's "throwaways" have been replaced by squares of modern plastic.

Storage is a cinch in a home of pole and thatch. Almost anything can be hung from the walls with a bit of wire or string. Bottles, cups, gourds and tin cans adorn the sides of every Maya home. Foods that need to be protected from domesticated animals or pesky pests are arranged on a *peten*, a woven basket that is safely suspended from the housetop rafters.

Every Maya kitchen has a built-in area for grinding. Usually the metal hand-mill is supported on a heavy wooden crossbeam so that corn, chilies, squash seeds or other crushables can easily be ground into a waiting bucket. Several decades ago most of the grinding was accomplished on a *ca* (Maya) or *metate* (Nahuatl), a low sloping grinding stone. The handstone that looks somewhat like a rolling pin with tapered ends is the *u-kab-ca*—the "hand of the metate." Today, all corn and squash seeds are ground with a metal hand-mill. Only onion, garlic, chili and condiments for a recado are stoneground. In other Mexican provinces a volcanic rock metate accompanies the hearth, but in the lowland Maya region many of the grinding stones are smooth, fine-grained and light-colored. The surface of a Yucatecan metate is so shiny, it looks as if it has been laquered. Occasionally a *molcajete* and *tejolote* is used to crush small amounts of onion or chili with a little water. This is a volcanic rock mortar and pestle that is not local to the region, but must be purchased from the market. In pre-Conquest times, volcanic stone was a vital trade import from other regions of Mexico and Guatamala.

One of the most useful tools ever invented in Mexico is the plastic mesh shopping bag that comes in a kaleidoscope of colors. These market totes schleppe fruits, vegetables and an assorted hodge-podge of items on a daily basis, but their most creative chore is unrelated to transit. The truth of the matter is that they make a dynamite sieve. I tried to think of something a little more aesthetically pleasing to substitute for these plastic totes, but could not improve upon Maya ingenuity one whit. Whatever needs to be strained or sieved is placed into the bag and held over a bucket or stewpot. With a little wringing and squeezing, the contents of the tote are miraculously crushed and strained. Even more amazingly, this magical invention holds a greater quantity of food than a blender or food processor, thus eliminating the necessity of sieving ingredients in several batches.

Some of the larger Maya families have constructed a raised counter that holds a few dishes, some pots and pans and a few buckets of water. This auxilary counter keeps everything a little more protected than if the items were simply set upon the floor. The counter is usually too rough to be used for anything but storage, for it is constructed of small timbers or split logs.

Maya cuisine is sometimes simple, sometimes lavish, but always exquisite. Yucatecans know how to extract every last bit of flavor from each ingredient and utilize it to its full potential. Toasting is one of their primary culinary secrets. It is an extremely easy technique that usually adds little time to the total cooking process.

The Maya hearth is made for toasting. While a stewpot simmers on the fire, it is no trouble for the cook to nestle an onion, chili, or tomato into the glowing embers. The only way to appreciate the incredible difference that toasting makes is to actually try it. The aroma is truly tantalizing and the enriched flavor enhances the sauce. Once the vegetables are toasted, they are removed from the fire and tossed into the cooking pot. Because fire is essential to cooking, there is really not an extra step—at least for the Maya.

Toasting vegetables may be accomplished in modern kitchens on all kinds of stoves or ranges, but it is faster, easier and less messy with a gas stove or portable gas burner. Toasting small seeds and spices is a simple process that requires only a heavy-bottomed skillet with either gas or electricity.

The second culinary secret is grinding or crushing. The Maya kitchen is designed for grinding with both metal and stone. Seeds and chilies smell marvelous after they've been toasted, but the flavors literally burst once these condiments are ground. Again, the only way to appreciate the difference that grinding makes is to try it and see.

Sesame seeds or pumpkin seeds make a wonderful example. Take a handful and smell them. The aroma is rather bland as they come from the package. Now give them a light toasting, just enough to turn the seeds a delicate gold—the nutty flavor is much more pungent. While the seeds are still warm, place them in a grinder and pulverize them ever so slightly. The marvelous smell literally jumps to the nostrils. The essence of chili is extracted in the same manner, usually in a *molcajete* and *tejolote* —or mortar and pestle.

Most contemporary kitchens contain everything necessary for Yucatecan cuisine. The only checklist I recommend is:

1. A portable gas burner—nice, but not essential

2. A small electric grinder, the kind that is suitable for coffee beans and small seeds. I have three of them: one for coffee, one for spices and one for chili and black pepper—at least one is essential

3. A *molcajete* and *tejolote* or mortar and pestle make perfect companions for grinding a very small amount of chilies or spices —nice, but not essential

4. A blender—essential

5. A large sieve—essential

6. A wooden-handled fondue fork or barbecue fork—essential for toasting with gas

7. An unglazed pitcher for making chocolate; the earthy flavor cannot be duplicated with modern ceramics—nice, but not essential

The Maya kitchen is so simple, the techniques are easy to duplicate—or at least, approximate. For anyone who wishes to speed up the cooking process, these toasting steps can be eliminated. It truly does make a difference, but Maya recipes are magnificent, regardless of the cooking method.

To duplicate a Maya hearth, the ideal would be to have a lovely wood fire to coax the meals to perfection. Most of us do not have the opportunity or patience to prepare our foods in this manner, so ... a very close second to the hearthfire is a gas stove or portable gas burner. Toasting may be accomplished with electrical equipment, but the results take a little more time and are a little more messy.

Do not feel discouraged if you feel that toasting is too much trouble with any method. Just eliminate the extra step, enjoy the delicious menus and do something really exciting with the time saved.

Instructions for Toasting

SEEDS AND SPICES:

Heat a heavy skillet to "low" or "medium low." Be ready to turn the skillet down if the fire gets too hot. Heat the seeds or spices, one layer at a time, just until they show a very slight change in color and start to exude their pungent oils. If the seeds become too dark, they will taste burned and spoil the sauce. Turn off the heat.

Most seeds are more easily ground if they are still warm from toasting.

WITH A GAS STOVE:

Use a wooden-handled barbecue fork or wooden-handled fondue fork. Turn the heat on high. Spear the vegetable and hold it in the flame until the skin begins to blacken. Turn until all sides are nicely charred. Notice the wonderful aroma.

Tomatoes. I like my tomatoes really charred, particularly if the tomatoes will be puréed in the blender. If the tomatoes will be mashed or crushed, I cook them a little more lightly. Experiment to discover your own taste. As a general rule, the toastier the tomato, the tastier the sauce. Prepared in this manner, tomatoes retain all of their juices.

Time: about 2 to 3 minutes

Garlic Bulbs or Cloves. Leave the garlic unpeeled. I rarely toast the garlic one clove at a time. My usual method is to spear the whole bulb and toast the garlic until most of the outer papers have disintegrated. I continue toasting until the bulb is charred, rather than completely blackened.

If the garlic is going into a soup or stew, the papers can remain on the bulb. If the individual cloves are going into a *recado* or salsa, peel the papers from the garlic after charring.

Time: about 1 and ½ minutes

Chilies. Chilies will singe and blacken almost immediately. I let them blister and char but remove them from the flame before they really turn black.

Time: about 1 minute for small hot chilies, about 3 minutes for large green peppers

Chilies for Recado de Chilmole or Relleno Negro. Please see Note at end of this chapter.

Onions. Leave the onions unpeeled. Spear the onion and toast it until most of the outer papers have disintegrated. Continue to toast until the onion is well charred. If the onion is going into a soup or stew, do not remove the peeling. If the onion is going into a salsa, peel it after charring.

Time: about 5 minutes

WITH AN ELECTRIC STOVE:

I have cooked tomatoes, onions (peeled first) and garlic (peeled first and separated into cloves) directly on the coils of an electric stove, but the process creates a bit of a mess. In the case of the garlic cloves, I had a hard time fishing them out of the coils when they slipped through. It is a rather frustrating challenge. As an alternative, select an old heavy bottomed skillet—cast iron is perfect. Use a wooden handled spatula or a pair of tongs.

Tomatoes. Have the skillet hot. The more quickly the tomatoes char, the juicier they will be. There is a tendency for the tomatoes to "roast," rather than "toast" in a skillet. They lose a lot of liquid and get soft and mushy if cooked too long. Turn the tomatoes with a spatula as they blacken on each side.

Time: about 8 minutes

Garlic Bulbs or Cloves. Peel the garlic and separate it into cloves. Have the skillet hot. Drop in the garlic cloves and toast them on one side. Turn them with a spatula or tongs and toast them on the other side.

Time: about 1 minute

Chilies. Have the skillet hot. Drop in the chilies and toast them on one side. Turn them with a spatula or tongs and toast them on the other side.

Time: about 2 to 3 minutes for small hot chilies, about 4 minutes for a large green pepper

Onions. Peel the onions and cut them in half. Have the skillet hot. Place the onions in the skillet with a spatula or tongs and cook until charred on one side. Turn and cook on the other side. If possible, try to char the sides of the onions, also.

Time: about 5 to 6 minutes.

Chilies for Recado de Chilmole or Recado de Relleno Negro (Most Yucatecans buy these from the market already prepared). Place the barbecue grill far from the house and neighbors. Allow the fire to burn until the flames have died down, but the coals are still glowing. Arrange the chilies in a single layer in a heavy skillet, griddle, or other utensil that has a flame-proof handle. Stay away from the fire, and do not breath the smoke. Allow the chilies to burn to a lovely sooty black. Hold your breath and turn the chilies with a long wooden-handled spatula, fork or spoon.

When the chilies are completely blackened, but not burned to ashes, again hold your breath and remove them from the fire using gloves for safety. Set the chilies aside to cool. In case of disaster, have a hose handy to cancel the whole cooking process.

THE HEARTHRITES OF ACABCHEN

Don Casellano, the xmen of Acabchen.

*T*here were eight families who lived in Acabchen when I first began my visits there. Over a period of years they have shared many of their traditions and allowed a glimpse of their gentle way of life. A decade of friendship means some changes not only in the appearance of Acabchen, but in its many inhabitants. The old schoolhouse is in ruins and has never been replaced. Any of the children who attend school now do so in Chan Kom, boarding during the week with relatives and returning to their own families on the weekends. One house has been abandoned and allowed to disintegrate, another stands vacant, and a new dwelling has been constructed atop a grassy knoll. For many years there were hopes and prayers for a road leading from Xanla to Acabchen. In 1993 this road became a reality.

I have mixed feelings about progress because the ease of transport will hasten the eroding of ancient ways. These fragile traditions are already rapidly evaporating, generation by generation. A number of festivals are no longer practiced because no one remembers the necessary rituals. In another decade or so, many of the remaining ceremonies will be but a memory. There have been a number of births to celebrate and several deaths to mourn over the years in this little pueblo, but I have written these pages from the past as if it were the present, to introduce the Maya who first gave me love and shelter. The accompaning hearthrites are traditional rites of the hearth that have been prepared in the same manner for many centuries—and perhaps in some cases, for several millenia.

TS'ANCHAK BI KAX
Chicken Cooked in a Peppery Broth

From the Hearth of Rosita and Casellano

Don Casellano is the *xmen*, the shaman, healer, and spiritual leader of Acabchen. His wife, Doña Rosita, is his friend, his love, and his helpmate.

Rosita and Casellano have always tried to patiently answer my barrage of questions about their garden, their foods, and their menu patterns. Rosita seems to be slightly amused at my fascination with her kitchen, perhaps not quite comprehending how something so ordinary for her could be so extraordinary for me.

One of my favorite remembrances of Acabchen is a fragrant pot of *Ts'anchak bi Kax*, a spicy chicken stew in a piquant black pepper sauce that Rosita and Casellano would prepare as a present for me whenever I returned for a sojourn in the village. Within hours of my arrival, Casellano would point to a plump hen dangling from the rafters of his home, as if to point out that my welcome was being sanctioned with this ritual offering. This delicious gesture was one I always enjoyed and greatly appreciated.

To Prepare Ts'anchak Bi Kax:

If the recado has been made ahead of time, this recipe is a snap to whip up on a busy afternoon or evening. The chicken simmers to perfection in a delightfully seasoned broth—and is topped at the last minute with a handful of *fideos* (spaghetti). A topping of pasta may seem a bit out of place in a traditional Yucatecan menu, but the Maya have been borrowing the best from foreign customs for many a century.

Ts'anchak is served with a stack of hot tortillas and a chili salsa.

Have on Hand:

> *Recado de Escabeche*, page 56
> Tortillas
> Chili salsa—such as *Salsa Indio, Mojo*, or other favorite salsa

Ingredients:

> 2½ pound roasting chicken
> 8 cups, or more water
> 2 onions, chopped
> 4 tablespoons *Recado de Escabeche*

¼ cup lard (optional)
4 ounces *fideos* (spaghetti)

Method:

Place the chicken in a large stockpot with the water. The chicken should be completely covered. Add more water if necessary. Add the onions and enough *recado* to season the broth to taste. Use a bit more *recado*, if necessary. Add the lard for an extra-rich stock, if desired. Cover the chicken and simmer until it is tender—approximately 45 minutes.

Remove the chicken from the pot and cut it into serving-sized portions. Return the chicken to the pot.

Add the spaghetti to the cooking pot and continue cooking until the pasta is done. Do not overcook.

To Serve:

Fill each bowl with some broth and a piece or two of the chicken. Top with a portion of *fideos*. Serve with a chili salsa and tortillas.

Serves 4.

ONSIKIL BI CHAY
Chaya in a Squash Seed Sauce

From the Hearth of Eulogia and Luis

Don Luis, the comisario of Acabchen, and his wife, Eulogia, have a one-room home tranquilly perched on a rocky incline overlooking the plaza.

Eulogia invited me to join the family for one of their favorite meals prepared with *chaya* leaves and squash seeds—*Onsikil bi Chay*. Arriving early to witness all aspects of the preparation process, I received a lesson in life, as well as the culinary arts. I noticed for the first time that the Maya have a love affair with their food. It is never wasted or taken for granted. Every morsel, every drop is treated with reverence. The food is even fondled and gently caressed. When Eulogia harvested the *chaya* leaves, she plucked each leaf from the tree, gave it a careful inspection and several loving pats. Once she had collected five or six of the leaves, she lined them up very carefully, one atop the other, taking care that the edges were meticulously matched. She then arranged them in a bucket, one small packet after another. The collection process was slow and the task pursued in a focused meditative manner. It appeared as if the plucking were not a means to an end, but was actually an end in itself.

The entire process, from start to finish could be termed a religious ritual for the Maya. I have come to realize that each act of the day, from dawn to sunset, might be termed a religious ritual. Each daily rite serves to connect the individual with his family, his fellow man, his earth, his gods—and his universe.

To Prepare Onsikil Bi Chay:

Onsikil (many squash seeds), or *pipian*, in Spanish, is the name of a recipe that requires a base of toasted and ground squash seeds. Combined with an array of spices and tossed into the stewpot amidst other vegetables, this delectable stew may be combined with *chaya*, black beans, lima beans, squash, lentils, or eggs.

Have on Hand:

> Hot freshly made or packaged tortillas
> A favorite salsa such as *Tsah bi Yax Ik* or *K'ut bi Ik*
> ½ recipe of *masa*, prepared as for tortillas, page 116

Ingredients:

> 2 pounds *chaya* or spinach, washed and trimmed
> 10 cups water
> 8 ounces squash or pumpkin seeds, toasted and ground
> Salt to taste
> 8 cloves garlic, toasted
> 1 tablespoon oregano
> 1 tablespoon black peppercorns
> 2 cloves
> 1 inch stick cinnamon
> 1/3 cup *achiote*
> 4 cups water
> 2 cups *masa* (from tortilla recipe)
> 2 cups water

Method:

Place the *chaya* or spinach in the stockpot with the water and bring the pot to a boil. Reduce the heat and simmer for one hour.

Sieve the ground toasted squash seeds with 1 quart of water, letting the mixture drain into the stockpot. Sieve the remaining seeds (those trapped in the sieve) with another quart of water. Repeat once again with 3 cups of water. Any bits of seed left in the sieve at this point may be thrown away.

Prepare the *recado* by toasting the garlic cloves. Throw away the blackened skins and purée the garlic cloves to a fine paste in a blender.

Grind the oregano, black pepper, cloves, and cinnamon in a spice grinder. Add the ground spices to the blender with the garlic and process the mixture well.

When the *chaya* or spinach has simmered for one hour, add the *recado* to the pot.

Crush the *achiote* slightly. Add two cups of water to the *achiote* and mix thoroughly with the fingers, coaxing the deep red color from the seeds. Run the mixture through a sieve and into the stockpot. Repeat the process with one more cup of water. Repeat the process a third time with one cup of water. Throw the seeds away.

Mix the *masa* and water together. Strain the *masa* through a sieve and into the stockpot. Stir the mixture occasionally for the next 30 minutes. *Masa* has a tendency to stick. Check the seasoning.

To Serve:

Eat with hot tortillas as the spoon or scoop.

Serves 6.

TS'ANCHAK BI VETCH
Armadillo (or substitute) Cooked in a Seasoned Sauce

From the Hearth of Eleutaria and Valentin

Don Valentin and his wife, Eleuteria live in a two-house compound atop a hilly ridge that overlooks the plaza. One afternoon, Valentin had a successful hunt and I was invited to an armadillo banquet. I had never eaten armadillo and would rather have one for a pet than a dinner, but accepted the invitation graciously, nonetheless. I immediately scampered up the path with my notebook and camera to find them all smiles with their catch of the day—a wonderfully fat and soon to be sacrificed armadillo. I was able to capture a photo of the hunters home from the hunt—and scribble the cooking directions. The meal was interesting and the company fascinating, but I doubt that this recipe prepared with wild game will have much interest. Where will anyone ever find an armadillo? Fortunately, any kind of meat would be delicious in Eleuteria's sauce.

To Prepare Ts'anchak Bi Vetch:

The ancient Maya associated the armadillo with bee ceremonies and apiculture in their rituals. I find the flavor of this beautiful creature a bit gamey for my taste, but the presentation of an armadillo certainly makes for an interesting meal. Any kind of meat, beef, pork, venison, or chicken may be substituted for the armadillo in preparing this meal. *Rice and Beans*, a favorite of the coastal Maya, makes a wonderful accompaniment to this recipe.

Have on Hand:

> *Recado Colorado*, Red Spice Paste, page 51
> 18 hot freshly made or packaged tortillas

Ingredients:

> 3 pounds armadillo meat, cleaned, trimmed of fat, or a
>   substitute meat
> 6 cups water
> 1 onion, toasted
> 1 bulb garlic, toasted
> 1 chili, toasted
> ¼ cup *Recado Colorado*, Red Spice Paste
> 3 large tomatoes, cut into eighths

Method:

Place the armadillo or other meat in a large saucepan with the water, toasted onion, garlic, and chili. Bring the water to a boil, reduce the heat, add a cover, and allow the meat to simmer for 1½ hours. If using armadillo, or other "gamey" meat, throw out the cooking water at this point and add 4 cups of fresh water. Otherwise, the meat may continue to simmer in the same broth.

Add the *Recado Colorado* and tomatoes to the cooking liquid and once again bring the pan to a simmer. Cook for another hour or until the meat is tender.

To Serve:

This meal is especially good with some form of rice and a stack of hot tortillas. Be sure to pass a bowl of extra sauce.

Serves 6 to 8.

BU'ULIWAH
Black Bean Tamales

From the Hearth of Alberta and Pablo

I know Don Paulino by his nickname—Pablo. He and Alberta have the largest family in Acabchen. Pablo invited me to share in the abundance of his *milpa* as he offered the first fruits of his bean harvest in a *Primicia* ceremony. He had invited friends and family members to aid in the digging of the *pib* and join him in a feast of *Bu'uliwah*, bean tamales offered as a "thank you" to the gods.

The tamales are small, individually sized, and take only a few hours to roast to perfection. It is fascinating to watch the uncovering of these little breads as they are brought fragrant and steaming from ground to surface. Pablo placed a portion of tamales on an altar for the gods, then turned to serve his guests. It was a delightful repast and everyone returned for seconds.

To Prepare Bu'uliwah:

I adore these smoky/chewy breads when they emerge from their long smoldering in the oven, but they are also delicious cooked on top of the stove or in a regular oven. Try them with any of the tomato or chili salsas.

Have on Hand:

> *Ts'anchak bi Bu'ul*, Yucatecan Black Beans, page 171
> *Masa for Tamales*, as directed in *Basic Masa Preparation*, page 116
> 2 banana leaves, prepared for cooking, page 120, or parchment paper or aluminum foil
> Banana strings or household string for wrapping
> *Salsa Ranchera, Xnipek*, or other salsa

Ingredients:

> 2 cups *Ts'anchak bi Bu'ul*, Yucatecan Black Beans, drained
> 1 recipe Basic Masa for Tamales
> 2 large banana leaves, prepared for cooking and cut into 10-inch pieces

Method:

Mix the drained black beans into the *masa* with the fingers.

Place a banana leaf section, ribbed side down (or parchment paper or aluminum foil), on a work surface.

35

Form ½ cup of *masa* into a ball, then pat it into a football shape. Fold the banana leaf (or parchment paper or aluminum foil) around the *masa*, as though wrapping a package. Tie the package with banana strings or household string. Make the remaining breads in the same manner. Place all of the tamales in a steamer or on the rack of a baking pan. Fill the steamer or baking pan with about an inch or two of water—not enough to touch the breads. Cover the steamer or baking pan and bake for 1 hour.

To Serve:

Serve with *Salsa Ranchera, Xnipek,* or other chili salsa.

Serves 6 to 8.

TOKSEL
Toasted Lima Beans and Squash Seeds

From the Hearth of Isabel and Victor

Victor and Isabel have a house with such a lovely view. Isabel has adopted me and goes out of her way to show me the culinary crafts of her village.

Toksel is a toasted lima bean mixture that I had never tasted, only read about, and it was my search for this elusive recipe that led me to the isolation of Acabchen. *Toksel* means "burned and coarsely ground," and requires the use of special heated stones. People in the cities prepare *Toksel*, but without going to the trouble of using the stones. They admit that this modern shortcut results in a somewhat different flavor. I asked Isabel where she had gotten her cooking stones and she motioned to her front yard. I told her that I would love to have my own cooking stones so that I could prepare *Toksel* with the true flavor of Acabchen. When I left the village after my first visit, Isabel handed me a carefully wrapped package, and embraced me with tears in her eyes. It was a selection of stones, lovingly handpicked, to add a taste of the Yucatan to the Mexican foods I prepare in my kitchen.

To Prepare Toksel:

Toksel might be thought of as a pre-Columbian form of "trailmix" because it keeps for weeks without refrigeration when cooked in the traditional manner. It is lovely, whether served as a side dish vegetable or starred in a main course tortilla or tamale.

Note: Please do not try the recipe with stones, for it can be dangerous. I have included the information about the tradition of using the stones for information only. Rocks from various sources can explode and may cause injuries. I've had rock flying from the pot and crashing all around my kitchen.

Have on Hand:

> 16 hot freshly made or packaged tortillas
> *Tsah bi Ik, Salsa Verde* or other chili salsa

Ingredients:

> 10 ounces lima beans, fresh or frozen
> ½ cup water
> 1 cup squash seeds

1 hot green chili, toasted and chopped
3 green onions, chopped
Salt and pepper to taste

Method:

Place the lima beans in a saucepan with the water and bring the ingredients to a simmer. Cover and cook until just tender, about 6 or 7 minutes. Drain the limas well.

Toast the pumpkin seeds in a heavy skillet until they are golden brown, stirring frequently so that they do not burn. Place them in a blender or food processor and grind them coarsely. Return the pumpkin seeds to the skillet with the lima beans and add the chili and green onions. Cook the mixture over low heat, stirring very carefully so as to not crush the beans. Cook until the beans and seeds are very dry, about 15 minutes. Season with salt and pepper.

To Serve:

Tuck some of the *Toksel* into a tortilla and add a touch of salsa.

Serves 4.

PP'AK I TSIKIL
Toasted Tomatoes and Squash Seed Sauce (Vegetable Dip)

From the Hearth of Severiana and Lucas

Lucas and Severiana live next door to Casellano and Rosita. Lucas is related to half the village, as is obvious from their physical similarities. The other half of the village is related also, as there are only two main family lineages.

One beautiful autumn morning, Severiana took Soco, Apolinaria (daughter of Pablo and Alberta), and me to her *milpa* to fetch some squash seeds for preparing *PP'ak i Tsikil*, a marvelous tomato/toasted squash seed concoction. We left early to avoid the midday sun. It was not easy work to break open the squash and scoop out the seeds, for we were using our hands as tools. I was covered with orange stains—even my denim skirt had taken on a golden hue. By the time we had finished the chore, each of us had collected a bucket of seeds. Severiana selected some of the nicest *calabaza* (squash) to make into a honeyed dessert, then threw the refuse to the pigs as a special treat.

Pp'ak i Tsikil is a delicious sauce that can serve as appetizer or main dish. Imagine the heady fragrance of pumpkin seeds, juicy tomatoes, and a bite of chili, all carefully toasted to enhance their flavor essence. This is a versatile combination that brings pleasure each Fall, an eagerly awaited dish that celebrates the onset of autumn and the joy of an abundant harvest. This recipe dates from the pre-Columbian era, although cilantro is a more modern addition.

To Prepare Pp'ak I Tsikil:

Have on Hand:

     18 corn tortillas, either warmed on a griddle or fried in oil

Ingredients:

     1½ cups pumpkin or squash seeds, toasted and
ground
         5 medium tomatoes, toasted
         1 hot green chili, toasted
         3 scallions, chopped
         3 tablespoons cilantro, chopped
         Salt to taste

Method:

Toast the pumpkin seeds until golden. While they are still warm, place them in a spice grinder and grind rather finely—but do not grind them to a sticky paste.

Toast the tomatoes. Remove any large pieces of charred skin. Toast the hot green chili.

Place all of the ingredients in a blender. Blend until the sauce is smooth.

To Serve:

The sauce may be spooned into a soft tortilla, or fried crispy tortillas may be used as a scoop.

Serves 8 to 10 as an appetizer or 6 as a main course.

CHA'CHAKWAHES
Chicken Tamales in a Fragrant Sauce

From the Hearth of Vasilia and Ilario

Ilario is a son of Valentin. He was born in Kunkunul and is married to Vasilia, a lovely Maya woman with the same birthplace.

Vasilia taught me how to make *Cha'chakwahes*, wonderful chicken tamales in a thick fragrant sauce, that she carefully wrapped in banana leaves and steamed atop her hearth. She enlisted the help of her mother-in-law, Eleutaria, and set about the task of toasting banana leaves, simmering the chicken, and grinding *masa*. When Vasilia strains her corn to make the *masa*, she uses a plastic mesh shopping bag to act as the "sieve." She fills the bag with cooked ground corn, then twists and squeezes the bag until its contents are strained into a waiting bucket. I tried to think of a gadget to bring to Acabchen that would do the work more efficiently, but finally came to realize that the simple mesh bag is a truly amazing tool. It does the job as well, perhaps better, than a fancy electric blender.

To Prepare Cha'chakwahes:

The Maya name for this delicious recipe means, "red bread steamed in water." The bread is "red" because *achiote* has been added to the *masa* mixture. These tamales are wonderfully moist and delicious, a result of the *K'ol*, a thickened broth made with *masa*. This is a favorite tamale for *Hanal Pixan* (All Souls Day), Christmas, and any other time the family gathers for a special meal.

Have on Hand:

> *Recado Colorado*, Red Spice Paste, page 51
> 1 recipe *Yucatecan Masa* for tamales, page 118
> 2 banana leaves, prepared for cooking, page 120, or parchment paper or aluminum foil
> *Xnipek* or other favorite salsa—or chopped chili

Ingredients:

> 3 to 4 pound roasting chicken
> 8 cups water
> 1 onion, toasted
> 1 bulb garlic, toasted
> 1 chili, either mild or hot, toasted

41

2 tablespoons *Recado Colorado*, Red Spice Paste
Salt to taste
4 cups chicken broth resulting from the above recipe
1 cup *Masa Harina*
2 large tomatoes, toasted and skinned
2 banana leaves (or parchment paper or aluminum foil), pre-
    pared for cooking and cut into twelve 10-inch sections

Method:

Place the chicken in a Dutch oven or stockpot and cover it with the water. Add the toasted onion, garlic, chili, *Recado Colorado,* and salt. Bring the water to a boil, reduce the heat and cover the chicken. Let the chicken simmer for 1 hour and 15 minutes, or until the meat is done.

Remove the chicken from the broth and let it cool. Debone the chicken and shred the meat.

Strain and degrease the broth. Four cups of it will be needed to prepare the thickened *K'ol.* Any remaining broth may be used as a liquid for the tamale dough or it may be set aside for use as a soup.

To prepare the *K'ol,* blend 2 cups of the broth in a mixing bowl with the *masa.* Whip with a wisk until all of the lumps disappear. Bring the remaining 2 cups of broth to a simmer. Slowly add the *masa*/broth mixture. Simmer until the sauce is blended and thickened. It should be the consistency of thin pancake batter.

Toast the tomatoes and remove the skins. Chop the tomatoes and add them to the *K'ol.* Set the *K'ol* aside.

Place a banana leaf, dull side facing upward (or parchment paper or aluminum foil), on the work space in front of you. Place about ¼ cup of *masa* in the center of the leaf and pat it into a rectangle about ¼ inch thick. Arrange a few pieces of chicken on one side of the *masa* rectangle—the side furthest away from you—and top it with a tablespoon of *K'ol.* Fold the banana leaf over so that the *masa* rectangle is doubled back on itself. Make a package by tucking in the sides and ends. Tie the tamale with a banana string or household string. Prepare all of the tamales in the same manner.

Arrange the tamales in a steamer, ends pointing up and down. Add water to the steamer, cover the tamales and let them cook for 1½ hours. The *masa* should flake and pull away from the sides of the banana leaf when it is done. The tamales may also be cooked on the rack of a large baking pan—fill the pan half full with water and cover the entire pan with aluminum foil, taking care to seal the edges. Bake at 325 degrees for the same amount of time.

When the tamales have about 30 minutes more to cook, bring the *K'ol* back to a simmer and let it cook until the tamales are done. Stir the *K'ol* frequently to keep the sauce from sticking.

To Serve:

Serve the tamales with an extra helping of *K'ol* and offer some chili or other salsa on the side.

Serves 6 to 8.

JOROCHES DE FLOR DE CALABAZA Y CALABAZA
Stew of Little Dumplings with Pumpkin Flowers and Pumpkin

From the Hearth of Anita and Leondro

Leondro and Anastasia (Anita) live in a double house complex between the schoolhouse and Luis and Eulogia. One bright November morning, Anita invited me to share in *Joroches de Flor de Calabaza,* some little corn dumplings cooked with squash blossoms. I had waited for a long time to taste this wonderful stew, but my visits seemed to fall either before or after the squash blossom season. Anita had harvested a whole bucket of blossoms, enough to feed the entire village. She showed me how to form the little hollow cups to make the dumplings, a much easier task than making tortillas. The dumplings and flowers are cooked together to make a thick soup, a superb autumn meal.

To Prepare Joroches De Flor De Calabaza Y Calabaza:

Joroches are representative of the one pot meals that are so typical of ancient Maya cuisine. Tiny little dumplings simmer with the vegetables, eliminating the need for making tortillas or messing up a second pot. One may use squash, beans, *chaya* or spinach—whatever happens to be on hand.

Ingredients:

> 3 pounds pumpkin or winter squash, peeled and cut into 2-inch slices
> 12 cups water
> Salt to taste
> 2 cups *Masa harina*
> 1 teaspoon salt
> ½ cup lard or shortening
> 1 cup chicken stock, vegetable stock, or water
> ¼ cup cilantro, chopped
> 24 pumpkin or squash blossoms, stamens removed
> ½ cup pumpkin or squash seeds, toasted and ground
> 6 quartered limes or lemons
> 2 or 3 hot green chilies, such as the jalapeño or *jabanero*

Method:

Place the cut pumpkin pieces in a large stockpot. Add the water and salt. Cover and cook for 1½ hours, or until quite tender.

Meanwhile, prepare the *joroches*. Add the salt to the *masa harina*. Mix in the lard or shortening and the broth. Knead the mixture well with the fingers. Pinch off a piece about the size of a large walnut. Form the *masa* into a little ball. With the thumb, make an indentation in the top and mold it into a little cup.

When the pumpkin is tender, drop the *joroches* into the broth and continue to simmer until they float to the top. Add the pumpkin flowers and the cilantro. Cook for five more minutes.

Arrange the ground pumpkin seeds, lime and chili in condiment bowls.

To Serve:

Each person adds a selection of condiments, to taste.

Serves 8.

RECADOS
Curries of Yucatan

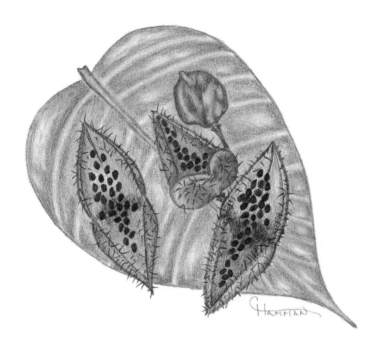

Achiote seeds.

$\mathcal{R}$*ecados* are subtly scented, vividly colored concoctions that fill huge washtubs in the central markets of Yucatecan towns and cities. Vendors offer a tantalizing variety of herbs and spices dressed in hues of pale celadon, burnt sienna, and inky black. Such magic potions can transform a simple meal into a culinary sensation. Although the use of these sticky pastes shows evidence of great antiquity, *recados* were unquestionably enriched after the Spanish Conquest with new blendings of herbs, spices, and condiments that found their way across the sea from China, India, and the Mediterranean.

Recados may have been one of the first innovations of early Maya women as they faced busy daily schedules and decided to plan ahead. This is one of their inventions that may be classified as an early convenience food, a pre-Columbian "pre-packaged mix." On those rare and wonderful days when no chores loomed heavy on the horizon, there were spare moments to wander through the bush, gathering sweet herbs and aromatic spices. Wild onions were native to the land, pungent bulbs that served as a binder for all of the other ingredients.

The condiments are crushed on a *metate*, then ground and reground to release their oils and flavor essence. The resulting aroma is much like a rare perfume. The Maya tuck their *recados* into a banana leaf and tie it securely with string. Carefully hung from the kitchen rafters, the tiny bundles dangle beyond the reach of marauding cats, dogs, and pigs. As the days pass by, a pinch of paste is removed for flavoring fish, poultry, pork, beef, venison, and vegetable soups and stews.

The name for a *recado* in Maya is *xak'*, a word referring to something that is repeatedly ground. The most prevalent spice mix in Yucatan is called *Recado Colorado* in Spanish and *Chak Xak'* in Maya. Both names allude to its vivid red/orange color. Dedicated cooks attribute to it almost as much importance as tortillas, chili, and beans in their diet. *Recado Colorado* is used in such famous dishes as *Pollo Pibil, Cochinita Pibil, Pollo a la Yucateca,* and *Tikinxik*. There are few foods that are not enhanced by a few tablespoons of this colorful seasoning.

Recado de Chilmole and *Recado de Relleno Negro* are also extremely popular, but present a real challenge for cooks who prefer to make everything from scratch. These *recados* require a significant portion of burned red chilies. The drawback is this: burning chilies create an acrid

48

smoke. The burning must take place outside in the open air. Even the Maya build an outside hearthfire when the time comes for preparing this coal-black sauce. Although several pounds of dried chili go into the stew pot, this *recado* is not terribly hot.

I have included a recipe that I adapted from the traditional one so that it may be prepared in urban kitchens. The resulting paste is delicious, but not as pungent and black as the original recipe. It does not require as much chili, either. There are few foods that do not benefit from a long slow simmer in these burned chili pastes.

Recado de Escabeche, known as simply *Xak'*, in Maya, is also extremely popular. Fish and chicken are often bathed in this piquant sauce.

Although most of the other *recados* go by the name of the principal recipe in which they are utilized, they are also called for in other dishes. Actually, the *Recados de Escabeche, Salpimentado, Mechado, Especie, Puchero, Chilaquil*, and *Alcaparrado*, are somewhat similar in many of their ingredients, but each contains one or more additional herbs or spices that add a unique character to the flavor. *Recado de Bistec* is delicious as a marinade on all types of beef. *Recado de Pepita*, a lovely pistachio-colored paste, is simply a mixture of finely ground large squash seeds—with nothing else added for flavoring. Utilized in *Papa'suules*, a recipe that features tortillas dipped in a squash-seed sauce, *Recado de Pepita* is at its best freshly made. For this reason, I have included the directions for toasting and grinding the seeds in the recipe for *Papa'suules*.

City *recados* bear little resemblance to their country cousins, but they do serve a wide market. Not everyone, even in Yucatan, wants to take the time and trouble to prepare their own, although a blender and spice grinder make the task almost effortless. Acabchen is a rare village where the women still grind their own *recados* on a *metate*. Their *recados* are also free from additives such as vinegar, ground tortillas, and flour that add extra bulk—and sometimes color—to expensive ingredients.

Recados made with the traditional recipes will keep for a year in the refrigerator, while the commercial variety will develop mold within a few months. One reason for this phenomenon is that any liquid added to the ingredients tends to reduce the keeping quality, and *recados* from the market are usually made with vinegar. *Recado de Pepita* is the only paste that is best prepared shortly before it is needed because the delicate seeds tend to lose their flavor rather quickly.

When experimenting with one of these seasoning pastes, try adding one or two tablespoons at a time, let the flavors simmer for a bit, then check to see if more of the *recado* is needed. Most meats, soups and stews will benefit from the addition of one of these flavorings.

Visitors to Yucatan who wish to purchase a supply of *recados* in one of the markets will have no problem with United States Customs. Try to buy them the day before departure: most hotels will be happy to keep a small package refrigerated overnight.

RECADO COLORADO
Red Spice Paste

Rosita showed me how to make *Recado Colorado* (*Chak Xak'*) on a *metate* while I carefully noted the directions for her recipe. It took about 45 minutes for her to grind all of the ingredients into a smooth mass. She prepares it quite often, for this is the seasoning used in daily meals, as well as agricultural ceremonies. Whenever Casellano offers a gift of chicken or turkey to the gods, it is bathed in this aromatic paste. *Recado Colorado* can be used on chicken, beef, pork, and fish—or added as a flavoring to soups and stews.

Ingredients:

> 1-inch piece cinnamon stick, crushed
> 10 cloves
> 5 allspice berries
> 2 tablespoons black peppercorns
> 2 tablespoons *achiote*
> 1 pinch cumin
> 1½ teaspoons oregano
> 1 large onion, toasted
> 2 bulbs garlic, toasted

Method:

Place the cinnamon, cloves, allspice, black pepper, *achiote*, cumin, and oregano in a spice grinder. Grind the spices to a fine powder.

Toast the onion and garlic. Peel the onion and cut it into quarters. Peel the garlic cloves and place them in the blender with the onion. Blend the vegetables to a thick purée. Add the ground spices and blend thoroughly.

Place in an airtight container and store in the refrigerator.

CHILMOLE
Chili Spice Paste

Chilmole is a *Nahuatl* word meaning "chili sauce." The technique of making *Chilmole* seems to have been borrowed from central Mexico where chilies are first toasted, then ground with other condiments and spices. Perhaps the recipe was introduced during one of the Toltec invasions of Yucatan. When properly prepared, there are no words to do *Chilmole* justice... the sauce just floats over the tongue and tantalizes the mouth.

For years I ordered pork simmered in *Chilmole* whenever possible in all of the restaurants. It is a glossy black sauce, somewhat garlicky, and hints of all the good tasting things that have gone incognito. No one, however, could tell me how to make the seasoning paste. Everyone bought it readymade in the market.

Imagine my delight in Acabchen to find that *Chilmole* was often prepared, and not just as a sauce for pork, chicken and turkey, but for beans as well. I begged for someone to show me the chili burning process. Isabel offered to be my cooking instructor. With the help of my translator, Amelia, she assembled a new hearth just outside the kitchen door. An early morning trek to the family milpa produced a basket overflowing with brilliant crimson chilies.

Amelia started the fire and balanced a griddle atop the three-stone hearth. Isabel began to toast the chilies while Amelia lit several corn-husks and tossed them onto the griddle. It didn't take long for acrid smoke to assail our lungs. Isabel gingerly stirred the chilies that were now aflame and turning from red to black. When the mixture was properly charred, she removed the griddle from the hearth and allowed the chilies to cool. The next step was a chili bath, several dunkings in fresh clear water. Rinsing removes most of the gritty soot and fiery seeds. After the last rinse water was clean enough to suit her, she ground the chilies with garlic, onion, and spices and added them to the stewpot. Isabel then added a healthy portion of black beans, topped the pot with a lid, and we settled back in our hammocks to enjoy the spicy odors, and to gossip. Or rather, Isabel and Amelia gossiped and I listened to Amelia's translations.

After returning home, I could hardly wait to try my hand at burning chilies. I had no backyard hearth, nor any great hatred for my neighbors, so I opted for my kitchen and an ordinary gas stove. It would not be difficult, I thought, to toast the chilies while holding my breath. It would be a cinch, I reasoned, to spread a towel over my nose, run to the front door for a fresh breath of air and dash back to stir the chilies again. I had underestimated the amount of smoke that would billow in an enclosed space. I had not even thought of what searing chili oils would do to skin and eyes.

My first three trips for a gasp of air didn't go too badly, but soon thereafter the situation turned ghastly. I snatched up my two Siamese cats, Maya and Mixtec, and made a hasty escape to the outside and a breath of fresh air. It was several hours before we could go back into the house again, and several days before the place began to smell normal.

I have adapted Isabel's recipe to non-Mexican resources and kitchens. She used more than a pound of dried red chilies, an amount that is not always available, even in rural Yucatan. When chili is scarce, burned tortillas add a touch of bulk and blackness to the sauce. Corn will be added to the sauce, anyway, so the flavor of the tortillas is not really noticible. An extra amount of chili will, however, result in a richer sauce. The adapted recipe calls for 1 to 4 ounces of chili, an amount that is not too fiery for even the most timid of palates.

There is an alternative method to making this wonderful *recado*, but it requires a trip to Yucatan or the generosity of travelling friends. *Recado de Chilmole* is easily purchased in the markets and will keep beautifully in the refrigerator for at least a year. The paste is so delicious and versatile it will probably disappear long before that.

Ingredients:

> 1 to 4 ounces dried red chili, burned black on a charcoal grill
> 3 corn tortillas, burned black on a charcoal grill
> 2 bulbs garlic, toasted
> 2 large onions, toasted
> 4 allspice berries
> 6 cloves
> 1 1-inch piece cinnamon stick
> 1½ tablespoons oregano
> 2 tablespoons *achiote*
> 1 teaspoon black pepper

Method:

Wear long flame-resistant barbecue gloves for this task and be very careful.

As a charcoal grill will be necessary to toast the chili, it may be used to toast all of the other vegetables, as well.

Place the chilies in a cast iron skillet and set the skillet directly on the red coals. The chilies will begin to smoke and then turn black. Stir them with a long-handled barbecue utensil or wooden spoon until there is no red color remaining on the chilies. Remove the skillet from the coals and set it aside to cool.

With long-handled tongs, toast the tortillas until they are black. Toast the garlic and onion until they are charred. Bring all of the toasted foods inside the house.

Wash the chilies in a pot of water and scoop out any burned seeds that float to the surface. Throw the seeds away. Wash the chilies a second time, drain them and set them aside. If the chilies are extra sooty, wash them a third time.

Grind the allspice, cloves, cinnamon, oregano, *achiote* and black pepper in a spice grinder. Grind them to a fine powder.

Peel the garlic cloves and onions and throw the skins away. Quarter the onion and place it in the blender with the garlic. Break the tortillas into pieces and place them in the blender. Blend the vegetables to a smooth purée. Add the ground spices and blend until everything has become a smooth paste.

Place in an airtight container and store in the refrigerator.

RELLENO NEGRO
Toasted Chili Spice Paste—Fiesta Version

Some Yucatecans consider *Recado de Chilmole* and *Recado de Relleno Negro* to be the same. In Acabchen, people make some minor distinctions between the two. *Relleno* is the ultimate celebration dish, *Chilmole* the less elaborate country cousin. *Recado de Relleno Negro* often requires more chili and spices, but perhaps that is due to the difference between daily cooking and fiesta cuisine, when cost is not a factor.

Alberta gave me this recipe which makes plenty of *recado*, enough to cook an entire pig under the ground or on top of a stove. *Recado de Relleno Negro* is made to flavor fiesta foods, most specifically, pig or turkey that simmers underground in an earthen oven or *pib*. *Relleno Negro* is the typical celebration food for a Maya wedding, to honor a village saint, or to pay homage to ones ancestors on the anniversary of a death. In this latter instance, a departed soul is not offered *Relleno* until the second anniversary of a death: the soul is considered too delicate at this point to deal with an abundance of chili.

To duplicate the exact flavor of this *recado*, *chili seco* is necessary. There is no problem in bringing chili into the United States: simply declare it when checking through Customs at the airport. The dried chili freezes quite beautifully for future use, so buy plenty—and plant some of the seeds.

Ingredients:

> 6 bulbs garlic, toasted
> 6 large onions, toasted
> 1 cup *achiote*
> ¼ cup black peppercorns
> ¼ cup cloves
> 6 ½ -inch pieces cinnamon sticks
> ¼ cup oregano
> 2½ pounds *chili seco*, toasted

Method:

Follow directions for the preceding recipe, but omit the burned tortillas.

Place in an airtight container and store in the refrigerator.

RECADO DE ESCABECHE
Piquant Chili Spice Paste

Rosita uses *Recado de Escabeche*, (*Xak'*), almost as much as *Recado Colorado*. She uses it in her recipe for *Ts'anchak bi Kax*, chicken cooked in a peppery sauce, as well as various soups and stews. It is a lovely chocolate color and adds a zest to everything. Rosita wraps her *Xak'* in a banana leaf and places it in a *peten*, a large flat storage basket that swings from her kitchen rafters. This *recado* derives its name in Spanish from the fact that vinegar is added to the cooking liquid in many of the recipes—hence a piquant or pickled sauce.

Ingredients:

> 1-inch piece cinnamon stick, crushed
> 10 cloves, whole
> 2 tablespoons black peppercorns
> 1 teaspoon oregano
> 1 pinch cumin
> 1 onion, toasted
> 1 bulb garlic, toasted

Method:

Place the cinnamon, cloves, black pepper, oregano, and cumin in a spice grinder. Grind the spices to a fine powder.

Toast the onion and garlic and remove the skins. Cut the onion into fourths. Place the onion and garlic in a blender. Blend the vegetables to a fine purée. Add the ground spices to the onion/garlic mixture and process until well blended.

Place in an airtight container and store in the refrigerator.

RECADO DE SALPIMENTADO
Salt and Peppered Spice Paste

The name of this *recado* translates as "a salt and peppered spice paste," but the salt goes into the stew, not the recado. *Recado de Salpimentado* adds a lovely flavor to almost anything.

Ingredients:

> 1 bulb garlic, toasted
> 1 onion, toasted
> 1 tablespoon black pepper
> 1 1-inch stick cinnamon
> 6 cloves
> 1 teaspoon oregano

Method:

Toast the onion and garlic and remove the skins. Cut the onion into quarters. Put the onion and garlic in a blender and purée the vegetables until smooth.

Place the black pepper, cinnamon, cloves and oregano in a spice grinder. Grind the spices to a fine powder and add them to the onion and garlic. Purée once again until the spices and vegetables are blended.

Place in an airtight container and store in the refrigerator.

RECADO DE MECHADO

Mechado refers to something that has been "stuck" or "pierced" with another ingredient, such as a roast with garlic, ham, or lard inserted for flavoring. However, *Recado de Mechado* may be used without going to the trouble of "sticking" the meat with something else.

The directions for this *recado* were given to me by Ernestina Hereria, the grand dame of San Pedro, Ambergris Caye, Belize. An amazing lady, she is well into her nineties, but still manages to preside over all of the local doings. San Pedranos greet her every afternoon as she waves from the second story of her balconied dwelling. Ernestina's mother emigrated to San Pedro with the Maya influx from Bacalar, an area just north of Chetumal or *Chactemal*, during the War of the Castes. Many of the Maya in San Pedro are descended from the refugees of this brutal conflagration.

This *recado* is very similar to *Recado de Especie*, but it contains no saffron. With that in mind, for saffron is very expensive, *Recado Mechado* may be considered a substitute for the *Recado de Especie* when cost is a factor.

Ingredients:

    1 tablespoon black pepper
    1-inch cinnamon stick
    1 teaspoon oregano
    4 cloves
    1 pinch cumin
    5 allspice berries
    1 medium onion, toasted
    1 bulb garlic, toasted

Method:

Place the black pepper, cinnamon, oregano, cloves, cumin, and all-spice in a spice grinder. Grind the spices to a fine powder.

Toast the onion and garlic. Remove the skin from the onion and cut the onion into quarters. Remove each clove of garlic from the bulb and place the garlic and onion in a blender. Blend until the vegetables are a smooth purée. Add the ground spices and blend well.

Place in an airtight container and store in the refrigerator.

RECADO DE ESPECIE

This recado is very similar to *Recado de Mechado*, but it contains saffron.

Ingredients:

1 tablespoon black pepper
1 1-inch cinnamon stick
1 teaspoon oregano
4 cloves
1 pinch cumin
5 allspice berries
2 pinches saffron
1 medium onion, toasted
1 bulb garlic, toasted

METHOD:

Prepare the *Recado de Especie* by placing the black pepper, cinnamon, oregano, cloves, cumin, allspice and saffron in a spice grinder. Grind the spices to a fine powder.

Toast the onion and garlic. Remove the skin from the onion and cut the onion into quarters. Remove each clove of garlic from the bulb and place the garlic and onion in a blender. Blend until the vegetables are a smooth purée. Add the ground spices and blend well.

Place in an airtight container and store in the refrigerator.

RECADO DE PUCHERO

This *recado* is sometimes called *Recado de Adobo Blanco* or *white seasoning paste*. The name does not seem to fit since this *recado* is not white, but it is delicious nonetheless. I find it exceptionally good with almost any kind of vegetable, soup, or stew.

Ingredients:

1 teaspoon oregano
1 tablespoon black pepper
8 cloves
½ teaspoon cumin
1 ½-inch piece cinnamon stick
2 pinches saffron
1 onion, toasted
1 bulb garlic, toasted

Method:

Place the oregano, black pepper, cloves, cumin, cinnamon and saffron in a spice grinder. Grind to a fine powder.

Toast the onion and garlic. Peel the onion and cut it into quarters. Peel the garlic cloves and place them in the blender with the onion. Process the mixture until the vegetables are a smooth paste. Add the ground herbs and spices to the onion/garlic purée and blend well.

Place in an airtight container and store in the refrigerator.

RECADO DE CHILAQUIL

This is a handy *recado* to have for an all-purpose seasoning. Because it does not contain cinnamon or cloves and is flavored with *epazote*, this *recado* has a distinctive flavor.

Ingredients:

     3 cloves garlic, toasted
     1 small onion, toasted
     5 allspice berries
     1 tablespoon black peppercorns
     1 tablespoon *achiote*
     2 sprigs *epazote*

Method:

Toast the onion and garlic. Peel the onion and cut it into quarters. Peel the garlic cloves and place them in the blender with the onion. Blend the vegetables to a thick purée. Add the ground spices and blend thoroughly.

Place the allspice, black pepper, *achiote*, and *epazote* in a spice grinder. Grind as finely as possible. Add the ground spices to the garlic/onion purée and process until smooth and well blended.

Place in an airtight container and store in the refrigerator.

SALSAS
The Salsas of Yucatan

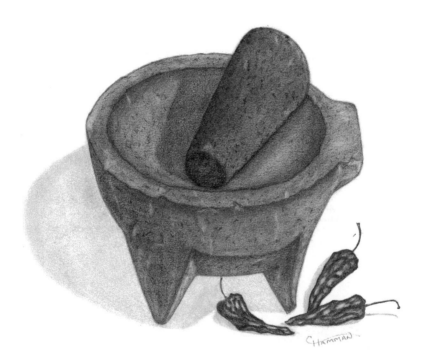

Molcajete and Tejolote

*T*he vividly colored salsas of Yucatan are more than just a topping for a taco, tamale, or a savory soup or stew. For the rural Maya, they are often the culinary focus, the entire meal itself, for many a breakfast, lunch, or dinner. Imagine a pile of toasty hand-patted tortillas, hot from the griddle and ready to dip into a vibrant red chili paste—or a luscious tomato salsa. *Naranja Ik*, an orange and chili dip, is aromatic with a handful of toasted squash seeds and provides an ideal way to launch an autumn morning.

Most of the local restaurants feature three or four salsas on each table so that one may sample a variety of different flavors at the same meal. There is always a bowl of *Xnipek*, perhaps my favorite goes-with-every-thing salsa, a blend of tomato, onion, cilantro, jabanero chili and sour orange. Sometimes, one of the selections is *K'ut bi Ik*, an offering of pure chili, crushed and blended with water, vinegar or lime. *Salsa Verde* is another popular choice, a lovely green salsa made with the husked *tomatillo*. It is possible to change the entire flavor of a meal simply by adding a different topping.

Most of these salsas are at their best when freshly made, although they may be stored for several days in the refrigerator. Any leftover sauce will transform a daily breakfast lunch or dinner into a Mexican fiesta.

XNIPEK
Nose of the Dog

This is Yucatan's most famous sauce, the one that sits out on every table at breakfast, lunch, dinner, and in-between. It is very similar to the fresh chili salsa of Mexico, *Salsa Mexicana*, except that the *jabanero* chili is substituted for the tamer varieties. Oh my, and therein lies the name of this salsa, which is so hot it will make any nose moist—just like the nose of a puppy dog. The jabanero is my favorite chili and has a wonderful addictive flavor, but beware. It is said to be 20 times hotter than any other chili.

Xnipek is best when allowed to marinate for an hour, if time permits, but the tomatoes begin to lose their crisp texture fairly rapidly. The salsa is still delicious (although the texture is not the same) for another day or two, but it is best to make small quantities of *Xnipek* so that it may be enjoyed at its peak.

Ingredients:

> 3 large tomatoes, chopped
> 1 medium onion, chopped
> 1 chili *jabanero*, chopped—or any hot green chili
> 3 tablespoons cilantro, fresh, chopped
> 1 pinch salt
> $1/3$ cup juice from the sour orange—or lime or lemon juice

Method:

Chop all of the vegetables and place them in a mixing bowl. Add the chopped cilantro, salt, and citrus juice. Mix thoroughly.

Store in the refrigerator for an hour or so to let the salsa season.

Makes about 3 cups of salsa.

SALSA VERDE WITH TOMATILLOS
Green Sauce with Tomatillos

I love this sauce. It's easy to prepare and tastes marvelous on everything. Although it originated in central Mexico, rather than the Yucatan, it has been lovingly adopted and is almost as popular as the ubiquitous *Xnipek.*

Note: Two 11 ounce cans of *tomatillos* may be substituted for the fresh ones. They will not need to be covered in water and simmered. Drain the *tomatillos* and place them in the blender with the remaining ingredients.

Ingredients:

> 3 cups water
> 1 pound tomatillos, fresh
> 1 medium onion, quartered
> 1 hot green chili
> 2 tablespoons cilantro
> 2 large garlic cloves
> ½ teaspoon sugar

Method:

Bring the water to boil in a medium sized saucepan. Add the tomatillos and simmer them for three minutes. Drain the tomatillos and add them to the blender with the onion, chili, cilantro, garlic, and sugar. Coarsely chop all of the ingredients in the blender. If the salsa thickens too much when refrigerated, thin it with a little water.

Makes about 6 cups of salsa.

SALSA VERDE CON AGUACATE
Green Sauce with Avocado

Salsa Verde is a beautiful pale green salsa, almost the color of celadon, but its delicate color is a camouflage for the fire concealed within. This recipe from *El Tacolote* in Cancun, Quintana Roo, specifies the bite of a *jabanero*, but a tamer chili, such as the jalapeño, may be substituted.

Ingredients:

   1 small avocado, peeled and seed removed
   1 small *jabanero* or other hot green chili
   2 tablespoons cilantro
   1 very small onion, chopped
   1 clove garlic

Method:

   Place all of the ingredients in the blender. Blend until liquified.
   This salsa is thin and fiery.

Makes about 2 cups of salsa.

SALSA RANCHERA
Cooked Country-style Sauce

This is a delicious all-purpose cooked salsa. I like to keep a jar of it on hand in the refrigerator because hardly a day goes by that I can't think of something to put it on. Toasting the vegetables makes a difference and really brings out the flavors. For dynamite results, buy the biggest, reddest, juiciest tomatoes you can find. Or grow your own.

Salsa Ranchera will keep three or four days in the refrigerator.

Ingredients:

> 4 large tomatoes, toasted
> 1 large onion, toasted
> 3 cloves garlic, toasted
> 1 hot green chili, toasted
> Salt to taste

Method:

Toast the tomatoes, onion, garlic and chili. Place the vegetables in a blender or food processor and blend them until they are coarsely chopped.

Transfer the mixture to a saucepan and add salt, if desired. Simmer the salsa for 30 minutes.

Makes about 6 cups of salsa.

CHILTOMATE
Chili and Tomato Salsa

This is a lovely fragrant salsa made with crushed toasted tomatoes and chilies.

Ingredients:

2 large tomatoes, toasted
1 chili jabanero or other hot green chili, toasted
2 tablespoons cilantro, fresh, chopped
½ cup juice from the sour orange—or regular orange juice with a tablespoon of lime juice added for tartness

Method:

Toast the tomatoes and chili. Crush the tomatoes in a molcajete or mortar and pestle. If nothing is available to crush the tomatoes, chop them with a knife. Do not use a blender or food processor. Chop the chili and add it to the tomatoes. Stir in the chopped cilantro and add the sour orange juice.

Makes about 2½ cups of salsa.

SALSA INDIO
Indian Sauce

Salsa Indio is a variation of *Chiltomate* that contains garlic and omits the citrus. It's a spicy refreshing sauce that goes especially well with any kind of meat, fish, or fowl that does not already contain tomato.

Ingredients:

> 2 large tomatoes, toasted
> 2 cloves garlic, toasted and chopped
> 1 hot green chili, toasted and chopped
> 3 tablespoons cilantro, chopped

Method:

Toast all of the vegetables. Remove any large pieces of burned skin from the tomatoes.

Crush the mixture with a wooden masher or with a mortar and pestle. A blender will not do, because the tomatoes should be mashed, rather than pulverized.

Add the cilantro and serve.

Makes about 2 cups of salsa.

MOJO
Orange, Onion and Chili Salsa

This is a wonderful salsa to add some zip to any soup, vegetable or meat. *Mojo* presents a lovely color contrast with pale orange citrus and sharp green chili. My friend from Acabchen, Anastasia, always makes a little jícara of this beautiful salsa to add to her wonderful stews.

Ingredients:

> 1 large onion, finely chopped
> 2 cloves garlic, chopped
> 1 hot green chili, chopped
> ½ cup juice from the sour orange—or lime or lemon juice

Method:

Mix all of the ingredients together.

Makes about 2 cups of salsa.

K'UT BI IK
Crushed Red Chili Sauce

K'ut means mashed or crushed and *ik* is the general word for chili. When there is plenty of dried chili in the fields, a simple *k'ut* provides a pungent dipping sauce for tortillas. *Chili seco* has a lovely smoky flavor unlike any other chili to be found in Mexico.

K'ut bi Ik brings back memories of steaming hot coffee, heavily sweetened and served in a bowl, a napkin-filled stack of hot breads, and the flickering warmth of a hearth fire. One early summer morning I went to Alberta and Pablo's to have breakfast. Alberta was feeding their youngest, a beautiful two-year old child. The little one was ecstatic, dabbing bits of toasted tortilla into a small bowl of chili paste, grinning broadly and happily popping it into his mouth. The baby was literally covered with it. When I asked Alberta if the chili ever made him cry, she replied, "The only time he ever cries is when he doesn't get his chili."

There are two ways to utilize *K'ut bi Ik*. Sometimes liquid chili drops, rather than crushed chili bits are needed, particularly if the chili is used to garnish *atole*. When only the liquid is to be used, the *k'ut* is strained to get the brick red chili broth. Slow hand grinding is needed for this salsa to yield its full rich flavor. There is no short cut.

Ingredients:

    15 dried red chilies
    1 tablespoon water

Method:

Tear the chilies into two or three pieces. Crush the chilies using a mortar and pestle. Be patient. This process may take ten minutes to complete.

To use only the chili liquid, add an additional three tablespoons of water to the crushed chilies and strain the liquid into a container. Use this liquid as a garnish—just as you would tabasco sauce.

Makes less than ¼ cup of a very potent salsa.

TSAH BI IK
Enriched Sauce of Dried Red Chili

The Maya love their chili and don't consider a meal complete without it. It is held in such high esteem that Don Luis, the *comisario* of Acabchen, once commented, "If a meal does not contain chili, we do not feel as if we have eaten." The word *tsah* in the title indicates that lard has been added to the chili—*Tsah bi Ik* is a rich, fullbodied chili salsa.

Ingredients:

> 1 small onion, toasted and chopped
> 2 cloves garlic, toasted and chopped
> 10 dried red chilies, toasted
> 2 tablespoons lard or oil
> ¼ cup juice from the sour orange—or lime or lemon juice
> Salt to taste

Method:

Toast the onion. Toss out the outer skin and chop the onion.

Toast the garlic. Peel the cloves of garlic and chop them.

Toast the chilies and mash them in a molcajete or mortar and pestle, or grind them in a blender or food processor.

Heat the oil in a heavy skillet and sauté the onion and garlic until the onion is translucent. Add the ground chilies and sauté the mixture for another 2 minutes.

Mix in the sour orange juice, or lime or lemon juice and salt.

Makes about 1 cup of salsa.

TSAH BI YAX IK
Enriched Sauce of Fresh Green Chili

This chili salsa is very much like the preceeding one, only fresh green chili is used instead of dried red chili. It adds a beautiful green color to dishes that are made with tomatoes.

Ingredients:

> 1 small onion, toasted and chopped
> 2 cloves garlic, toasted and chopped
> 5 fresh green hot chilies, toasted and chopped
> 2 tablespoons lard or oil
> ¼ cup juice from the sour orange, or lemon or lime juice
> Salt to taste

Method:

Toast the onion. Toss out the skin and chop the onion.

Toast the garlic. Peel the cloves of garlic and chop them.

Toast the chilies and crush them in a *molcajete* or mortar and pestle, or grind them in a blender or food processor.

Heat the oil in a heavy skillet and sauté the onion and garlic until the onion is translucent. Add the chilies and sauté for another 2 minutes.

Mix in the sour orange juice, or lime or lemon juice and salt.

Makes about 1 cup of salsa.

NARANJA IK
Orange Chili Salsa

Oh, what a heavenly salsa this is. It is delicious spooned on almost any main dish recipe or may be used as the focus of a meal. One of the specialties of Acabchen, *Naranja Ik* is often used as the dip for a stack of tortillas, thus making it an ideal appetizer. Sour orange trees proliferate in Yucatan and bear produce throughout the year. This useful citrus can be seasonal in North American markets, so it may be necessary to improvise when they are unavailable.

Ingredients:

> 15 dried red chilies, toasted
> 1 small onion, toasted
> 3 tablespoons lard or oil
> ¼ cup pumpkin or squash seeds, toasted and ground
> ½ cup juice from the sour orange, or lime or lemon juice

Method:

Toast the chilies. Mash them with a *molcajete* or mortar and pestle, or grind them in a blender or food processor.

Toast the onion. Toss out the skin and chop the onion.

Sauté the chilies and onion in the shortening for five minutes, stirring occasionally.

Toast the pumpkin or squash seeds. Grind them in a blender or food processor.

Blend the pumpkin/squash seeds with the chili/onion mixture. Stir in the orange juice.

To Serve:

Fill a small bowl with the *Naranja Ik* and scoop up the salsa with toasty tortillas—or use it as a topping on something else.

Makes about 1¼ cups of salsa.

APPETIZERS

"A first course for the gods, Pokbilnales and Atole Nuevo."

$\mathcal{Y}$ucatecans, like all Mexicans, love to munch. It is hard to walk down the city or village streets without being tempted by vendors purveying all sorts of intriguing tidbits. Salty, sour, or sweet, there is something to appeal to every appetite. Restaurants and bars offer a tantalizing array of *botanas, bocadillos,* or *aperetivos,* as the Mexicans call their appetizers or snacks. Chilied peanuts or olives are often served with a cocktail or *cerveza* (beer) in many establishments. Some restaurants automatically present a basket of crisp *Tostaditas* and a bowl of *Xnipek* to start the meal.

The traditional Maya in rural areas have not acquiesed to modern habits for they do not have a first course before their entree. One hearthfire and one pot limit the display of dishes a Maya matron sets upon her dinner table. Whatever the culinary presentation might be, it usually has top billing and is the only featured attraction. A Maya appetizer is really a between-meal-snack, a bit of fruit, leisurely scavenged from the nearest tree, or a small bowl of something preserved in honey from last month's or last week's harvest.

Many of the Yucatecan delicacies that could be considered an appetite-whetter are in reality an entre offered in smaller amounts, or regular portions to be shared by convivial diners. Three or four tacos, *Quesadillas, Salbutes* and *Panuchos* are more than enough for a regular meal, yet a portion of just one per person makes an ideal appetizer. *Queso Fundido* is a favorite first-course in the local cafes, but it easily serves as an entre when the ingredients are doubled or tripled.

The following appetite teasers represent just a sampling of many possible choices for beginning a meal. To supplement this selection, remember that most recipes featuring tortillas make marvelous *bocadillos.* Anything resembling a salsa or dip, such as *Naranja Ik, Pp'ak i tsikil* or *Salsa Indio* makes a delicious *apperitivo* presentation.

GUACAMOLE
Sauce of Avocado

There is probably no one left in the world who does not have a favorite recipe for Guacamole. Although the name, which means *avocado salsa* in *Nahuatl*, indicates that the recipe probably originated somewhere in central Mexico, an itinerant warrior or merchant must have divulged the secret in Yucatcan. The Maya then added their own interpretation, a version that is unsurpassed. They use the same ingredients as everyone else in the country, but the reason for the flavor difference is simple. They toast.

Have on Hand:

   Tostaditas, page 93, use 12 tortillas

Ingredients:

   2 avocados, ripe
   1 medium onion, toasted and quartered
   1 small tomato, toasted and quartered
   3 cloves garlic, toasted
   1 or 2 hot chilies, toasted
   1 lime
   3 tablespoons cilantro, chopped
   Salt to taste

Method:

Spoon the avocado pulp into a bowl and crush it; the mixture should have some texture to it and not look puréed.

Place the onion, tomato, garlic, and chilies in a *molcajete* or a mortar, and crush them also, or place the ingredients, one at a time on a chopping block and chop them with a heavy knife.

Scoop the vegetables into the mixing bowl with the avocado. Add the juice from the lime and stir in the cilantro and salt.

To Serve:

Guacamole looks exotic when served in a *molcajete*. If one is not available, choose a serving dish that will accentuate the vivid colors of this salsa. Serve with *Tostaditas* as a scoop for the *Guacamole*.

Serves 4 to 6.

MALAKOF A LA HOTEL COLON
Hot Crusty Cheese Squares

The Hotel Colon is a sentimental landmark in Mérida that holds many special memories. It has always been customary in my family to pay homage to the canine host who so bravely guards the front entrance. My dad informed me on my very first visit to Mérida that it was his custom to greet "Old Charlie Black and Tan" with a few pats on the head. I have henceforth adhered to the ritual and find it impossible to cross the threshhold of the hotel without delivering a few furtive caresses to the faithful statue. On several cross-country bus ventures, I've arrived long past midnight at Mérida's Estación de Camioneros, then hailed a taxi to career through the slumbering streets. The doors to the Colon were always closed and securely locked, but a light tap, tap, tap awakened the sleeping concierge. I said my hello's to Charlie, patted his wise old head, and asked for one of the Colon's high-ceiling abodes. I don't remember lodging in the same room twice and for many years the hotel was a home away from home.

The Colon boasts a number of exquisite old steam baths, *Baños de Vapor.* The larger baths have individual swimming pools, all tiled in beautiful Talavera. I have grown to love my "one bucket baths" in Acabchen and have artfully developed the task of bathing with soap and pail. However, I would be stretching the truth a bit if I didn't admit to a slight hankering for an unlimited supply of water, hot or otherwise after a few days or weeks in the hot buggy jungle. My first destination, after roughing it a bit with my companions, the mosquitoes and *garapatas,* is a luxurious *baño* in the Hotel Colon. As La Carreta is located just across the street, I stop there first and ask Teodoro for a frosty margarita *para llevar*—to go. I can then bask in the lap of luxury while sipping a perfect margarita. When I finally emerge, relaxed, renewed and squeaky clean, I head for the dining room and a platter of *Malakof.*

This recipe was at one time a well-loved appetizer on the menu of the Hotel Colon. To my disappointment, it disappeared rather suddenly from the menu. Eddie Vasquez, one of the friendly "fixtures" of the hotel, volunteered to personally resurrect these crusty squares of melted cheese. He disappeared into the kitchen, then returned and beckoned me to follow. Eddie had arranged for the kitchen staff to make a batch of *Malakof* so that I could note the necessary details. Even though

Malakof may no longer be offered on the menu of the Colon, thanks to Eddie, it may be recreated for a fiesta at home.

Have on Hand:

A favorite chili salsa

Ingredients:

1 egg, beaten
6 ounces beer
1 cup flour
Salt to taste
Black pepper, freshly ground, to taste
3 cups oil, for deep frying
12 ounces cheddar cheese, cut in ¾ inch cubes

Method:

Mix the beaten egg and beer.

Season the flour with salt and pepper, if desired.

Heat the oil in a heavy skillet. Dip each piece of cheese into the beaten egg/beer mixture. Roll it in the seasoned flour and drop it into the hot oil. Repeat this procedure with all of the cheese squares. Cook until golden brown on one side. Flip and cook until golden brown on the second side. Remove the *Malakof* with a slotted spoon and drain them on paper towels.

To Serve:

They are delicious as is or with a favorite dipping salsa.

Serves 4 to 6.

TORTILLAS AND TAMALES
The Breads of the Yucatan

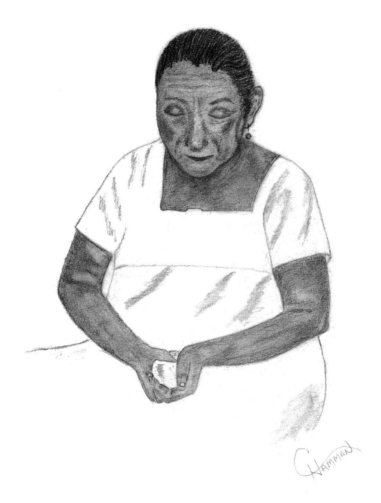

Forming an Ibewah

"They make good and healthful bread of different kinds, except that it is bad to eat when it is cold and so the Indian women take a great deal of trouble making it twice a day."
—Bishop Diego de Landa,
Landa's Relación de las Cosas de Yucatan (circa 1566)

*B*read is basic to any civilization: for many ancient cultures it formed the basis of their daily cuisine and the bulk of their calories. As Landa points out, the Maya made use of various types of bread but his description leaves everything to the imagination. I think of the tortilla as an item ubiquitous to the Mexican table, yet there is a debate among archaeologists as to whether the Maya actually made use of them or not.

The *Manche Chols*, a Maya linguistic group in Guatemala, had to be taught by Spanish priests how to fashion a tortilla, an art the invaders learned in central Mexico. Most of the archaeological sites of Yucatan seem to lack a *comal*, the griddle employed today atop every Maya hearth. Without the *comal* some argue there would be no way to toast a fragile tortilla. Thomas Gann, an early archaeologist/adventurer in the Maya area, found a few of these griddles in southern Yucatan and Belize, but recent excavation teams have not recovered any of these items from their digging sites. Only further fieldwork will provide answers to the ongoing debate. Whether the Maya patted their ground corn into a fat cake or *pim*, or worked it into a thin tortilla, research indicates that corn breads were the staple of ancient Maya cuisine, just as they are today.

Modern breads from the Yucatan Peninsula can be divided into two principal groups: *tortillas*, thin flat cakes, or *pimes*, fat flat cakes; and *tamales*, breads enveloped in a wrapper, such as a corn husk or banana leaf.

The traditional way to begin making any of these breads is to place dried corn into a large cooking pot with plenty of water and some powdered limestone or "lime." After the corn has simmered for about an hour, it is allowed to sit, usually overnight, until it is quite soft and the outer skin of each kernel can be easily removed. This cooked corn (*k'uum*) is given four or five separate rinses to make sure that the last traces of limestone and outer skin have been cleansed away. The soft plump corn kernels are now ready to be ground.

Before the use of hand or machine grinders, corn was ground on a large flat grinding stone known as a *metate* in Mexico, or *ca'* in Yucatan. The long cylindrical stone used to crush the corn is known as the "hand of the metate" (*k'abka'*). The *ca'* rested on a special table (*payonché*) so that women did not have to kneel when grinding corn. The first grinding results in a mixture called *tse*, coarsely crushed corn kernels. The second grinding is accomplished with more force and results in *sakan* (Maya) or *nixtamal* (Nahuatl), finely crushed kernels.

The *sakan* is now ready to make into any type of bread, but as the quality of each batch of tortillas is dependent upon the fineness and delicacy of the *masa* (finely ground corn), conscientious wives repeat the grinding process once again. Tortillas may then be patted out on a broad leaf such as that of the banana tree that flourishes just outside the kitchen door. Sometimes, each of these leaves is given a light toasting before it is pressed into service, then stored in water pails near the hearth. This toasting is said to strengthen the delicate leaf fibers so that they will stand up to a morning of strenuous tortilla making. Nowadays, small pieces of waxed or plastic paper take the place of a banana leaf.

The basic word for bread in Maya is *wah*, but various definitive words are employed to distinguish differences in flavor, ingredients, form, usage, and cooking technique. For example, *petwah* is the common name for a thin tortilla cooked on a griddle. As nothing is allowed to go to waste, a leftover *petwah* is given new life and a new name, (*chu-chulwah*), when it is toasted over the coals of a hearthfire. A leftover tortilla that is set aside for several days to "age," will develop a beautiful fuzzy orange mold known as *kuxum*. Such a bread is called *kuxumiwah*, a delicacy highly revered and known for its *penisulina* (penicillin). Evidently, this mold is site specific, for I have not been able to grow orange mold on any tortillas made in Miami. My tortillas develop a green or black mold, just as a regular loaf of bread does in my kitchen.

A *pim-pim-wah*, more simply known as a *pim*, is a fat tortilla cooked on a griddle and can range anywhere from three tortillas in thickness to half an inch or so. The pim becomes a *penchuk* when cooked directly on the ashes of a fire. If a griddle were truly lacking many centuries ago, the pim might prove to be one of the earliest forms of Maya bread.

When masa is embellished with any additional ingredients, the names of these items are added to the basic word, "wah." *Bu'ul*, for instance, is the word for black beans. *Wahi-bu'ul* is a pim mixed with black beans. *Wahi-sikil* is a pim mixed with squash seeds. A favorite delicacy is *Is-wah*, a tortilla prepared at harvest time from tender, newly plucked corn, rather than the hard dried kernels shucked from older ears. Breads also derive special names that are dependent upon the time of cooking. The very first batch of tortillas made each day is the *pak'ach*. From this batch, *choko-wah* are the freshly made and piping hot tortillas offered to the husband or man of the house, who eats first. *Ok'inal'uil* are the leftover tortillas eaten by the wife and children.

Tamales, the third variety of breads, are festive fare and often require considerable time to prepare. They are reserved for holidays, holy days, or days programmed for leisure. Younger children, close relatives and friends often join in to help wrap the savory little packages and tend the hearth. An entire day is usually devoted to social activities with shared chores, and plenty of eating, drinking, and lively conversation.

Tamales consist of *masa* dough tucked into a leaf, then roasted or steamed until done. The manner of cooking depends upon the purpose of the celebration. If it is religious in nature, the *pib* or underground oven will be utilized. If the occasion is strictly social, the family hearth is employed, as well as one belonging to a neighbor. Most homes have only one hearth and, therefore, a place for only one pot. As the traditional beverage to accompany tamales is a corn porridge called *chok-osaka* (Maya) or *atole* (Nahuatl), a neighbor is often asked for assistance and the use of her fire. It is not a bad trade—the hearth lender gets to share in the tamales.

Tortillas and Tortilla Concoctions

It has been said that a Maya man relies so heavily upon his wife for making tortillas that if she should die, a replacement for her culinary expertise is sought even before the funeral is arranged and her body laid to rest. Mexican men would not even consider making their own tortillas, for they would be ridiculed and ostracized in traditional society.

Tortillas hand-patted from hand-ground *masa* are a fabulous invention, but these wonderful breads are usually available only in small villages. Larger villages and cities all have their *tortillería* where Maya women bring their freshly cooked corn to have it ground by a machine. Sometimes when in a hurry, they even purchase machine-made tortillas, a product that is similar to the packaged variety found in supermarkets throughout North America. Fresh masa is usually not available outside the Mexican community. Without access to a tortillería, one must rely upon *masa harina*, a corn flour produced by the Quaker Oats Company.

Tortillas hand-patted from fresh masa are truly an art, an art not easily mastered by the novice. Because tortillas hand-patted from commercially produced corn flour are even more difficult, I recommend the purchase of a tortilla press. The results are not the equivilent of a traditional tortilla made from fresh masa, but can pass as an excellent substitute. Quaker masa harina is available throughout the United States in regular supermarkets and specialty stores.

Tortillas are delicious alone, but they develop ambrosial qualities when doused in a pungent ground chili sauce or plunged into a wonderful soup or stew. They are the daily form of bread in Yucatan, often serving as both plate and spoon. A slightly folded tortilla provides a handy scoop for ladling ingredients from bowl to mouth, as knives and forks are still not used in remote areas. A tortilla is a delicious utensil, though not terribly dietetic or efficient. It is necessary to consume a six-inch pile of them at one sitting just to get the last flavorful morsel from the bottom of the bowl.

A soft floppy tortilla becomes a taco when it is embellished with any kind of filling. It may be folded, rolled, or served open-faced, as suits the whim of the eater. As a general rule, the wrapping may be tortillas of either corn or wheat, freshly prepared or reheated on a *comal*.

Tortillas should always be eaten hot, a characteristic that makes meals a fascinating show. Bread preparation does not begin until family and guests are seated. Tiny little cakes of masa deftly patted one at a time quickly materialize on a leaf or well-worn bit of plastic. Tortilla making is a precise art, a process requiring one hand to control the magical formation of each perfectly formed disk, the other to act as a pivot. Each golden circle is carefully placed on a hot griddle. By the time several tortillas are toasting, the first one is ready to flip, always with practiced fingertips, never a spatula. Once the second side is toasted, each bread is returned to the first side, then gingerly patted to make it bubble with air. Ready to be tucked into the hearth ashes for a final toasting, the thin layers separate and puff like a great balloon. After a quick slap between the palms, each tortilla deflates with a pop and is tossed into a waiting gourd. This sturdy gourd is known as a *lek* in Maya and serves as a surprisingly efficient pre-Conquest bun warmer.

A village homemaker must be endowed with endurance, for most adults consume at least thirty with each meal and even young children can eat a dozen. I was ecstatic to have the luxury of handmade tortillas and ate my fill of these marvelous breads until wrap-a-round skirts no longer wrapped around. After several weeks I set a quota for each meal—twenty was plenty.

BASIC CORN TORTILLAS

This basic recipe is very quick and easy to make from either fresh masa or masa harina. Strange as it may seem, the substitution of masa harina and water does not result in an exact substitution of measurements. Two cups of fresh masa equals two cups of masa harina and one cup of water.

Have on hand:

Tortilla press
2 plastic baggies or pieces of wax paper to sandwich the ball of
    masa or masa harina and keep it from sticking to the press
Griddle or heavy skillet
Basket or bowl lined with napkin or towel

Ingredients:

2 cups fresh masa,
    or
2 cups masa harina
1 cup water

Method for Fresh Masa:

Fresh masa needs no preparation or additional ingredients. Keep it moist by covering it with a damp towel.

Method for Masa Harina:

Mix the masa harina and water thoroughly.

For both masa and masa harina, have the tortilla press, baggies/wax paper, griddle or heavy skillet, and cloth-lined basket ready.

Heat the heavy skillet or griddle until a drop of water bounces from it.

Form a walnut-sized ball of dough from either the masa or masa harina. Place one baggie or piece of wax paper on the bottom section of the press. Place a ball of dough on the press just slightly above the center and top it with the second baggie. Press the handle down firmly on the press, peel off the plastic or wax paper and place the tortilla on the griddle.

Toast for approximately a minute and a half, flip and toast for about 45 seconds more. Flip the third time, pressing on the tortilla with fingers or spatula to encourage the bread to inflate. Cook on third side only about 30 seconds. Do not overcook—tortillas dry out quickly.

To Serve:
Place each tortilla in a cloth-lined basket to keep it warm and continue to cook the remaining breads.
Makes approximately 16 four-inch tortillas

CORN TORTILLA VARIATIONS

Three variations of corn tortillas are delicious and worth trying. Those made with beans and squash seeds can be traced back through the centuries. Those made with sesame seeds were introduced along with Spanish cuisine.

WAHI-SIKIL-PUS
Tortillas with Sesame Seeds

Lightly toast ½ cup sesame seeds. Add to the masa or masa harina in the basic tortilla recipe. Proceed as for regular tortillas.

WAHI-SIKIL (or WAHI-TOP)
Tortillas with Small Toasted Squash Seeds
(or Tortillas with Large Toasted Squash Seeds)

In the United States, peeled pale green pumpkin seeds are readily available. These are the ones I suggest to use in this recipe. In Yucatan, both a small and large variety of squash seed can be found in the markets. *Wahi-sikil* is the name for tortillas prepared with the small seed known as *pepita menuda*. These squash seeds are toasted and ground, peel and all. *Wahi-top* uses the large seeds, *pepita gruesa*, that are toasted, then peeled, before eating or cooking.

Lightly toast ½ cup peeled pumpkin seeds. Grind them very coarsely. Add seeds to the masa or masa harina in the basic tortilla recipe. Proceed as for regular tortillas.

WAHI-BU'UL
Tortillas with Black Beans

Add ½ cup of chopped drained black beans to the basic tortilla recipe. Proceed as for regular tortillas, but use less pressure on the tortilla press. A tortilla with beans will be thicker than a regular tortilla—in fact, it's more like a pim. Another name for *Wahi-bu'ul* is *P'ich*.

BASIC WHEAT FLOUR TORTILLAS

I am partial to wheat flour tortillas. Homemade ones are superior to the commercial variety, but there is less discrepancy between the home-made/machine made in wheat flour tortillas than in those made from corn. The difference in quality can generally be attritubed to fat—the type used, as well as the quantity. As a rule, the ratio of fat to flour in the most tasty ones is 1:4. Unfortunately, for those of us watching fat intake and calories, the tortillas that dry out and crack easily contain less fat. For anyone preferring vegetable shortening to lard, which is the traditional and most flavorful shortening, making tortillas at home allows a choice in both the type of fat and the amount used.

I often purchase flour tortillas from local restaurant supply stores, but prefer to purchase them from markets in Mexico, stuffing as many packages as space will allow into my protesting luggage. Flour tortillas freeze beautifully for several months, but there is method to madness in purchasing a smaller quantity. Then when the freezer supply runs out, one has a practical excuse for planning another trip.

For most gringos, flour tortillas take more time to make than corn, as they must be rolled, not patted or pressed into shape. When in Mexico, it is fascinating to visit a restaurant kitchen just to see the cook in action. An experienced tortilla maker can mix, form and flatten the dough in a lightning flash. Not having learned the art at mama's knee, my own tortillas will never be such poetry in motion. Thankfully, perfection of form is not essential. Even a pitifully misshapen attempt will taste just as good as a symetrical circle.

Flour tortillas keep well for several days in an airtight container in the refrigrator: for longer periods, seal tightly and freeze.

Have on hand:

    Plastic bag to keep finished tortillas hot
    Cloth-lined basket for serving
    Griddle or heavy skillet
    Rolling pin

Ingredients:

    1 pound flour, all purpose
    2 teaspoons salt
    4 ounces lard or other vegetable shortening

1 cup hot water
Flour on work surface as needed
Shortening in a saucer for greasing balls of dough

Method:
Place flour and salt in a mixing bowl. Add the lard or shortening and work it into the flour with the fingers, rubbing until the mixture has lumps the size of peas.

Add hot water and stir. When cool enough to handle, knead dough for three or four minutes. Place dough in a bowl, cover with a damp cloth and set aside for 30 minutes. This rest allows the dough to relax and become easier to handle.

Pinch off walnut-sized pieces of dough. Dip fingers into saucer of shortening and grease each ball of dough.

On a floured work surface, press each ball to flatten slightly with a rolling pin. Roll into a circle and proceed in the following manner:

Roll with the rolling pin twice, once back, once forth—then give the circle a quarter turn. Keep rolling and turning until the dough is very thin and about 7 inches in diameter.

Heat the heavy skillet or griddle until a drop of water dances when dropped upon it. Place each tortilla on the ungreased surface and cook for 30 seconds. The underside will just begin to brown. Press down any bubbles with a spatula or the fingers. Turn tortilla and cook for another 30 seconds.

As each tortilla is finished, place it in a plastic bag to keep it warm.
To reheat, lightly toast once again on the griddle.
Makes approximately 18 tortillas.

TOSTADITAS

Ingredients

3 cups Oil for frying
Tortillas, as needed

Method:
Cut tortillas into pie-shaped pieces, 4, 6, or 8, depending upon the size of the tortilla. Fry in hot oil until golden and drain on paper towels.
Tostaditas make wonderful "scoops" to be used in dips.

PAPA'SUULES
Tortillas in Squash-Seed Sauce

The name of these subtly flavored green-sauced tortillas comes from the words *papak'*, to anoint or smear, and *sul*, to soak or drench. *Papa'suules* are a complex creation made from soft corn tortillas dipped in a squash-seed sauce, filled with a slice of hard-boiled egg, covered with more squash-seed sauce, then liberally drenched in a tomato-chili salsa. One of my old Yucatecan cookbooks translates the title of this dish to mean "a dinner prepared for the Spaniards or hacienda owners." By whatever translation, Papa'suules are a wonderful lunch or dinner presentation, smooth in texture, rich in flavor.

In Yucatan, the squash seeds used for this dish are called *xt'op* (Maya), or *pepita gruesa* (Spanish). These are the large white seeds from the melon-sized, green and white *calabaza* named *xka'al*.

Many Yucatecan cooks buy their seeds in the *recado* section of the market, already skinned, toasted, and ground. *Recado de Pepita* is a beautiful pale lime-colored paste. For those with the inclination, there is a certain joy in preparing this recado at home. The seeds must be simmered in water the day before they're needed. When soft, the outer skin can be peeled away and the seeds spread out in the sun to dry. On the second day the pale green seeds are ready to be lightly toasted and ground.

In the United States, squash seeds are available with the skins removed and ready to toast.

Have on hand:

18 home-made corn or packaged tortillas

Ingredients:

1 medium onion, chopped
1 jabanero, jalapeño or other hot chili, toasted and chopped
1 or 2 cloves garlic, toasted and chopped
4 large tomatoes, toasted and chopped
3 tablespoons oil
2 sprigs epazote (optional)
6 cups water
1 pound large squash or pumpkin seeds (skins removed)
10 eggs, hard boiled and cut into slices

94

Method:

Toast and chop the onion, chili, garlic, and tomatoes. Heat the oil and sauté the onion until it is translucent. Add the chili, garlic, and tomatoes. Simmer for 30 minutes. Keep the mixture warm.

Simmer the *epazote* in 6 cups of water for 10 minutes. Set it aside.

Toast the squash seeds just until golden. While they are hot, process them to a fine grind in a blender. Add half of the epazote water (it should still be hot) to the squash seeds and stir until well blended. When cool enough to handle, mix and squeeze the seeds and water over and over again. After several minutes of "squishing" the mixture through the fingers, the seeds should release some of their oil. Spoon the oil into a small bowl and set it aside to use as a garnish. Add more of the epazote water, as necessary, to make a nice thin paste the consistency of pancake batter. Heat the sauce until hot but not simmering.

Have the tortillas warm and ready (don't let them overheat and dry out).

Have the serving plates handy.

Dip a tortilla into the squash-seed sauce and place it on a serving plate. Add several slices of hardboiled egg along the middle of the tortilla and roll it up. Place the tortilla seam side down on the plate. Prepare all of the remaining tortillas in the same manner. Spoon the rest of the squash-seed sauce on top of the tortillas.

To Serve::

Pass the bowl of squash-seed oil and tomato salsa.
Serves 6.

CODZITOS
Tiny Rolled Tacos

Codzitos take their name from the Maya *codz*, meaning "rolled," and *itos*, a Spanish term used affectionately for the diminutive. *Codzitos* are made from tortillas tightly wrapped around a spicy meat filling, fried in oil and topped with salsa and crumbly white cheese. Because I discovered the "word" *codz* before ever tasting *Codzitos*, they will always remind me of a wild jungle ride and the majestic ruins of Kabah.

I was visiting the Puuc, a hilly region south of Mérida, back in the days when a jeep was necessary for a tour of Sayil, Labná, and Kabah. The road, although it was sheer flattery to call it by such a name, was filled with holes and ruts. My driver was under the mistaken belief that at high speed his wheels would simply float over the crevices. To add to the adventure, his jeep had at some point in history lost its doors. I spent the day frantically clutching a seat and an empty door frame.

The first stop was Kabah, just off the main road to Uxmal and a lovely site to begin exploring. It was early in the day and other tourists had yet to arrive, just the atmosphere for pretending abandoned ruins are one's own. I was drawn to the intricate stonework of the temple of the Codz-Pop, the main structure at Kabah. Its facade was covered with row after row of carved cylinders, delicate yet powerful.

In Maya, *Pop* means "mat." A mat was considered a ruler or chief's symbol of office, similar one might say to a stately king and his throne. A *pop* has close associations with the jaguar and is often referred to as the jaguar mat. *Pop* is also the name of the first Maya month, represented, quite appropriately, by its patron deity, the jaguar.

My first stop back in Mérida was at Los Almendros, a restaurant well known for its typical Yucatecan dishes. It is one of the few places that offers its customers the luxury of hand-patted tortillas. A name on the menu immediately beckoned—*Codzitos*. I was surprised to have been presented with miniature cylinders from "my" temple, for neatly alined in a path across my plate were the lovely rolled mats of Kabah in miniature. They were so crisp and delicious I ate a double portion. Still filled with romantic adventure, I was certain those little *Codzitos* had been dubbed the namesake of my temple. It was not until several months later, while perusing a book on Maya language, that I came upon the real truth—my delicious new recipe and my own special temple were blessed with the same name, only because each bore the design of a rolled cylinder.

The *Codzito* is prepared much like the taco of central Mexico, rolled and fried until crisp. In Yucatan, most tacos are simply an open-faced tortilla with their filling spread enticingly across the top.

Have on Hand:

> 18 corn tortillas (packaged ones work best for this recipe)
> Wooden toothpicks

Ingredients:

> 8 ounces farmer cheese, crumbled
> 1 medium onion, chopped
> 2 tablespoons olive oil or other vegetable oil
> 2 cloves garlic, minced
> 3 large tomatoes, chopped
> 1 jabanero, jalapeño or other hot chili, chopped
> 1 inch stick cinnamon
> 4 allspice berries
> 6 cloves
> ¼ teaspoon cumin
> ½ teaspoon oregano
> ½ pound ground pork
> ½ pound ground beef
> 2 tablespoons olive oil or other vegetable oil
> ½ green pepper, chopped
> 1 medium onion, chopped
> 3 to 4 cloves garlic, minced
> 1 medium tomato, chopped
> 2 tablespoons dry sherry wine
> 2 tablespoons raisins, chopped
> 1 large pinch saffron
> 3 cups vegetable oil for frying

Method:

Sauté the onion in olive oil until it is translucent. Add the garlic, tomato and chili and simmer for 20 minutes.

Meanwhile, prepare the *Picadillo*. Place the cinnamon, allspice, cloves, comino, and oregano in a spice grinder and grind the spices to a fine powder.

Mix the ground pork and beef together and sauté the meat in olive oil until the fibers lose their raw color. Add the green pepper, onion, garlic, tomato, sherry, raisins, and saffron. Stir in the spices. Simmer the ingredients for 30 minutes taking care that mixture does not become too dry. Add more sherry or a little water if necessary, but when the *Picadillo* has finished cooking, the meat should be rather dry.

Note: If using homemade tortillas, make them while the *Picadillo* is simmering, setting each aside on a piece of waxed paper. Do not cook them on a griddle.

Place a tablespoon of meat on one side of a tortilla. Carefully roll up, jellyroll style and secure the tortilla with a toothpick. Prepare all of the tacos in the same manner.

Fry the *Codzitos* in hot oil until crisp and a deep golden color. Drain them well on paper towels.

To Serve:

Top each *Codzito* with a spoonful of salsa and a sprinkling of farmer cheese.

Serves 6.

CHILAQUILES

Chilaquiles is not a native Maya dish. Borrowed from the provinces of central Mexico, this famous chicken/tortilla/cheese concoction has been adopted with relish throughout the realm. It is a wonderful meal to prepare for a special breakfast, lunch, or dinner. Crispy tortilla strips and chicken simmer lazily in a zesty salsa. Brought to the table with a topping of sour cream and crumbly white cheese, Chilaquiles make a memorable presentation on any occasion. The recipe that follows is a special gift from Juan, the Maya cook at La Carreta who first showed me how to prepare them. His chilaquiles are moist, but not soggy, lovingly spiced and richly flavored. *Tsah bi Bu'ul* (*Frijol Colado*) or *frijoles refritos*—sieved black beans or refried beans—is an ideal accompaniment.

Ingredients:

> 12 corn tortillas, sliced in one-half inch slices
> 3 cups oil for frying
> 2 large tomatoes
> 1 large onion, chopped
> 4 slices onion, separated into rings
> 4 cloves garlic, minced
> 2 cups chicken stock
> 2 sprigs epazote
> Salt to taste
> ½ cup farmer cheese
> 2 to 3 cups cooked chicken, cut into bite-sized pieces
> 1 cup sour cream

Method:

Fry tortilla strips in oil until very crisp and medium brown. Drain and set aside.

Place the tomatoes, onion, garlic and water in a blender. Blend just until the sauce is somewhat liquified but still has chunks of vegetables.

Sauté the blended ingredients in 4 tablespoons of oil. Add the sprigs of epazote and salt to taste.

Place crisp tortillas in an empty skillet with the sauce and cooked chicken. Simmer until heated through.

To Serve:

Garnish with sliced onion and cold sour cream. Sprinkle with the farmer cheese.

Serves 4.

QUESO FUNDIDO
Cheese Fondue

This recipe is heaven on earth. It's an extremely versatile dish that is easily served as appetizer or entree, but do be forewarned if *Queso Fundido* is intended as a first course—guests may gorge themselves and have room for nothing else. This fabulous meal also has other merits: it's quick and easy to prepare, the perfect choice for a hectic day when there is no time to spend on dinner and the cook is tired.

Almost any kind of cheese can be used in an emergency, but the best combination is a selection of cheeses that string when melted. My favorite is a combination of monterey jack, muenster, mozzerella, and swiss. In Yucatan, many cooks prefer a Queso Manchego to prepare their fondue.

Have on Hand:

> *Xnipek* or other favorite salsa
> 12 tortillas, either wheat flour or corn — my choice for this recipe is the flour tortilla

Ingredients:

> 4 ounces monterey jack cheese
> 4 ounces muenster cheese
> 4 ounces mozzerella cheese
> 4 ounces Swiss cheese

Method:

Preheat the oven to 350 degrees.

Cut the cheese into ½ inch chunks and mix them together. Place the cheeses in a single shallow oven-proof dish—or individual ramekins. Bake the Queso for 20 minutes. It may brown ever so slightly, but do not let it overbake or the mixture will not be soft and stringy.

To Serve:

If using soft flour tortillas, each guest tears off a piece and uses it to pinch into a section of melted cheese. If preferred, a spoon may be used to spoon the cheese on top of the tortillas. With crisply fried tortillas, sometimes a spoon is easier. Top the queso with *Xnipek* or other salsa.

Any leftover cheese can be reheated and served in the same manner. The texture does not remain soft and pliable, but the taste is just as good.

Serves 4 to 6.

SALBUTES

Salbutes take their name from the words *sal*, meaning "light" and *but*, meaning "stuffing." As their name implies, *Salbutes* are light, slightly inflated tortillas, but their savory stuffing, at least in modern times, lies atop the tortilla. They are piquantly flavored with vinegared onions, slices of crimson tomatoes, bits of cabbage or lettuce, and a smidge of cooked chicken—roasted, then sliced or shredded. *Salbutes* can usually be found in the markets and restaurants of Yucatan. A *Salbut* is similar to a *tostada*, but the tortilla is not toasted on a *comal* before frying. It is deftly formed, then popped immediately into the hot oil to brown. There is one more difference — a small amount of wheat flour has in recent years crept into the corn mixture, adding a more delicate texture to the tortilla. Some cooks add a pinch of baking powder to their dough, but this is an even more modern addition. An exquisite example of country eating at its best, this is a dish to sample with gusto, good friends, and plenty of cold *refrescos* and beer.

I was first introduced to this famous Maya food in Kanasin, a little town on the outskirts of Mérida and on the road to Chichén Itzá. It was one of my first trips to Yucatan and I was especially interested in collecting ancient myths and legends. Alberto, a guide who led me to Kanasin, offered helpful information about the *x-tabai* (a wicked enchantress), the tiny *alux* (mischievous little pranksters), and other mythical creatures, as we munched local delicacies at La Susana, a local restaurant that specializes in regional foods.

Alberto entertained me that evening with stories of his own encounters with the *alux*. He had actually seen them, he assured me, dancing around his hammock one evening as he prepared to extinguish his campfire. Venturing into the jungle alone in search of *jabalí* (wild pigs), Alberto found no game, but encountered instead a trio of little tricksters who entertained him with their antics, then ran off with his favorite machete. Recollections such as these demonstrate that legendary *duendes* of the forest, tiny spirits of field and bush, are not frozen in some distant past, but continue to live on with vigor and vitality. In many ways, Kanasin was my gateway, not just to magnificent ruins, but to fascinating folklore and cuisine extraordinaire.

Have on Hand:

Cebollas Encurtidas, pickled onions, page 165
shredded chicken—leftover *Pollo a la Yucateca* is especially delicious
Xnipek or other favorite salsa
2 baggies or 2 pieces of wax paper
tortilla press

Ingredients:

2¾ cups fresh masa
¼ cup flour or 1¾ cups masa harina
¼ cup flour
1 cup water
3 cups oil, to deep fry
½ head lettuce or cabbage, shredded
Cebollas Encurtidas
2 large tomatoes, thinly sliced
3 cups chicken, shredded

Method:

If using fresh masa, mix the fresh masa with the flour.

If using masa harina, add it to the flour. Mix the water in well to make a dough.

Heat the oil. Place a walnut-sized bit of masa or masa harina dough between two baggies or pieces of wax paper on a tortilla press. The dough should be placed just slightly off center towards the top of the press. Press down the handle to make the tortilla, peel it from the baggie or wax paper and slide it into the hot oil. Cook the tortilla until the first side is golden brown. If the oil is hot enough, the *Salbut* should respond by puffing up beautifully. Carefully turn the tortilla with a pair of tongs and cook until golden brown on the second side. Remove the tortilla from the oil and drain it on paper towels.

Prepare the remaining breads in the same manner.

To Serve:

Garnish each *Salbut* with lettuce, *Cebollas Encurtidas*, tomato, and chicken. Offer *Xnipek* or other favorite salsa, if desired.

Makes about 16 and serves 4 to 6.

PANUCHOS
Tortillas Stuffed with Black Beans

Pan is from the Spanish word for "bread" and *uch* is a Maya term for mashed or crushed. Crispy tortillas filled with smooth black bean paste are topped with slivers of chicken, pickled onion, tomato, and lettuce or cabbage, then doused in *Xnipek*. *Panuchos* can be a great way to plan the use of leftovers, but are worth making all the necessary parts from scratch. In Yucatan, the black bean paste is tucked inside the pocket of a puffy tortilla. Some tortillas never develop this pocket and when this occurs, the beans are spread on top of, rather than within, each bread. In Campeche a variation called a *Panucho Sincronizado* is popular. A second tortilla tops the first one like a sandwich and both sides are lightly toasted.

Have on Hand:

> Shredded chicken, perhaps from *Pollo a la Yucateca*
> *Tsah bi Bu'ul (Frijol Colado)*, Enriched Black Bean Purée, page 172
> *Cebollas Encurtidas*, pickled onions, page 165
> *Xnipek* or other salsa to serve on the side

Ingredients:

> 12 corn tortillas
> ¼ cup oil
> 2 cups *Tsah bi Bu'ul (Frijol Colado)*
> 2 to 3 cups chicken, shredded
> 2 medium tomatoes, very finely sliced
> ¼ head lettuce, shredded or ¼ head cabbage, shredded
> *Cebollas Encurtidas*
> *Xnipek*

Method:

Heat the tortillas on a griddle or heavy skillet, pressing them with the fingers to get them to puff (if no pocket forms, black beans can go on top of the tortilla). If they puff, quickly slit a pocket on one side with a sharp knife.

Fill each tortilla with a spoonful of *Tsah bi Bu'ul*, pressing the filling so that it spreads across the inside. Dip the bottom of each tortilla in oil and place it on a griddle until it's sizzling hot and crispy. Top each panucho with tomatoes, lettuce or cabbage, and some *Cebollas Encurtidas*.

To Serve:

Top with *Xnipek* or any other chili salsa.

Serves 4.

Variation: Vegetarian Panuchos

When Yucatecos are in the mood for a light meatless meal, they often fill their tortillas with *Tsah bi Bu'ul* (*Frijol Colado*) and cook as in the previous recipe, but without the chicken. This vegetarian version is also a good choice for an appetizer or side dish to accompany meat.

GARNACHAS

A *Garnacha* is a messy tostada filled with thick black beans, topped with an array of crunchy fresh vegetables, and capped with a snowy dollop of sour cream. A *Garnacha* drips and makes an awful mess, but be assured that it will elicit ooh's and ah's of ecstasy with each bite.

The first *Garnachas* I ever tasted were served to me at the Ambergris Lodge, San Pedro, Belize. It was love at first bite and there is probably no other Maya food that I have prepared as much as this one. This culinary encounter happened long before my first visit to Mexico, but it whetted an appetite for more, both in the way of food and distant places. My travel for many years was strictly of the armchair variety, so I wistfully prepared *Garnachas*, dreamed, and read of other people's adventures. While flipping tortillas and stirring beans, I turned the pages and plotted future journeys. These crispy *Garnachas* were an impetus for journeying to fields afar.

Have on Hand:

> Tsah bi Bu'ul (Frijol Colado), Enriched Black Bean Purée, page 172
> *Xnipek* or other salsa to spoon on top

Ingredients:

> Oil for frying tortillas
> 12 corn tortillas
> 3 cups *Tsah bi Bu'ul (Frijol Colado)*
> ½ head lettuce, chopped
> 2 large onions, chopped
> 2 to 3 cups radishes, sliced
> 1 pound monterey jack cheese, shredded
> 2 cups sour cream
> *Xnipek*

Method::

Heat the oil in a heavy skillet. Fry the tortillas until golden brown and drain them on paper towels.

Arrange the tortillas, black beans, lettuce, onions, radishes, cheese, sour cream, and *Xnipek* in separate bowls.

To Serve:

Each person spoons black beans and a little bit of everything else onto a tortilla, then adds a topping of *Xnipek* or other salsa.

Serves 6.

TACOS DE COCHINITA

These are perhaps the best loved taco of Yucatan, eagerly devoured every day of the week, but most especially on the weekends. Many restaurants feature pork that has been cooked underground in a *pib*; patrons wait patiently in line to have their plates filled to overflowing with eight, ten, even a dozen or more of these rather substantial tacos. While driving through small towns, the smoky odor of roast pork wafts invitingly among the tiny cafes lining the roadside. Stopping for an *agua mineral, refresco,* or cold beer, I find it hard to resist the temptation. The traditional custom is to have plenty of sliced onions, liberally doused in sour orange—and of course, lots of chili, finely chopped or left whole. In the latter instance, one simply takes a large bite from time to time, a habit I've not yet been able to acquire.

The most delicious and authentic way to make these tacos is to utilize some leftover *Cochinita Pibil*. An alternate method produces excellent results when leftovers are not handy; pork chops—*Chuletas a la Yucateca*—make a very good, quick and easy substitute.

Have on Hand:

> *Cochinita Pibil*, page 244, or *Chuletas a la Yucateca*, page 250
> Assorted chili salsas

Ingredients:

> 1 large onion, sliced
> ½ cup juice from the sour orange—or lemon or lime juice
> 18 corn tortillas
> 3 cups *Cochinita Pibil* or *Chuletas a la Yucateca*, thinly sliced and
> in bite-size pieces
> 2 tablespoons oil
> 2 hot green chilies, such as a jalapeño or jabanero, chopped

Method:

Marinate the sliced onion in the sour orange juice for at least an hour. Several hours would be even better.

Have all of the ingredients ready to assemble.

Heat the tortillas on a griddle and keep them warm in a cloth-lined basket.

Heat the oil in a heavy skillet and toss in the pork pieces. Cook only until the pork is hot.

To Serve:

Place a spoonful of pork and the onion/orange mixture on each tortilla. Pass some of the chopped chili and salsa.

Serves 6.

POC CHUC
Tacos de Poc Chuc

Poc Chuk is traditionally accompanied by *Tsah bi Bu'ul* (*Frijol Colado*), or Enriched Black Bean Purée, and soft corn tortillas. When using packaged tortillas, heat them on both sides in a heavy skillet just before serving (do not let them cook enough to get crisp) and place them in a cloth-lined basket.

Ingredients:

> 2 pounds pork loin, cut into pork chops
> Salt to taste
> Pepper
> Juice of 4 sour oranges (divided)
> 1 tablespoon oil
> 2 large tomatoes
> 1 jabanero or other hot green chili
> 2 tablespoons cilantro, chopped
> 1 large onion, peeled
> 18 corn tortillas

Method:

Sprinkle the pork chops with salt and pepper to taste. Marinate the chops in half of the sour orange juice for three hours or overnight. Cook the chops on a charcoal grill or in a heavy skillet lightly coated with oil.

Toast the tomatoes and chili. Crush the tomatoes slightly. Chop the chili and add it to the tomatoes. Stir in the chopped cilantro.

Toast the onion until it is blackened. Cut it into eighths.

Pour the remaining sour orange juice into a serving bowl. Add the onion pieces.

Heat the tortillas on a griddle and place them in a cloth-lined basket.

To Serve:

Serve the pork chops with the chili/tomato (*Chiltomate*) sauce, onion, and some soft corn tortillas. It is customary to make a taco by placing a few pieces of meat into the tortilla, then adding the *Chiltomate*, some of the sour orange/onion, and *Tsah bi Bu'ul* (*Frijol Colado* or Enriched Black Bean Purée).

Serves 4 to 6.

XUX-I-CHAY
Wasp's Nest of Chaya

The name for this unusual recipe comes from *xux*, wasp's nest, and *chay*, or *chaya*. Torn bits of toasted chaya form a "nest," giving rise to the picturesque name. Spinach makes a fine substitute, but be sure to select large mature leaves that have toughened a bit. This dish has an unusual taste and texture and is a purely Maya dish that can only be encountered in the small pueblos of the countryside.

Severiana, my friend from Acabchen, introduced me to *Xux-i-chay*, but there was a small problem on the day of our luncheon. Pigs love chaya as much as the Maya, and the family sow and her nine baby piglets had devoured the chaya tree, leaves, branches, flowers, and all. Only one short scraggly stub remained, a pitiful testament to former glory. Undaunted, Severiana paid a little visit to Anita, her friend and sister-in-law who gladly gave her a bucket of leaves to feed the gringa.

I knelt at the hearth and watched with notebook in hand as Severiana used a dry griddle to give the leaves a light toasting. She crumbled the leaves slightly, then doused them in a bath of sour orange. Just before serving, she tossed the mixture with bright chunks of dried red chili, torn into tiny pieces. *Xux-i-chay* is eaten from a small bowl by dunking in torn pieces of tortilla.

After the meal we collapsed at last into our hammocks, rocking lanquidly in the lazy afternoon air. As our gauzy swings moved rhythmically, we glanced at the pigs and then at each other. We were both thinking the same thing and burst into spasms of laughter. The pigs had collapsed, right at the entrance to her front door. Both humans and animals were chaya-stuffed and ready for a serious siesta.

Ingredients:

    1 onion, chopped
    1 cup juice from the sour orange or a mixture of orange juice
        and ¼ cup lime
    36 chaya leaves or 72 large spinach leaves
    1 quart water
    1 teaspoon salt
    2 to 3 dried red chilies, toasted and torn into tiny pieces
    Salt to taste
    12 corn tortillas, freshly made or packaged

Method:

Mix the onion and sour orange juice.

Wash the chaya or spinach and remove any coarse stems. Mix the water and salt. Soak the leaves in the water for 10 minutes to add some additional flavor.

Toast the chaya or spinach until it is a very light golden brown. The toasting will occur in spots—portions of each leaf will remain green. Be careful not to burn the leaves.

Fill a soupbowl with 9 chaya or 18 spinach leaves, broken into bite-sized pieces. Add enough cold water to fill the bowl about ¾ of the way up to the top.

Prepare the tortillas from fresh masa or masa harina or heat packaged tortillas on a griddle.

To Serve:

Add some of the toasted red chili and onion/sour orange mixture. Season to taste with salt. Use pieces of tortilla as pincers to soak up the juice and pick up the bits of chaya or spinach.

Serves 4.

TAMALES

These wonderful celebration foods derive their name from the Nahuatl word *tamalli*. Like many of the names borrowed from Mexico's central highlands, tamales bear witness to the influx of foreign invaders who brought a strange language, new fruits, vegetables, and different cooking techniques to enrich the culinary repertoire of the pre-Conquest Maya. Tamale is a term favored by city dwellers and the inhabitants of larger villages, but smaller pueblos from Yucatan to Chiapas still prefer the Maya word *wah*. Maya tamales are usually enveloped in either corn husks or banana leaves, both prized for imparting their own special savour to the ingredients enclosed therein. The emerald leaves of the tropical banana seem to hold an edge over corn husks, perhaps because the ancient Maya were accustomed to wrapping their breads in a beautiful green leaf called the *bob* or *bob-che* (*Cocoloba Schiedeana*) in Maya. Still employed by the local *x-men* in agricultural ceremonies, *bob* leaves are prized for a remarkable ability to shield foods from the heat of underground ovens.

Some of the more unusual regional tamales are made with exotic leaves that are not easily encountered. In the area of Valladolid, local vendors offer *Xmakulam*, a tamale made with the leaf of a plant that bears the same name. The beautiful heart-shaped leaves are almost a foot in length and fragrant with the odor of anise. Another wonderful treat, *Ts'otobilchay*, consists of tiny fingers of masa wrapped in glossy *chaya* (*Jatropha aconi tifolia*) leaves. *Chaya* and *xmakulam* (*Piper auritum*) are delicate tropical bushes, but can be coaxed into prolific specimens wherever mild winters predominate. Both of these plants can be successfully propagated in certain parts of the United States. Although there is no substitute for *Xmakulam*, spinach serves as an acceptable stand-in for chaya.

Banana leaves and corn husks are available commercially in many specialty markets. Parchment paper or aluminum foil may be substituted for the leaves or husks in any of the recipes, however, and household string makes a quick and easy tie for the tamale packages.

The masa used in Yucatecan tamales is distinguished by a lovely pale orange color, a gift from the tiny seeds known as *achiote*. Achiote lends a subtle flavor and rich saffron hue to a melange of local specialties. Maya cooks knead the masa with enough lard so that when a bit of banana leaf is pressed into the dough, the leaf will not stick to it. The amount of fat specified in each recipe may be reduced, but the resulting product will be heavier and not as flaky and moist. Tamales encountered along the coastal regions of Quintana Roo and neighboring Belize are sometimes enhanced with the rich flavor of coconut milk. It adds a slightly nutty taste to the corn masa and evokes an island mood with its delicate perfume.

Though somewhat timeconsuming, tamales are easy and enjoyable to make. Almost everything can be prepared a day or two in advance. Only the masa needs to mixed on the same day that the tamales are cooked. As these tasty breads have a way of disappearing all too rapidly, it is worth the effort to make enough for leftovers. Because they freeze beautifully, tamales make an ideal choice for dinner parties. They are also the perfect answer for picnic and lunchbox foods. Neat, portable, and able to withstand long hours without refrigeration, they provide a delightful addition to almost any menu. Any extras may be eaten at room temperature, as the Maya do, or gently reheated in a steamer, heavy skillet, or microwave.

Tamale Preparation

There are usually four basic steps in preparing tamales:
1. Mixing the masa, or corn dough
2. Preparing the leaves, husks, parchment paper or foil wrappings and the ties from banana leaves or corn husks—or, you can use household string (some of the smaller tamales do not need to be tied)
3. Making the filling
4. Making a sauce or salsa for the topping

In Mexico, all cooks have access to masa made from freshly ground corn. As traditional masa is not available in most parts of the United States, all of the recipes in this book may be made with a masa dough mixture based upon 4 cups of masa harina and two cups of liquid, unless otherwise noted. Masa harina is made by the Quaker Oats Company and is available throughout the United States in regular supermarkets and specialty stores. Freshly ground masa is usually moist enough that it is not necessary to add additional liquid. Most localities with Mexican residents have a tortillería or Mexican restaurant where fresh masa may be purchased. It is advisable to call the restaurants a day in advance to place an order, for many of them prepare only enough for their own use.

The traditional shortening for tamales in Mexico is lard. Unfortunately, commercially available lard is rather tasteless. Home-rendered lard has a lovely smoky taste and is surprisingly easy to make. It adds a wonderful aroma to the masa and is more than worth the extra bit of trouble to make it. Solid or liquid shortening may be substituted for the lard.

Most tamales are served with a tomato or chili salsa. Experiment with the various salsa recipes to determine which ones are favorite palate pleasers. For a gala gathering, an offering of several different salsas allows guests to taste and sample. The salsas suggested in the tamale recipes present only one or two of many possibilities.

BASIC MASA PREPARATION

Masa is best when prepared on the same day that it will be needed. The amount of shortening added by most Yucatecan cooks will vary, but most use approximately 1 part shortening to 4 or 5 parts of masa. If the shortening used is vegetable oil, the amount called for in the recipe may be cut in half. Otherwise, it will be difficult to work all of the oil into the masa. Less lard or other shortening may be used, but the resulting masa will not be as light, moist and tender.

Many Maya cooks add a hot green or yellow jabanero chili, finely chopped, to their masa. It adds a lovely bite to the finished tamale. Any hot fresh chili may be substituted for the jabanero.

Ingredients using freshly ground masa:

> 4 cups (2¼ lbs.) freshly ground masa
> 1 teaspoon salt
> 1 cup lard or other shortening, very soft (or use ½ cup vegetable oil)
> 1 hot green chili, finely chopped (optional)

Ingredients using masa harina:

> 4 cups masa harina
> 1 teaspoon salt
> 1 cup lard or other shortening, very soft (or use ½ cup vegetable oil)
> 2 cups chicken broth or water
> 1 hot green chili, finely chopped (optional)

Method:

For fresh masa, place the masa and salt in a large mixing bowl. Beat the lard until it is fluffy (liquid shortening may be added directly to the masa. Work the lard into the masa. Add the chopped chili, if desired. The mixture should be well incorporated. Some Maya cooks recommend mixing the dough for as long as 10 minutes to obtain the best results.

For masa harina, place the masa harina and salt in a large mixing bowl.

116

Beat the lard or other shortening until it is fluffy (liquid shortening may be added directly to the broth). Stir in the broth and add the mixture to the masa harina. Blend the ingredients well with the fingers. Add the chopped chili, if desired, and mix it in well.

YUCATECAN MASA

Red achiote seeds are added to the basic masa recipe to impart a deep marigold glint to the dough. The ancient Maya used these seeds in their ceremonial broths and breads as a plea to the *Chacs* for rain. Achiote lends a subtle but distinct aroma to any breads and adds a striking color contrast to banana leaf wrappers.

Less lard or other shortening may be used, but the resulting masa will not be as tender.

Ingredients using freshly ground masa:

> 4 cups (2¼ lbs.) fresh masa
> 1 teaspoon salt
> 1 cup lard or other shortening(or ½ cup vegetable oil)
> 2 tablespoons achiote seeds
> 1 hot green chili, finely chopped (optional)

Ingredients using masa harina:

> 4 cups masa harina
> 1 teaspoon salt
> 1 cup lard or other shortening (or ½ cup vegetable oil)
> 2 tablespoons achiote seeds
> 2 cups chicken broth or water
> 1 hot green chili, finely chopped (optional)

Method:

For fresh masa: Place the masa and salt in a large mixing bowl. Melt the lard in a skillet. Add the 2 tablespoons of achiote seeds. Cook for five minutes on low heat, until the seeds have released their color. Strain the seeds from the lard and discard them. Let the lard cool to lukewarm and add it to the bowl of masa. Work it in well with the fingers. Add the chopped chili, if desired, and mix it in thoroughly.

For masa harina: Place the masa harina and salt in a large mixing bowl. Add the broth or water to the masa mixture. Blend the ingredients well with the fingers. Prepare the achiote seeds as stated in the step for fresh masa. When the mixture has cooled to lukewarm, add it to the bowl of masa harina. Incorporate the chopped chili into the dough, if desired.

COASTAL MAYA MASA

This masa mixture goes well with any filling and adds a tropical flavor to any menu.

Less lard or other shortening may be used, but the resulting masa will not be as light, moist and tender.

Ingredients using fresh masa:

>   4 cups (2¼ lbs.) fresh masa
>   1 teaspoon salt
>   1 cup lard or other shortening (or ½ cup vegetable oil)
>   ½ to 1 cup coconut milk
>   1 hot green chili, finely chopped (optional)

Ingredients using masa harina:

>   4 cups masa harina
>   1 teaspoon salt
>   1 cup lard or other shortening (or ½ cup vegetable oil)
>   2 cups coconut milk
>   1 hot green chili, finely chopped (optional)

Method:

For fresh masa: Place the masa and salt in a large mixing bowl. Beat the lard until it is fluffy. Stir in ½ cup of coconut milk and add the mixture to the masa. Blend the ingredients well with the fingers. If the masa still holds its shape, an additional ½ cup of coconut milk may be added. Add the chopped chili, if desired, and blend well.

For masa harina: Place the masa harina and salt in a large mixing bowl.

Beat the lard until it is fluffy. Stir in the coconut milk and add the mixture to the masa. Add the chopped chili, if desired. Blend the ingredients well with the fingers.

TAMALE PREPARATION

Tamale Wrappers

Any tamales may be wrapped in either banana leaves, corn husks, parchment paper, or aluminum foil. *Chaya* or *xmakulam* are exotic leaves that will not usually be available unless you import your own tropical tree. Corn husks, although not traditional for many of these recipes, may be substituted for any of the smaller tamales. It is possible to make any of the large tamales in miniature. As a general rule, each of the larger banana leaf tamales require 2 cups of masa, while the smaller ones utilize only ½ cup. Corn husk tamales need about ¼ cup of masa. A recipe that makes 2 large banana leaf tamales will yield approximately 16 when made with corn husks.

Using Banana Leaves

Every Maya homesite has its own supply of banana trees. The leaves are used as a wrapping for tamales, for lining cooking pots—they add a soft subtle flavor—and they often serve as a base for forming tortillas. As banana leaves are available in such abundance, they are the traditional Mayan kitchen wrap. All of the *recados* are tucked into banana leaves for storage, as are small amounts of most any ingredient that is destined for use at a later date.

A banana leaf has two sides. The glossy green side or top of the leaf is visible when the tamale is served. The masa is placed on the dull green side.

Method:

Wash the banana leaves.

Pass the leaves quickly over a flame or electric burner. The leaves will change from dusty to shiny green as they become softened. Small charred spots will not matter, but take care not to burn any holes in the leaves. However, in case of disaster, any hole can be patched with leaf scraps when the tamales are assembled.

Place the toasted banana leaf on a large flat surface. With a sharp paring knife, cut the center rib from the banana leaf. Starting at the thick end of the rib, run a sharp paring knife as close as possible to the edge

120

of the rib and follow it all the way down the leaf to the tip end. Repeat the cutting procedure on the other side. Save the ribs to prepare banana strings for tying up the tamale packages.

Cut the toasted banana leaves to proper size—if a large piece is needed, two or three smaller pieces can be overlapped and arranged together. The banana leaves may be wrapped in plastic wrap or foil and frozen for later usage if they are not needed immediately.

Preparing Banana Leaf Ties

Method:

Starting at the thick end of each rib, cut a strip about $1/16$ to $1/8$ inch wide. Continue cutting as far as possible down the length of each rib. If the strips break, tie them together. Repeat until there are enough strings to tie up all of the tamale packages.

Preparing Other Leaves

Chaya leaves may be used without any cooking. They are soft and flexible. The leaves from a *xmakulan* tree should be steamed for two or three minutes to make them more pliable. I have used them, however, by simply snipping them from the tree and giving them a quick rinse. Remove any coarse stems from either chaya or *xmakulan* before using them.

Preparing Corn Husks

Corn husks (*holoches*) may be purchased in packages, already dried. They will need to soak for about an hour in hot water to soften them.

To dry fresh corn husks, cut them from the corncob at the base with a sharp knife. Thread them onto a string and hang from a hook in the kitchen until dry. The amount of time necessary for drying will vary according to the climate. If there is no chance of rain, the process may be hastened by drying the husks in the sun. The dried husks may be stored in plastic bags for several months.

To use fresh corn husks without drying them, cut them from the corncob with a sharp knive. Place the corn husks in a pan with water to cover. Bring the husks to a simmer and cook them for about 10 minutes—until they are soft and pliable. Drain the husks well and pat them dry with a soft towel or paper towels.

To make corn husk ties, start at the top of a corn husk and make an initial cut about ¼ inch from the edge. Beginning at the initial cut, tear carefully down the entire length of the husk. Continue making additional corn husk strings in the same manner. Two short ones may be tied together. Make enough ties to wrap up all of the tamale packages.

Using Parchment Paper or Aluminum Foil

When using parchment paper or aluminum foil as a substitute for banana leaves, exotic leaves, or corn husks, simply cut the paper or foil into pieces of the appropriate size. Corn husks are usually about 8 X 10 inches. A prepared banana leaf (allowing for overlap where the rib or spine is removed) may measure about 18 X 28. Follow the instructions for banana leaves in making tamales. If the recipe is for a large tamale which calls for two overlapping banana leaves (because the leaf must have its center rib removed for cooking), the parchment paper or foil substitute remains as one single sheet. Foil is especially easy to use because the ends may be crimped or twisted just before the package is tied.

Wrapping Tamales

Tamales are easier to wrap than a simple birthday package. They are extremely forgiving—if a leaf has a hole in it, simply patch it with another bit of leaf. If the tamale has too much filling in it and begins to leak, just tuck in an extra bit of masa over the leaky area. If, in trying to get the masa to wrap around the filling and it won't wrap around, add a masa extention on one of the sides. If, after the tamale is wrapped, a new leak appears, don't worry. As the tamales cook, the masa and filling become more firm and everything seems to hold together miraculously.

To wrap tamales with banana leaves, cut the banana leaves to size if the recipe is for small tamales. If the recipe is for a large tamale, two or more banana leaves must be overlapped. Place the banana leaves, shiny side down, dull side up on the work surface.

Place the required amount of masa in the center of the leaf. Flatten the masa in the center of the leaf area, shape it into an an oval or rectangle and pat it until smooth. Place the filling in the middle of the masa, taking care to use only a small amount so that the sauce or meal will not leak out when it is wrapped.

There are two ways for a banana leaf tamale to be formed. Any variations will be noted in the individual recipes.

1. With the fingers of each hand, lift the sides of the leaf closest to you up and toward the center. This should lift the masa up toward an imaginary halfway line running horizontally across the tamale. The masa should easily pull away from the leaf if enough shortening has been added. Let the masa rest on the halfway line. Then lift the sides of the leaf farthest away from you toward this imaginary halfway line, but bring it down just a little bit further to create an overlap. Smooth the masa and press it over the filling if any leaks occur. Patch any bad leaks.

Wrap the tamale just like a package—fold the two leaves back across the horizontal line, overlapping slightly. Then fold the ends over and pick the tamale up and set it down on the folded sections. Tie the tamale with banana or household string, as if tying a package.

2. Some tamale recipes, such as *Ibewahes*, require the masa dough to be patted into a circular or tortilla shape. Place the filling in the center of the masa. Lift the sides of the banana leaf closest to you up toward the imaginary halfway line so that the tamale is folded in half. Pick up the tamale and mold it into a football shape with tapered ends. Wrap it in a banana leaf as instructed above.

To wrap tamales with exotic leaves, the first step is to arrange the leaves. *Chaya* leaves are arranged three to a tamale, their ends overlapping and pointed toward the center. Spread ¼ cup of masa in the center of the leaves. Add the filling and lift each of the sides and ends to make a package, as described above. Place the tamales seam side down in a steamer.

Xmakulam leaves are delicate and usually cooked within a banana leaf. To make small tamales, place a leaf on top of a 10-inch square piece of banana leaf and proceed as above. To make a large tamale, arrange three xmakulam leaves, stem ends pointing toward the center, in the middle of two overlapping banana leaves. Proceed as above.

To wrap corn husk tamales, place a large corn husk in the center of the work area, the longest side running right to left. Put ¼ cup of masa slightly to the right of the middle of the corn husk and spread it evenly into a circle. Spoon the filling into the center of the masa. Lift the side of the corn husk closest to you towards the center, letting it rest upon the imaginary line. Lift the opposite side towards the center, allowing it to overlap a little. Tuck in the ends and turn the package over, seam side down. Tie with corn husk string or household string, as if tying a regular package, if desired, although corn husk tamales do not need to be tied. When filling the steamer, arrange the tamales so that the side with the longest end wrapper will point toward the bottom. This way, if the shorter end of the wrapper should not hold, the filling will not leak.

To wrap tamales in parchment paper or aluminum foil, follow the instructions for wrapping banana leaf tamales. The paper or foil can be cut to size and will not need to overlap.

Cooking Tamales

In the Yucatan, any ceremonial tamales that will be dedicated to the gods must be cooked in a *pib*. These earth ovens give the breads a long slow smoldering that results in a rather firm, somewhat chewy tamale with a lovely smoky flavor. Most tamales prepared for secular occasions are steamed in a pot that rests on the three-stone hearth. Steamed tamales are soft, moist, and delicate.

There are three popular ways in which to cook tamales in a modern kitchen.

1. Tamales may be baked in a regular oven by placing them in a baking pan and covering the pan securely with aluminum foil. This method will result in a firm tamale similar to those baked in a pib.

Tamales wrapped in banana leaves are larger than corn husk tamales. They are usually placed on the rack of a baking pan and steamed, tightly covered, in the oven. If the rack fits the pan, place the tamales on top of it in a single layer. Fill the pan with approximately 1½ inches of water. The water should not touch the bottom of the rack. Place the rack of tamales on the pan and cover with a lid. If there is no lid to fit the pan, make a "lid" by covering the top very securely with aluminum foil.

If a rack does not fit the baking pan, it may be propped up with 3 or 4 overturned ovenproof cups.

2. The smaller banana leaf, exotic leaf, and corn husk tamales may also be steamed on top of the stove in a regular covered steamer. Fill the bottom part of the steamer with about 2 inches of water—but do not allow the water to reach the upper part of the steamer. If a corn or spaghetti pot is used (with a very deep steamer section) there will be room for only a little water. You will have to check the water level from time to time throughout the cooking process to make sure that the pan does not run out of water.

3. Tamales wrapped in parchment paper or aluminum foil may be cooked by any of the previously mentioned methods.

The masa dough should flake and pull away from the sides of a leaf, husk, or wrapper when it has cooked a sufficient amount of time.

TAMALES DE ESPELON

These were the first banana-wrapped tamales I ever sampled in Yucatan. They are made with a savory little bean known as the *espelon* or *peron*. It is not available in the United States, but the black-eyed pea is rather similar in appearance and flavor. The filling for this version boasts chunks of juicy pork in a spicy masa-thickened broth called *K'ol*. It is a magnificent repast. Chicken may be substituted for the pork as a variation.

Have on Hand:

> *Recado de Chilaquil*, page 61
> 1 recipe of Yucatecan Masa for Tamales, page 118
> 2 or 3 large banana leaves, prepared for baking, page 120, or
>   substitute wrappings
> Banana string ties or household string
> *Salsa Ranchera, Salsa Verde, Mojo,* or a favorite salsa

Ingredients:

> 1½ pounds pork butt
> 4 cups water
> 1 onion, toasted
> 1 bulb garlic, toasted
> 1 hot green chili, toasted
> 1 sprig *epazote*
> ¼ cup *Recado de Chilaquil*
> 2 cups *espelones* or fresh or frozen blackeyed peas
> 1 cup water
> Salt to taste
> 4 large tomatoes, chopped
> 1 cup fresh masa, or ½ cup masa harina
> 1 cup water

Method:

Place the pork in a Dutch oven with the water, onion, garlic and chili. Add the *Recado de Chilaquil* and bring the ingredients to a simmer. Cook on low heat for 45 minutes. While the meat is cooking, prepare the beans.

Place the *espelones* or black-eyed peas in a saucepan and cook until tender. Drain them well and salt to taste.

Remove the pork from the broth when it has finished cooking and let it cool; cut the meat into bite-sized pieces. Remove the chili and toasted garlic bulb from the broth and discard them. Strain the broth and return it to the pot. Remove 2 cups of broth and set it aside to let it cool.

Return the meat to the broth with the chopped tomatoes.

If using fresh masa, mix it with the reserved broth. With a whisk, stir to remove any lumps. Strain the masa/broth back into the pot and stir. If using masa harina, mix it with the water, blending well with a whisk. Strain the mixture back into the pork broth and stir it in thoroughly. Bring the ingredients to a simmer. Cook for 30 minutes, stirring frequently to keep the masa from sticking. When thoroughly cooked, the mixture should resemble a rather thin pancake batter. If the mixture does not thicken sufficiently, add a little more masa, following the preceeding instructions.

Add the *espelones* to the masa dough mixture.

Preheat the oven to 350 degrees.

Arrange a 12-inch long section of banana leaf on the work surface. Press ½ cup of masa into a circle about 1/3 inch thick. Top with some of the pork mixture. Lift each long section of the banana leaf toards the imaginary halfway line, overlapping slightly. Press the edges together to seal them. Wrap the tamale like a package and tie it with banana string or household string. Repeat the process until all of the masa has been used.

Place the tamales on the rack of a large baking pan. Fill the pan halfway with water, but do not allow the water to touch the rack or the tamales. Cover the entire pan with aluminum foil and bake for 1 hour. The tamales may also be placed ends down in a steamer and cooked on top of the stove for the same amount of time.

To Serve:

Adorn with a favorite salsa.

Serves 8.

MUKBIL POLLO

Mukbil is a Maya term for "cooked underground" and *pollo* is Spanish for "chicken." This famous tamale is a favorite for *Hanal Pixan,* Dinner of the Souls. This is a special celebration during the first week of November when the dearly departed are welcomed back to share with the living in a week of feasting and reverent celebration.

The masa used in this recipe is flavored with achiote, bits of chili, and flecked with a bean called the *espelon.* Juicy chunks of pork and chicken, slowly simmered in a enticing broth, provide the filling for this well-loved tamale. *Mukbil Pollo* is truly an exceptional meal.

My search for someone who could prepare this famous tamale launched an enduring friendship with the Peraza/Menendez family and initiated my apprenticeship at La Carreta Restaurant. While lunching at La Carreta one summer afternoon, I checked to see if *Mukbil Pollo* was on the menu. It wasn't. When I inquired if it would be possible to order it, Rommel Menendez suggested I return at 8:00 the following evening. I was beside myself with anticipation, never having tasted any tamale that was usually prepared for the palates of departed spirits.

I arrived at the appointed hour and Rommel greeted me with a bottle of red wine. "Your dinner has not yet arrived," he commented rather cryptically, and disappeared into the kitchen. It seemed a puzzling statement, but I settled contentedly back into my chair, sipped the wine, and watched strolling tourists and local residents as they passed back and forth from the *Zocalo.* No more than fifteen minutes had passed before a car pulled up to the restaurant's entrance and stopped. Three little girls piled out, each quite elegantly dressed in patent leathers and party whites. Heavily laden with baskets and carefully wrapped packages, they too, disappeared into La Carreta's kitchen. Moments later, Rommel returned to my table, this time accompanied by a steaming platter. His favorite aunt, Melva Menendez Diaz, had been called upon to gratify my quest for this ancient Maya dinner. It was a grand and lovely feast.

The following recipe for *Mukbil Pollo* has been adapted from Melba Menendez Diaz' recipe. Markets in the United States do not carry espelon, but the black-eyed pea is a good substitute. *Mukbil Pollo* is delicious served with a tossed vegetable salad or a light fruit combination such as *Xek de Naranja* or *Pico de Gallo.*

This recipe makes two large tamales. They freeze beautifully.

Have on hand:

Recado Colorado; Red Spice Paste, page 51
A double portion of Yucatecan Masa, page 118
2 banana leaves, prepared for cooking, page 120, or substitute
   wrappings
Banana leaf ties or household string
Xnipek, *Salsa Ranchera*, or other favorite salsa

Ingredients:

1 3-4 pound chicken
1 pound pork butt
12 cups water
1 onion, toasted
1 bulb garlic, toasted
1 hot green chili, toasted
1 teaspoon oregano
½ cup *Recado Colorado*, Red Spice Paste
¼ cup sour orange juice (optional)
2 large tomatoes, chopped
2½ cups fresh masa, or 1 cup masa harina
2 cups water
3 large tomatoes, very thinly sliced
2 hot green chilies, chopped
2 sprigs *epazote* (optional)

Method:

Place the chicken and pork in a large stockpot with the water, onion, garlic, chili, oregano, and recado. Bring to a simmer, cover and cook for 1 hour or more—until the meats are tender. Remove the meats from the broth and let them cool. Strain the broth and return it to the pot. Remove 2 cups of the strained broth and set it aside.

Skin and debone the chicken. Cut the pork into bite-sized chunks.

If using fresh masa, blend it with the 2 cups of strained broth. With a whisk, stir well and whisk away as many of the lumps as possible. Pour the masa mixture through a strainer back into the stockpot. If using masa harina, blend the masa harina with the water and mix it into the reserved broth. Strain the mixture back into the pot and cook for about 30 minutes, until thickened, stirring frequently. If the mixture does not thicken sufficiently, add a little more masa, following the preceeding directions. Check the seasoning.

Preheat the oven to 325 degrees.

Select two round or square casseroles, each about 10-inches in diameter. Arrange one of the prepared banana leaves with halves overlapping in the center of the casserole.

Mix one of the chopped chilies into the masa (if a chili has been used when making up the recipe of masa, this step may be omitted unless an extra chili is desired). Divide the dough into quarters. Place two banana ties or pieces of household string at right angles to one another in each of the pans (they must be long enough to wrap around the tamale). Line the baking pans with banana leaves, making sure that there is enough overlap to completely wrap the tamale. Take one piece of the masa and press it into a 10-inch round or square to fit the baking pan. Add ½ of the meat and cover it well with the thickened masa broth. Decorate the tamale with thin slices of tomato, bits of chili, and sprigs of epazote. Top with another slab of masa, flattened on the worktable, then lifted onto the tamale and fashioned into the same shape as the bottom section. Seal the edges and wrap the tamale with the banana leaves to tightly enclose the package. Tie with the banana strings or household string. Repeat with the second tamale.

Place the two *Mukbil Pollos* on the rack of a large baking pan. Pour water halfway up the sides of the pan and cover the top with aluminum foil. Bake for 1½ hours.

To Serve:

Offer extra chili, more thickened broth—and a bowl of *Xnipek, Salsa Ranchera*, or other favorite salsa.

Serves 16.

A TAMALE TRIO

The next three tamales require basically the same ingredients. The difference is mainly in size—and the type of wrapper. *Brazo de Indio* is the grandaddy of the bunch. It is big and brawny, like an Indian's arm, and can be made by anyone with regular market produce. The smaller renditions, *Tamalitos de Ts'otobilchay*, come in two versions, one wrapped in chaya and one wrapped in banana leaves. The small banana leaf *tamalito* may be prepared with either regular masa or coconut masa.

BRAZO DE INDIO
The Indian's Arm

This is a gorgeous chaya or spinach tamale, lavished with sliced hard-boiled eggs, toasted pumpkin seeds, and a zesty tomato salsa. I usually prepare the *Brazo* as an entree, but it makes a spectacular vegetable sidedish.

This recipe makes two large tamales.

Have on Hand:

> 1 recipe Basic Masa for Tamales, page 116
> 2 large banana leaves, prepared for cooking, page 120, each yielding a wrapper approximately 18" x 24", or substitute wrappings
> Banana leaf ties or household string

Ingredients:

> 3 tablespoons oil
> 2 medium onions, toasted
> 8 large tomatoes, chopped
> 1 or 2 hot green chilies, chopped
> 3 large cloves garlic, toasted
> Salt to taste
> 16 ounces fresh chaya or spinach
> 6 eggs, hardboiled and sliced
> 8 ounces pumpkin or squash seeds, toasted and ground

Method:

Heat the oil in a heavy skillet and sauté the onion until it is translucent. Add the tomatoes, chili, and garlic. Season with salt, if desired, and simmer the mixture (covered) for 30 minutes.

Carefully wash the chaya or spinach and remove all of the thick stems. Place the leaves in a cooking pot. It is not necessary to add additional water, for a sufficient amount will cling to the leaves. Cook, stirring occasionally, until the chaya is cooked — or the spinach wilted. Drain the chaya and coarsely chop it. With the fingers, mix the chopped chaya with the masa. Cover the masa with a moist towel and set it aside.

Set the hard-boiled egg slices and toasted ground pumpkin seeds nearby.

Preheat the oven to 325 degrees.

Arrange the banana leaves in the middle of the work area. Position two long leaves together, slightly overlapping. Divide the masa mixture in half and press the dough into a ½ inch thick rectangle. The banana leaf should extend about 3 inches on all sides of the flattened dough. Spread a generous portion of the pumpkin seeds down the middle of the rectangle. Add half of the slices of hardboiled egg, overlapping them slightly. Spoon on a layer of sauce, taking care to not use too much. Otherwise, when the tamale is folded, the filling will ooze out.

Starting with the long side closest to you, carefully lift the banana leaf away from you and towards the center—this will fold the tamale from one side onto the other side. The masa should pull away from the leaf and rest upon an imaginary middle line that runs the length of the tamale. Repeat with the other half of the leaf, the side furthest away. Allow the masa to overlap slightly so that the filling is completely sealed and covered.

Carefully fold the banana leaf, as if for a package. Patch with extra pieces of leaf, if necessary. Tie up the tamale with banana strings. Prepare the second tamale in the same way.

Place the tamales on a rack in a baking pan. Fill the pan halfway with water and cover the top of the pan with aluminum foil. Bake for 2 hours.

To Serve:

Open the *Brazo de Indio* at the table. Slice the tamale and serve it with extra helpings of toasted pumpkin seeds and chili/tomato salsa.

Each tamale serves 4 to 6.

TAMALITOS DE TS'OTOBILCHAY I
Small Chaya Tamales

Ts'otobilchay is a tiny tamale or tamalito of masa filled with toasted pumpkin seeds and wrapped in chaya leaves. It is served with chopped egg, more toasted pumpkin seeds and a chili/tomato salsa. Some Maya cooks chop the chaya, blend it into the masa, and cook the package in a banana leaf, as in *Tamalitos de Tsotobilchay II*. Whether the chaya is mixed or wrapped, the flavor is very much the same—spectacular. In the absence of chaya, spinach serves beautifully, but follow the instructions in *Tamalitos de Ts'otobilchay II*.

I was introduced to *Tamalitos de Ts'otobilchay*, at the Hacienda Uxmal, my favorite watering hole and home base when exploring the ruins of Uxmal and the rolling Puuc region south of Mérida. Uxmal, that magnificent jewel in a jungle setting, is the abandoned city of a powerful family bearing the name of Xiu. Uxmal, meaning "thrice built," once was a grand metropolis that joined with the formidable powers of Chichén Itzá and Mayapan to form a triumvirate known as the Triple Alliance of Mayapan.

I owe this recipe to the courtesy of Alfredo, a waiter who worked at the Hacienda. He lives in the neighboring hamlet of Santa Elena, a picturesque little village snuggly nestled in the gently sloping hills of the Puuc. When he learned of my fascination with chaya, Alfredo stopped off to make the necessary purchases at a local market, then directed the Hacienda's staff in the preparation of a platter of these tiny tamales. His masterpiece was a colorful presentation of small green chaya fingers accompanied by bowls of ground toasted pumpkin seeds, tomato salsa, chopped chili, and slices of hard boiled eggs to be heaped on as a topping. Alfredo added a gift of several chaya cuttings from the family tree, giving careful instructions for their planting and care.

Note: A chaya leaf is not large enough to make a tamale, but by overlapping three of them it is possible to make a small, tidy, finger-shaped package that is entirely edible.

Have on hand:

1 Basic Masa for Tamales, page 116
72 large chaya leaves

Ingredients:

> 3 tablespoons oil
> 2 medium onions, toasted
> 8 large tomatoes, chopped
> 1 or 2 hot green chilies, chopped
> 3 large cloves garlic, toasted
> Salt to taste
> 6 eggs, hardboiled and chopped
> 8 ounces pumpkin or squash seeds, toasted and ground

Method:

Heat the oil in a heavy skillet and sauté the onion until it is translucent. Add the tomatoes, chili, and garlic. Season with salt, if desired, and simmer the mixture (covered) for 30 minutes.

Pat the masa into a rather thick patty or use a press lined with plastic wrap or baggies to make a tortilla. Do not press down hard—the tortilla should be rather fat. Sprinkle toasted and ground pumpkin seeds across the middle of the tortilla. Beginning at one end, roll the patty or tortilla into a tamalito like a jelly roll and place it in the center of two or three overlapped chaya leaves. If the tortilla is hand pressed and rather large (about 6 inches), then three chaya leaves will be needed. If the tortilla is rather small because it is pressed from a tortilla press (about 4 inches), two leaves will be sufficient. Wrap the tamales like a package and set them aside, seam side down. It is not necessary to tie these breads with string. Continue making all of the remaining breads in the same fashion.

Place the tamalitos in a steamer and cook them for one hour.

To Serve:

Arrange some chopped hard-boiled eggs, toasted pumpkin seeds, and chili/tomato salsa in separate serving bowls. Spoon some of each on top of the tamalitos.

Makes about 3 to 4 dozen tamalitos, and serves 10 to 12.

TAMALITOS DE TS'OTOBILCHAY II

These luscious little bits of bread may be made with Basic Masa for Tamales or Coastal Masa for Tamales. The coastal or coconut version is favored along the turquoise waters of southern Quintana Roo and Belize.

Have on hand:

> 1 recipe Basic Masa for Tamales, page 116, or Coastal Masa for
> Tamales, page 119
> 3 banana leaves, prepared for cooking, page 120, cut into 8-inch
> squares, or substitute wrappings

Ingredients:

> 3 tablespoons oil
> 2 medium onions, toasted
> 8 large tomatoes, chopped
> 1 or 2 hot green chilies, chopped
> 3 large cloves garlic, toasted
> Salt to taste
> 1 pound chaya or spinach
> 6 eggs, hardboiled and chopped
> 8 ounces pumpkin or squash seeds, toasted and ground

Method:

Heat the oil in a heavy skillet and sauté the onion until it is translucent. Add the tomatoes, chili, and garlic. Season with salt, if desired, and simmer the mixture (covered) for 30 minutes.

Carefully wash the chaya or spinach and remove all of the thick stems. Place the leaves in a cooking pot. It is not necessary to add additional water for a sufficient amount will cling to the leaves. Cook stirring occasionally until the chaya is tender—or the spinach wilted. Drain the chaya (spinach) and coarsely chop it. With the fingers mix the chopped chaya (spinach) into the masa.

Shape the masa into tiny cylinders and roll them in banana leaf wrappers. Tuck in the ends and set them aside on their seam. The tamalitos are small and don't need to be tied with string. Place the tamalitos, ends pointing downward, in a steamer and cook them for one hour.

To Serve:

Arrange some chopped hard-boiled eggs, toasted ground pumpkin seeds, and chili/tomato salsa in separate serving bowls. Spoon some of each on top of the tamalitos.

Makes about 3 dozen tamalitos, and serves 10 to 12.

CHAY-WAH
Chaya Bread

Chaya is one of the Maya's favorite vegetables. It yields its bounty of leaves throughout the year and appears on their table in numerous manifestations. A variation of the preceeding recipe omits the hard-boiled eggs and toasted pumpkin seeds. Add 1½ cups of drained black beans to the chaya/masa mixture. Form the dough into fat little tortillas or *pimes*, using ½ cup of masa for each of them. Wrap the breads in banana leaves cut into 8 x 10 inch pieces and bake or steam them for 1 hour. Serve the Chay-wah topped with the chili/tomato salsa.

BU'ULIWAH
Black Bean Tamales

These little black bean tamales are traditionally cooked in a pib—underground oven—and offered to the gods during a *Primicia*. This is an annual rite of forest and field when the Maya proffer their thanks for the first black beans that are harvested from the milpas. I love these smoky breads when they emerge from their long smoldering in the earth oven, but any kind of steamer or baking pan will do. Try them with any of the tomato or chili salsas.

Have on Hand:

Ts'anchak b i Bu'ul, Yucatecan Black Beans, page 171
1 recipe Basic Masa for Tamales, page 116
2 banana leaves, prepared for cooking, or substitute
Banana leaf ties or household string
Salsa Ranchera, Xnipek, or other salsa

Ingredients:

2 cups *Ts'anchak bi Bu'ul,* Yucatecan Black Beans, drained

Method::
Mix the drained black beans into the masa with the fingers.
Place a banana leaf section, ribbed or top side down, on a work surface.
Form ½ cup of masa into a ball, then pat it into a football shape. Fold the banana leaf around the masa, as though wrapping a package. Tie the package securely with banana strings. Make the remaining breads in the same manner.
Place all of the tamales in a steamer or on the rack of a baking pan. Fill the steamer or baking pan with about an inch or two of water—water should not touch the breads. Cover the steamer or baking pan and bake for 1 hour.

To Serve:
Serve with *Salsa Ranchera, Xnipek,* or other chili salsa.
Serves 6 to 8.

TAMALES DE ESPECIE

One lovely spring weekend I explored the streets and bustling market of Bolonchen and had a fascinating conversation with several of the ladies in the central market. I questioned them about their favorite tamales and found that *Tamales de Especie* were a starred attraction in this region. These delicate little masa breads, filled with a spicy picadillo, tomato salsa, and sliced hardboiled eggs, are served anytime of year, but especially at Easter. This recipe is a compilation of the several versions I collected from the Maya matrons.

Have on Hand:

> 1 recipe Basic Masa for Tamales, page 116
> 2 or 3 large banana leaves, prepared for cooking, page 120, cut
> into 24 eight-inch squares, or substitute wrappings

Ingredients:

> 3 tablespoons oil
> 1 onion, chopped
> 3 cloves garlic, chopped
> 1 hot green chili, chopped
> 6 large tomatoes, chopped
> 1 pound pork, ground
> 2 cloves garlic, chopped
> 1 onion, chopped
> 1 tomato, chopped
> 2 tablespoons capers
> ¼ cup raisins
> 1 teaspoon oregano
> Salt and pepper to taste
> 4 cups chicken stock or water
> 3 hard boiled eggs, sliced

Method:

Heat the oil in a heavy skillet. Sauté the onion until it is translucent. Add the garlic and chili. Sauté for a few moments more. Add the chopped tomatoes and simmer, covered for 30 minutes.

Brown the pork in a skillet and add the garlic and onion. Sauté for five minutes and add the tomato, capers, raisins, oregano, and salt and pepper. Cover and cook on low heat for 15-20 minutes. The mixture should be quite dry, but check to make sure that it does not stick.

Place the fresh masa dough or masa harina dough in a mixing bowl and add 1 quart of chicken stock, whisking to make sure there are no lumps. Sieve the masa into a saucepan and cook over medium heat until thick. Stir frequently to keep the masa from sticking.

Place about ¼ cup of masa on a banana leaf, add a spoonful of pork and top with some tomato salsa. Add 2 slices of hard-boiled egg on top. Fold the leaf to make a package, but the tamale will not be steamed, so it does not have to be tied. Prepare all of the tamales in the same manner and arrange them on a platter.

The K'ol has been cooked and the tamales are now ready to serve at room temperature. If you wish to serve them hot, they may be placed on a heavy skillet or griddle and warmed over a very low heat.

To Serve:
Serve with extra salsa.
Serves 10.

IBEWAHES
Lima Bean Breads

These are delicious little breads, filled with lima beans and toasted ground squash seeds, then adorned with a sauce of tomatoes, onions, and chili. Football shaped and steamed in banana leaves, they are lovely vegetarian tamales that look just as beautiful on a banquet table as in a lunchbox. Eulogia Chay Uk, of Acabchen, prepared these lima-bean tamales for me. She worked with the deft fingers of an artist, fashioning each tamale with careful practiced pats. I volunteered my services to help. Although everyone laughed, my tamales didn't look too bad, even though somewhat misshapen. They are certainly much easier to form than tortillas and are such fun to unwrap.

Have on hand:

> 1 recipe of *Toksel*, page 37
> 1 recipe of Basic Masa for Tamales, page 116
> 2 or 3 large banana leaves, prepared for cooking, page 120,
>   12 pieces, 12 x 12 inches, or substitute wrappings
> Banana string ties or household string
> *Salsa Verde, Salsa Ranchera, Xnipek,* or other favorite salsa

Method:

Preheat the oven to 350 degrees.

Place a prepared banana leaf on a work surface. Pat ½ cup of the masa mixture into a "tortilla" or *pim* 5 or 6 inches in diameter and ½ inch thick. Mound 2 tablespoons of *Toksel* in the center of the tortilla, fold the tortilla in half and seal it around the edges. Pat the masa into a football shape, fat in the middle and pointed at the ends. Fold the banana leaf around it like a package and tie it securely with string.

Arrange the *Ibewahes* on the rack of a baking pan. Fill the pan about halfway with water, but do not allow the water to touch the rack or the tamales. Cover the pan with a lid or aluminum foil and bake for 1 hour. The tamales may also be cooked in a steamer for the same length of time.

To Serve:

Accompany with a tomato or chili salsa.
Serves 6 to 8.

TAMALES COLADOS A LA JAVIER LUNA
Quivering Pork and Chicken Tamales

Whenever I return to Mérida, my friend and mentor at La Carreta, Javier Luna, always prepares these fabulous tamales especially for me. He knows they are on my list of favorite Yucatecan foods and likes to watch me stuff myself silly. Their name is an indication of the technique that contributes to their unusual texture; the masa is first sieved, then slowly simmered, before being placed in the banana leaf. It emerges as a light, quivering mass, almost translucent in appearance. It is possible to find *Tamales Colados* in the central market and a few typical restaurants near the Zocalo, but Javier's recipe is unsurpassed.

Have on Hand:

> 1 recipe *Recado Colorado*, Red Spice Paste, page 51
> 1 recipe Basic Masa for Tamales (for the tamales) plus 1 cup
> fresh masa or ½ cup masa harina (for the *k'ol*)
> 3 large banana leaves, prepared for cooking, page 120, cut into
>   16 pieces, 10- by 10-inches, or substitute wrappings
> *Xnipek* or other salsa

Ingredients:

> 1 chicken
> 1 pound pork
> 10 cups water
> 1 onion, toasted
> 1 bulb garlic, toasted
> 1 teaspoon oregano
> 1 sprig epazote (optional)
> 1 recipe masa for tamales
> 1 quart water
> 1 sprig epazote (optional)
> 1 cup lard or shortening
> 3 tablespoons oil
> 1 onion, chopped
> 3 cloves garlic, chopped
> ½ teaspoon oregano
> 3 large tomatoes, chopped

2 sprigs epazote (optional)
2 tablespoons *Recado Colorado*
1 cup fresh masa or ½ cup masa harina
1 cup water
Salt and pepper to taste
3 tablespoons oil
2 large tomatoes, sliced
1 onion, sliced and separated into rings
Epazote (optional)

Method:

Place the chicken and pork in a stockpot with 10 cups of water. Add the onion, garlic, oregano, and epazote. Bring the water to a simmer and cook for an hour, or until the meats are very tender. Remove them from the broth and let them cool. Skin and bone the chicken. Shred the pork. Set the meats aside.

Mix the fresh masa or masa harina dough with 1 quart of water. Stir the mixture well and pass it through a sieve into another bowl. Pour the masa through 2 layers of cheesecloth and into a heavy Dutch oven. Add a sprig of epazote. Add the lard or shortening a little bit at a time and cook over low heat, stirring frequently, for 20 to 25 minutes—until the mixture pulls away from the sides of the pan.

Heat the oil in a heavy skillet. Sauté the onion until it is translucent. Add the garlic, oregano, tomato, epazote and *Recado Colorado*. Sauté for 5 more minutes.

Stir the fresh masa or masa harina into the water. Use a whisk to stir out any of the lumps and sieve it into the vegetable mixture. Add salt and pepper to taste. Add the 3 cups of reserved broth from the meats. Simmer until thick. Let the mixture cool.

Preheat the oven to 325 degrees.

Place a 10 x 10-inch piece of banana leaf in the center of a work area. Put several spoonsful of masa in the center of the leaf. Add some chicken and pork, a few rings of onion, a slice of tomato, and a sprig of epazote. Add some of the sauce. Fold the tamales as if wrapping a package and tie with some string. Make them fat, tight, and somewhat squared.

Place on the rack of a large baking pan and fill the pan half full with water. Form a cover for the tamales with aluminum foil and bake for 1½ hours.

To Serve:

Tamales Colados are delicious with any salsa, but my favorite is *Xnipek*. *Serves 6 to 8.*

TO'BIHOLOCH

To'obil means "that which is wrapped" and *holoches* are corn husks. Corn husk tamales are more difficult to find in the Yucatan than those wrapped in banana leaves. These little packages are filled with a tantalizing mixture of spicy pork simmered in a corn-thickened broth (*K'ol*). The bright red tomatoes make a lovely color accent against the achiote-tinted masa.

Have on Hand:

> *Recado Colorado*, Red Spice Paste, page 51
> 1¼ recipe Yucatecan Masa for Tamales, page 118 (1 recipe for the tamales, ¼ recipe for the *K'ol*).
> 24 corn husks, prepared for cooking, page 121, or substitute wrappings
> Corn husk strings or household string
> *Salsa Ranchera*, *Xnipek*, or other favorite salsa

Ingredients:

> 1½ pounds pork loin, boneless
> 6 cups water
> 3 tablespoons *Recado Colorado*, Red Spice Paste
> 1 onion, toasted
> 1 hot green chili, toasted
> 1 bulb garlic, toasted
> 1 teaspoon oregano
> 2 sprigs epazote
> 4 large tomatoes, toasted, peeled and chopped
> 1 cup fresh masa or ½ cup masa harina
> 1 cup water

Method:

Place the pork slices in a large saucepan with the water, *Recado Colorado*, toasted onion, chili, garlic, and oregano. Bring the meat to a boil and reduce the heat to a simmer. Cover the pan and cook the pork until it is fully cooked and tender—about 1 hour. Remove the pork from the broth, let it cool and cut the meat into tiny pieces. Strain the broth and set aside two cups of it. Return the remaining broth to the saucepan.

Prepare a nice thick *K'ol* to flavor the tamales. Add the epazote and chopped tomatoes to the reserved broth in the saucepan. Bring the mixture to a simmer. Mix one cup of the reserved broth with the fresh masa or the masa harina mixed with water. Stir until the mixture is well blended. Slowly add the remaining one cup of broth, whisking the mixture to remove any lumps. When the broth/masa is smooth, add it to the liquid and vegetables in the saucepan, stirring until the mixture thickens. Add the pork pieces to the saucepan and continue to cook for 30 minutes on very low heat, stirring on occasion to keep the *K'ol* from sticking.

Meanwhile, ready the masa and corn husks. Form little elongated—about 2 inches—patties with the masa, no more than ¼ inch thick. Place each patty in the middle of a large corn husk, or—if the husks are small, piece together several smaller ones. Add a tablespoon of *K'ol* in the center of the masa rectangle and close it carefully to seal in the liquid. Wrap the tamale like a package and tie it with corn husk strings or household string. Continue forming all of the tamales in the same manner.

Place the tamales in a steamer, ends pointing up and down. Add water to the steamer (do not allow the water to touch the tamales), top with a cover and cook the tamales for 1 hour. The tamales may also be cooked on the rack of a large baking pan. Add water halfway up the sides of the pan and cover the tamales with foil, sealing the pan securely so that the tamales will not dry out. Bake at 325 degrees for 1 hour.

To Serve:

Serve with extra *K'ol* and plenty of salsa.

Serves 6 to 8.

TAMAL DE HOLOCH
Tamale With Corn Husks

Tamales made with corn husks—*holoch*—are great fun to make. This is a lovely vegetarian tamale that may be eaten as an entree or vegetable dish. As I am such an afficionado of *Toksel*, with its toasted lima beans and pumpkin seeds, this little tamale is often the star attraction on my dinner plate. A *Tamal de Holoch* is similar to the *Ibewah*, but is wrapped in a layer of fragrant corn husks, rather than banana leaves.

Have on Hand:

> 1 recipe *Toksel*, Toasted Lima Beans and Pumpkin Seeds, page 37
> 1 recipe Masa for Tamales, page 116
> Corn husks, prepared for tamales, page 121, 24 large ones, or
> substitute wrappings
> *Salsa Ranchera, Salsa Verde*, or other favorite salsa

Method:

Place one large corn husk on the work table in front of you. Spread a heaping tablespoon of masa on the middle of the husk, extending it in all directions, but not to the edges. Leave about ½-inch of margin. Add a rounded teaspoon of *Toksel* to the center of the masa and fold the corn husk like a package. Tie it securely with corn husk string or household string. Prepare the remaining tamales in the same manner.

Arrange the tamales in a steamer, ends pointing up and down. Add water to the steamer, top with a cover and cook the tamales for 1 hour. The tamales may also be cooked on the rack of a large baking pan. Add water halfway up the sides of the pan and cover the tamales with foil, sealing the pan securely so that the tamales do not dry out.

Bake at 325 degrees for one hour.

To Serve:

Serve with plenty of a favorite salsa.
Serves 6 to 8.

VEGETABLES AND SALADS

Doña Eulogia harvesting chaya.

VEGETABLES

I am always dazzled by the incredible artistry of a Mexican market. All of the fruits and vegetables are meticulously arranged, as if each were posing for a still life. Radishes are never just tossed into a bucket, but tucked oh so carefully into a neat little nosegay. Strings of garlic are tightly braided and lovingly displayed, like well-coifed children sporting their party manners. Mounds of varicolored root vegetables form tight little pyramids and bouquets of herbs and spices nestle against a background of leaves. Nothing is ever tossed haphazardly, but deftly placed with a creative eye.

Mexican produce is offered in such an astounding profusion of shapes and colors that it is easy to be seduced. Squash may be so small that it sits upon the palm of one's hand (*mehen ku'um*), or large enough to resemble a Halloween pumpkin (*ku'um*). While living in Mexico it is so easy to eat like a vegetarian. There are few other places where one can find such a magnificent variety of ingredients and cooking techniques. In rural areas, the Maya diet is based almost exclusively upon the diverse abundance one finds in the plant kingdom. One of my favorite pastimes is to amble through a Yucatecan market with a pen and notepad in one hand and a market tote in the other. When something new and intriguing catches my fancy, I have to stop and wangle an introduction to the strange commodity. Maya vendors love questions and are eager to discuss their wares and how to use them. They are delighted to see someone ecstatic over the beauty of a chayote or jícama and never fail to offer a favorite recipe.

Fortunately, for budding botanists, most vegetables may be brought safely back into the United States—only fruits are on the forbidden list. Such a generous policy on the part of the U.S. Customs Department makes it possible to return home with a cache of beans, roots and seeds to plant in one's own garden for future tasting and sampling.

TS'ANCHAK BI CHAY
Chaya Simmered in a Light Broth

Almost every Maya homestead has at least one chaya tree. The plant is more like a large bush than a tree and is so happy in tropical climates it can overtake a yard. Bishop Diego de Landa observed:

> They have a little tree with soft branches and which holds a great deal of milk, the leaves of which are eaten cooked and are like cabbages to eat, and good with much fat bacon. The Indians plant it at once wherever they are going to stay and during the whole year it has leaves to gather.

Other ancient texts reveal that the Maya employed chaya as a medicine almost as much as a food source. Whether food or medicine, chaya lends itself to a multitude of preparation techniques. The following recipe is an extremely simple one that goes well with meat, fowl, or fish. Served ala carte with a basket of tortillas, it makes a light vegetarian meal for luncheon or supper enjoyment. Because chaya is usually unavailable in the United States, spinach may be substituted.

Have on Hand:

Freshly made or packaged tortillas

Ingredients:

1 pound chaya or spinach, chopped
2 cups water
2 dried red chili peppers, toasted and chopped
¼ cup pumpkin or squash seeds, toasted and coarsely ground
2 limes

Method:

Cook the chaya or spinach in a small amount of water. Chaya cooks in about 25 minutes. Spinach will be tender in five minutes or less.

Toast the chilies on a griddle or heavy skillet and grind them in a spice grinder. Set them aside.

Toast the pumpkin or squash seeds until golden brown. Grind them in a spice grinder. Set them aside.

Cut the limes into quarters. Arrange chili, pumpkin seeds, and limes in condiment bowls.

To Serve:

Serve these tender greens with a sprinkling of chili, pumpkin seeds, and a squeeze of lime. They may be removed from the cooking liquid and served as a vegetable, or left in the broth and served as a soup.

Serves 4. (Spinach may serve only 3, for it has less volume than chaya.)

TS'ANCHAK BI K'UM
Pumpkin or Squash Cooked in a Light Broth

It is difficult to find anything more delicious than a freshly picked winter squash, still tinged with dew from the fields. The Maya often cook it quite simply, with only water, then add garnishes such as lime, toasted squash seeds and chili at meal time. I love to eat it, as they do, with plenty of hot tortillas.

Have on Hand:

Hot freshly made or packaged tortillas

Ingredients:

4 pounds pumpkin or winter squash, cut into 2-inch pieces
10 cups water
salt to taste
2 dried chili peppers, toasted and chopped
¼ cup pumpkin or squash seeds, toasted and coarsely ground
2 limes

Method:

Place the squash pieces in a large saucepan or Dutch oven with the water. Bring the water to a simmer, cover and cook until the pumpkin is quite tender when pierced with a fork—approximately one hour. Season with salt.

Toast the chilies on a griddle or heavy skillet and grind them in a spice grinder. Set them aside.

Toast the pumpkin or squash seeds until golden brown. Grind them in a spice grinder. Set them aside.

Cut the limes into quarters. Arrange the chili, pumpkin seeds, and limes in small serving bowls.

To Serve:

Place the pumpkin in a dish with some of the broth—pasta plates work perfectly in this recipe. Each portion is garnished with a sprinkling of chili, some pumpkin seeds, and a squeeze of lime.

Serves 8.

KUM YACH'
Mashed Pumpkin

Yach' is the Maya word for something that is mashed or kneaded. This is a refreshing vegetable dish, spicy, colorful and fragrant with the aroma of cilantro.

Ingredients:

> 3 pounds pumpkin or winter squash, cut into 2-inch pieces
> 6 cups water
> Salt to taste
> ¼ cup cilantro, chopped
> 1 or 2 hot green chilies, such as the jabanero or jalapeño, chopped
> ¼ cup juice from the sour orange, or lime or lemon juice

Method:

Place the pumpkin pieces in a large saucepan with the water and salt. Bring to a boil and simmer for about 1½ hours, until very tender. Drain the pumpkin, peel it and mash it with a fork.

Mix the cilantro, chilies, and sour orange juice and add it to the mashed pumpkin. Stir all ingredients to blend well.

To Serve:

Garnish with a few sprigs of cilantro.
Serves 6 to 8.

TON LUCH
Dulce de Calabaza con Maiz Tierno
(Sweet Squash and Corn)

My friend, Javier Luna, manager of La Carreta, introduced me to this beautiful Maya vegetable combination. The calabaza utilized in this recipe is called *Ts'ol*, a rather small green squash that is usually eaten while young and tender. The flavor is mild and delicate. New corn, also fresh from the harvest, simmers along with the squash. Javier showed me how to hold a knife between the rows of corn to *desgrana*—or lift the kernels of corn from the cob. With a little wiggling motion, it is possible to lift out the first row or two. This little hollowed out part is called a *camino*—a road. Once the *camino* has been forged, a knife can easily be inserted to lift out the remaining kernels of corn. The corn should not just be sliced off the cob unless one has reached the limits of one's patience.

Have on Hand:

Pimes or freshly made or packaged tortillas

Ingredients:

3 ears corn on the cob
3 pounds small tender winter squash, cut into 2-inch pieces
1 cup water
1 to 2 tablespoons sugar

Method:

Place the ears of corn and squash pieces in a saucepan with the water. Cover the vegetables and simmer them for about an hour.

Drain the vegetables and let them cool. Insert a knife length wise between two rows of corn kernels. Press down with the knife and wiggle it until a row of kernels dislodge. After this *camino* has been made, it is possible to remove the remaining kernels with the fingers.

Add the sugar to the calabaza and corn kernels and blend well.

To Serve:

Serve as a vegetable side dish or light entree with tortillas or *pimes*.
Serves 8.

CHULIBU'UL
New Corn and Vegetable Medley

This is a lovely harvest meal that blends new corn, new beans and new tomatoes. It is a delicious melange that can be enjoyed for only a few weeks in late September and October when *milpas* give birth to their early autumn crops. This is another one of Javier Luna's pre-Hispanic recipes.

Most of us have access to only dried black beans, rather than the "new" ones called for in the recipe. They must be cooked for much longer and the results will not be exactly the same. The meal will be outstanding, nonetheless.

Have on Hand:

Dried red chili, chopped green chili, or chili salsa

Ingredients:

1 pound tender black beans (if using dried black beans, soak them overnight or bring them to a simmer for 10 minutes and let them sit for 1 hour before continuing with the recipe)
8 cups water
1 sprig epazote
4 tablespoons oil
1 large onion
2 large tomatoes
12 ounces fresh corn kernels
Salt and pepper to taste
½ cup pumpkin or squash seeds, toasted and ground

Method:

Wash the beans and place them in a large saucepan with 8 cups of water and a sprig of epazote. Cover them and simmer until they are tender — about 1 hour. (Simmer for about 3 hours, if using dried black beans)

Heat the oil in a heavy skillet and sauté the onion until it is translucent. Add the tomatoes and simmer for two or three minutes. Add the onion/tomato mixture to the beans. Cook until there is very little liquid left in the pan.

Place the corn in a hand grinder, blender or food processor and purée. Press the purée through a sieve into the beans. Simmer until the

Chulibu'ul is thick, stirring frequently so that the corn does not stick. Season with salt and pepper, if desired.

To Serve:

Garnish with a sprinkling of toasted pumpkin seeds and some dried chili or a chili salsa.

Serves 6.

BUDÍN DE CHAYOTE
Chayote Pudding

This delicious recipe is wonderful served warm or cold and is one of those dishes that everyone seems to devour. It makes such a spectacular presentation at the table that I find it a perfect company dish—but don't wait for special guests to try it. The *budín* will make any dinner special. It may be prepared a day in advance, thus freeing the chef for other activities.

My version of this recipe is a little unusual. In Yucatan, the *budín* is either cooked in chayote shells—or the shells are dispensed with and the budín is cooked in a baking dish. When I was first experimenting with the presentation of this dish, most of the chayote shells maddeningly disintegrated. It was Christmas and the entire family had gathered for a feast that seemed destined for disaster. I decided to combine the two methods by using a shallow round baking dish and arranging the chayote shells, spoke fashion, with their tapered ends touching the edge of the dish. When the soft chayote budín was poured into the baking dish, the shells peeked out of the filling like a beautiful flower.

Ingredients:

> 6 chayote squash
> 2 cups flour
> 1 cup sugar
> 6 eggs, beaten
> 1 stick butter, melted and cooled
> ¼ cup cream

Method:

Place the chayotes in a Dutch oven or saucepan, cover with water and cook for approximately one hour, or until they can easily be pierced with a fork. Drain the chayotes and allow them to cool.

Split each chayote and remove the pulp from each half. Save 6 of the prettiest of the chayote shells and set them aside. Chop the chayote pulp. With your hands, pick up the pulp and squeeze some of the liquid from it. Place the pulp in a large mixing bowl.

Mix the chayote with flour and sugar. Add the beaten eggs, melted butter, and cream.

Grease and flour a baking dish—a round one about 12" in diameter.

Pour all but 2 cups of the chayote mixture into the baking dish. Arrange the chayote shells, spoke fashion, on top of the *budín*. Fill the shells with the reserved chayote mixture.

Bake at 350 degrees for about 35 to 40 minutes, or until firm.

To Serve:

Serve hot or cold.

Serves 8 to 10.

CHOCHO
Baked Chayote

Chayote is known as *chocho* in the southern part of the Yucatan Peninsula, particularly in Belize. This recipe makes a rich casserole of brilliant colors. It's substantial enough to serve as a vegetarian main course or will blend well with almost any fowl, meat, or seafood entree.

To save time, the chayotes may be cooked early in the day or even the day before they will be needed. Once they have been simmered and cooled, the recipe is very easy to prepare and assemble.

Ingredients:

> 3 large chayotes
> Water, as needed
> ½ teaspoon salt (optional)
> 2 tablespoons oil
> 1 onion, chopped
> 2 cloves garlic, diced
> 3 tomatoes, cut into eighths
> 1 green pepper, chopped
> 4 ounces Swiss cheese, grated
> 4 ounces muenster cheese, grated

Method:

Place the chayotes in a saucepan with enough water to cover them. Add the salt and bring the water to a boil. Cover the pan and simmer the vegetables for about 1 hour, or until tender. Drain the chayotes and let them cool.

Peel the chayotes and cut them in half. Remove the seeds and any hard pithy parts. Cut each squash into ½-inch strips.

Preheat the oven to 375 degrees.

Heat the oil in a heavy skillet. Sauté the onion until it is translucent. Add the garlic and sauté for 2 or 3 minutes more. Add the tomatoes and green pepper. Cook for another 5 minutes.

Transfer the vegetable mixture to a baking dish. Sprinkle the grated cheese on top, cover, and bake the chayote for 30 minutes. Remove the cover and bake for another 15 minutes, or until cheese is bubbly and golden brown.

Serves 6 to 8.

FRIJOLES REFRITOS
Refried Beans

Frijoles Refritos is a popular way to use up any leftover *Tsah bi Bu'ul*, Puréed Black Beans. This thick bean paste is usually served with a garnish of crumbled white cheese, *Xnipek* or other hot chili salsa, and an assortment of *Tostaditas* to use as scoops.

The following recipe is not precise, for the necessary amount of lard or oil is left to the cook's discretion. Lard, of course, imparts a heavenly smoky taste to the beans, and the more lard one uses, the tastier the beans. Unfortunately, the more flavorful the beans, the higher the calories.

Have on Hand:

> *Tsah bi Bu'ul (Frijol Colado)*, Enriched Black Bean Purée, page 172
> *Tostaditas, Fried Tortilla Triangles*, made with 8 tortillas, page 93
> Chili or a favorite salsa, such as *Xnipek*
> ¼ cup or more lard or shortening
> 3 cups *Tsah bi Bu'ul* — Enriched Black Bean Purée
> ½ cup Farmer cheese, crumbled

Method:

Heat the oil in a heavy skillet and add the *Tsah bi Bu'ul*. Cook until the beans are thoroughly heated.

To Serve:

Garnish the *Frijoles Refritos* with some crumbled farmer cheese and *Tostaditas*. Serve with a bowl of *Xnipek*, dried chili, or chopped chili on the side.

Serves 4 to 6.

TSI BU'UL
Fancy Black Beans

Frijol Colado, the famous thick sieved black beans of Yucatan, can be found at almost every family meal and are exquisite in their simplicity. *Tsi Bu'ul* starts out with this famous dish, then adds a dressing of tomatoes, chilies, onions and crispy tortilla strips. It is an ingenious way to spruce up any leftovers.

Have on Hand:

> 1 recipe of *Tsah bi Bu'ul (Frijol Colado)*, Enriched Black Bean
> Purée, page 172

Ingredients:

> 3 tablespoons oil
> 1 onion, chopped
> 3 large tomatoes, chopped
> 1 hot green chili, such as the jabanero or jalapeño, chopped
> 10 corn tortillas, cut into strips
> 3 cups oil
> 1 recipe *Tsah bi Bu'ul*

Method:

Heat the 3 tablespoons of oil in a heavy skillet and sauté the onions until translucent. Add the tomatoes and green chili. Cook for another 15 minutes, stirring occasionally.

Heat the 3 cups of oil in a small skillet and fry the tortilla strips until golden brown and crispy. Drain the strips well on paper towels and set them aside.

Heat the *Tsah bi Bu'ul* until steaming.

To Serve:

Serve the *Tsah bi Bu'ul*, sauteed tomatoes and tortilla strips in separate bowls. Each person takes a serving of the frijoles and transforms them into *Tsi Bu'ul* by adding some of the tomato mixture and a handful of tortilla strips.

Serves 8 to 10.

RICE AND BEANS

The coastal Maya wax ecstatic over a simple meal of rice and beans, subtly enriched with the goodness of fresh coconut. A regional passion, this is a lovely menu choice for adding a tropical flavor to any entree of fish or meat. Steve Maestre, who owns *The Villa*, in Belize City, provided the instructions for preparing this famous dish.

Have on Hand:

Coconut Milk, page 276

Ingredients:

12 ounces dried red kidney beans, rinsed and cleaned
8 cups water
4 ounces salt pork or bacon, cut into small pieces
3 cloves garlic, chopped
Salt to taste
Black pepper, freshly ground to taste
2 cups Coconut Milk
1 large onion, sliced
2 cups white rice, rinsed

Method:

Soak the beans overnight in the 4 cups of water — or bring the beans and water to a boil. Let the beans boil for 10 minutes, cover them and turn off the heat. When the beans have steeped for 1 hour, they are ready to use.

Bring the beans to a simmer, cover them and cook until almost tender and still whole, about 2 hours. Do not let them cook to a broken mush. Add the salt pork, garlic, salt, pepper, *Coconut Milk* and onion. There should be about 4 cups of liquid in the pot. If not, add a little extra water.

Add the rice and cook very gently until the rice has cooked and the beans are tender. Check the seasonings.

Serves 8 to 10.

ENSALADAS
(*Salads*)

*I*n all of the years of traveling in Yucatan, I have never really encountered what I would consider a "salad." When I think of a salad, I think of a large bowl of mixed greens or a small to mid-sized bowl of some sort of vegetable or fruit concoction—maybe even something exciting served on a lettuce leaf.

Most of what I would label as a salad really classifies as a garnish in Yucatan. A magnificent platter of tacos, tamales, or meats might have a spoonful of guacamole or sliced avocado to add color, some fruit to add savour, or a small mound of vinegared lettuce, cucumber and tomato to serve as a garland for the main event. The farther one moves from the city, the less one is apt to encounter a crisp vegetable or fruit served to the side of something else. As a simple matter of custom and habit, most vegetables are cooked and used as a stuffing for a tortilla.

For example, in Acabchen there are several beautiful trees with cucumber-like appendages hanging from them. The villagers call the fruit *pepino cat* and it looks and tastes very much like a cucumber. I remembered reading that the ancient Maya had eaten these "cucumbers" raw and on one of those days when I hungered for something crunchy, asked my friend Alberta Chay Uk how this Mayan vegetable was usually prepared. She replied that the *pepino cat* was always heavily candied with honey as a dessert. I asked if anyone had ever tried to eat it raw. She looked at me rather strangely, but proceeded to pick a supply of *pepinos* for an experiment. The children brought out some chili and lime and I coached the entire family in a tasting session. Everyone looked at me as if I had been deranged by the hot tropical sun as they dutifullly munched away on my recipe suggestion. The gringa's salad has had no lasting effect. To this day, the only way that *pepino cat* is prepared in Acabchen is as a sweet dessert and a true salad is still a rarity in Yucatan.

ENSALADA DE AGUACATE
Avocado Salad

This is a delicious salad that is a wonderful treat when avocados are in season. Offered in small portions, this ensalada makes an artistic edible garnish.

The avocados that grow in my backyard in Florida are enormous, although their flavor is somewhat mild. The California avocados, as well as those grown in Mexico, are not quite as watery and have a more nutty aroma. They are also much smaller in size. Depending upon the variety available, substitute two or three of the smaller ones for the type grown in the "Sunshine State."

Ingredients:

       1 large avocado, cut into strips
       1 medium onion, sliced and separated
       4 dried red chilies, ground
       2 limes

Method:

Place the avocado strips on a platter or individual serving dish. Add the sliced onion rings. Add the dried red chili, to taste. Squeeze plenty of lime juice over the top.

Serves 4 to 6.

XEK' BI NARANJA
A Mixture of Stirred Up Things

I love to serve this colorful concoction as a salad or garnish. It is particularly beautiful when presented on a dark green leaf such as chaya, but only those living in tropical regions will have access to this Yucatecan vegetable. Avocado leaves, escarole, or romaine may be substituted. When oranges are in bloom, I add a few flowers as a garnish.

Severiana Tamay introduced me to this recipe, making use of the abundant sour oranges in Akabchen. I was aghast watching her prepare the chilies, for she tore each one into bits, rather than chopping it and the pieces appeared to be huge. I was sure my tastebuds would be destroyed after one bite, for the local chili, *chili seco*, is quite hot. Surprisingly, the fire did not singe, but because each variety of chili is different, experiment with a very small amount, then add more if necessary.

Ingredients:

> 10 oranges, preferably sour oranges, but sweet ones may be used
> 4 heaping tablespoons sugar (with sweet oranges, 3 heaping teaspoons of sugar—or to taste)
> 1 to 3 small dried red chilies, ground or finely chopped

Method::

Peel the skin from the oranges and cut the pulp into sections. Remove the seeds and place the oranges in a serving bowl.

Add the sugar and chopped chili. Mix all of the ingredients well and chill them in the refrigerator.

Serves 8.

Variation: XEK' BI NARANJA Y JÍCAMA (A Mixture of Oranges and Jícama)

One small peeled and julienned jícama may be added to six oranges for a variation.

CEBOLLAS ENCURTIDAS
Pickled Onions

These marvelous onions are not a salad in themselves, but they do serve as a salad-type garnish for practically everything. Maya cooks reach for a handful of these crunchy onion slices on a daily basis. Toss a handful onto a serving of meat, a sandwich, a taco, or a vegetable. There is hardly anything, save desserts, that don't benefit from their tangy flavor. They will keep for several weeks in the refrigerator, but a supply will probably not last that long. If red onions are unavailable, add a touch of beet juice to the vinegar to get the appropriate color.

Ingredients:

> 2 large red onions, sliced
> Boiling water to cover
> White vinegar, as needed
> Water, as needed
> 1 teaspoon oregano
> 5 cloves garlic, toasted

Method:

Slice the onions and place them in a heatproof bowl. Add enough boiling water to cover them. Let the mixture steep for one minute. Drain the onions and rinse them well with cold water.

Place the onions in a glass jar. Fill the container halfway with vinegar, then fill the remainder of the container with water. Add the oregano and toasted garlic. Set the onions aside for three days to marinate in the refrigerator.

Makes about 1 quart of pickled onions.

SOUPS AND STEWS

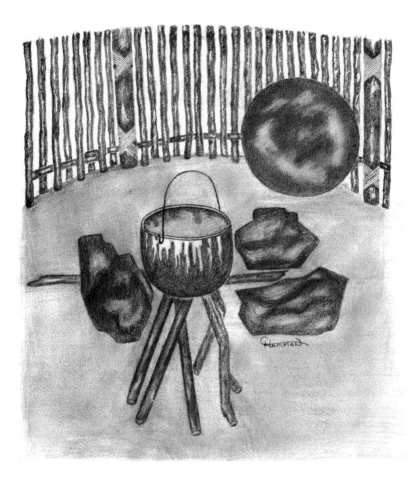

A Maya hearth and stewpot.

They prepare stews of vegetables and flesh of deer and of
wild and tame birds, of which there are great numbers,
and of fish of which there are large numbers.
—Diego de Landa, *Landa's Relacion de las Cosas de Yucatan*

*T*he soups and stews of Yucatan are glorious creations that may
contain only a single vegetable—or they may appear to be filled with
the contents of an entire village market. The Maya have evolved a
one-pot cuisine that elevates an ordinary soup or stew to a creative
work of art. The simmering broth might have a simple focus, a main
ingredient with a few condiments, as in the case of a *ts'anchak*. With the
addition of a little lard or other shortening to enrich the flavor, the
results are known as *tsahbil*. Other typical stews might be a *k'ol*, broth
thickened with freshly ground masa. Toasted dried red chilies, carefully rinsed and ground to a fine paste produce a *chilmole*, a beautiful
fire-blackened sauce that is mixed with beans or some type of meat.
Toasted squash seeds, finely ground and mixed with herbs and spices
make an *onsikil* (Maya) or *pipian* (Spanish), another rich stew that
simmers with whatever produce or meat that the forest or field has to
offer.

Daily provisions in a thatched Maya hut often revolve around some
form of simmered legume or vegetable and, of course, a mountainous
stack of toasty tortillas. A fiesta day or holy day calls for some form of
stewed or roasted animal. A simple fiesta celebration requires only a
chicken or turkey, but if the occasion is a momentous one, an entire pig
may be called upon to feed the whole village. In such a case, the single
stewpot gives way to enormous washtubs and the family hearth gives
way to an underground oven.

Sometimes it is difficult to categorize a rural Maya recipe as either a
vegetable, meat or soup. Most of the meals are simmered with a
seasoned liquid in a pot and served in a bowl to be eaten as a sort of
"taco" with tortillas holding a bit of the meat or vegetable—and at the
same time, scooping up the cooking broth. Even in the city, a Maya cook
will sometimes remove the vegetable from the broth, serve it separately
on a plate, and offer the liquid, with its accompaniments, as a soup. For
instance, a Yucatecan *puchero* calls for a stockpot filled to the brim with
beef, chicken, pork, an assortment of vegetables and both rice and

spaghetti. After the ingredients have happily simmered until tender, they are removed from the cooking liquid and arranged on a platter. The rich broth is then offered as a soup, temptingly garnished with a selection of crunchy condiments. Such an elaborate concoction is both meat, vegetable, salad and soup.

TS'ANCHAK
To Cook in a Light Broth

Ts'anchak is one of the principal cooking techniques that the Maya have utilized throughout the centuries. Sometimes the word is abbreviated to a simple chak, but by either name the definition is the same—to cook in water with a few condiments. It is easy one-pot cooking that is truly elegant in its simplicity. While living in Acabchen, I found that any embellishments added to the stockpot with the main ingredient would vary according to what is on hand. If *Ts'anchak bi Bu'ul* is on the menu, an early morning trip to the milpa may yield some dried chili to toss in with the black beans. An onion and a bit of garlic from the family garden may provide more flavor enhancement. Some juice from a tart sour orange plucked from a forest tree or a squeeze of lime gathered from a well-tended courtyard sometimes adds a piquant zest. If little else is available, at least a handful of salt is tossed into the pot to keep the beans from getting lonely.

Each of the following *ts'anchak* recipes is served with a squeeze of sour orange or lime juice and a bit of fresh or dried chili. Bowls of freshly chopped onion and radish add extra crunch and interest. If fresh cilantro is available, it adds a refreshingly cool tang.

TS'ANCHAK BI BU'UL
Yucatecan Black Beans

This hearthrite was my mainstay while living in Yucatan. I often enjoyed a bowl with my morning eggs and coffee, served with a stack of tortillas to dip into a salsa of ground red chilies. Sometimes there was a thick fried egg *torta* to accompany it. To this day, such a combination is my favorite breakfast. At mid-day, there was always plenty of lime and chopped onion to spoon into the beans and another pile of hot tortillas to serve as a spoon. If a kitchen garden was thriving, then a bright green jabanero added a bite to everything.

Have on Hand:

> Freshly made or packaged tortillas
> Onion, chopped
> Radishes, sliced
> Limes, halved
> Hot green chilies, chopped, or dried red chilies, ground

Ingredients:

> 22 ounces black beans, dried
> 12 cups water
> 1 or 2 hot green chilies, toasted
> 1 large onion, toasted
> 2 bulbs garlic, toasted
> Salt to taste

Method:

Wash the beans well; remove any pieces of dirt or stone. Place the beans in a large stockpot, add the water and soak overnight. Or, bring the beans and water to a boil, simmer for 10 minutes, cover and turn off the heat. Let the beans sit for one hour.

Add the toasted vegetables. Simmer the beans for three hours, or until they are tender. Add salt, if desired, after the beans have finished cooking.

Remove the garlic bulbs and chilies.

To Serve:

Ladle the beans and broth into a soup bowl. Offer the condiments in small containers and pass a basket of hot tortillas.

Variation: TS'ANCHAK DE LENTEJAS (Yucatecan Lentils)

Substitute lentils for the black beans in the above recipe.
Variation: TS'ANCHAK BI IB (Yucatecan Lima Beans)
Substitute lima beans for the black beans in the above recipe.

TSAHBIL
To Cook in an Enriched Broth

Tsahbil is a cooking technique employed by the Maya that enriches the flavor of the basic recipe with the use of lard or some other form of shortening. It is a method often used for flavoring soups, vegetables, and stews that contain little or no meat.

TSAH BI BU'UL (Frijol Colado)
Enriched Black Bean Purée

When served as a main dish, this thick black bean soup needs only some chopped onion, chili of choice, a squeeze of lime, and a stack of hot tortillas. It is a heavenly rich stew, thick, creamy and smoky in flavor. If there are by chance any leftovers, they take on new life when prepared as *Frijoles Refritos*, refried beans. Because beans freeze well, it may be worthwhile to make more than needed. There is hardly a Yucatecan meal that cannot benefit from a steaming bowl of thick black beans.

Have on Hand:

> Chopped onion
> Chopped radish
> Chili or chili salsa to use as a condiment
> Lime wedges
> Tortillas, freshly made or packaged

Ingredients:

> 22 ounces black beans, dried
> 12 cups water
> 1 hot green chili, toasted
> 1 bulb garlic, toasted
> ½ cup lard or oil
> 1 onion, toasted and chopped
> Salt to taste

4 limes, halved, or 2 sour oranges
2 hot green chilies, chopped or 6 dried red chilies, ground

Method:
Wash the beans well and remove any pieces of dirt or stone. Place the beans in a large saucepan, add water and soak them overnight. Or, bring the beans and water to a boil, simmer them for 10 minutes, cover and turn off the heat. Let the beans steep for one hour.

Add the toasted chili and garlic bulb. Simmer for two hours; additional water may be needed, as the beans must be covered with liquid.

Heat the lard or oil in a heavy skillet. Sauté the onion until it is translucent. Add the onion/oil mixture to the beans. Continue cooking for about an hour, or until the beans are done. Add salt, if desired.

Remove the garlic bulb and chili.

Place the beans in a blender or food processor and blend them to a purée. If the beans are to be served as a soup, the mixture should be thin. If the beans are to be served as a vegetable or refried, they may be thicker.

If the beans are too thick, add more water. If they are too thin, cook on low heat for a while longer, taking care to see that the mixture does not stick.

To Serve:
Serve with any or all of the suggested accompaniments.
Serves 8.
Variation: TSAH BI IB (Enriched Lima Bean Purée)
Until I went to live in Acabchen, I never associated lima beans with the Maya. Surprisingly, there are times when the lima bean is more easily found than the black bean when one travels throughout the countryside. The scarcity or abundance of a particular item is strictly a matter of what survives the vagaries of the weather in a *compesino's* vegetable patch.

This soup is especially pretty when garnished with bright red radishes and a dash of red chili. Cook in the same manner as *Tsah bi Bu'ul*, but substitute lima beans for black beans in the recipe.
Variation: TSAH BI LENTEJAS (Enriched Lentil Purée)
Lentils are a very popular legume in Yucatan. In the name for this dish, the preparation technique—*Tsah*—is Maya, while the principal ingredient is named in Spanish. The lentil is a post-Conquest product, and is so noted because there is no Maya word for it.

Substitute lentils for the black beans in *Tsah bi Bu'ul*.

K'OL BI BU'UL
Black Beans in a Thickened Corn Sauce

The Maya use corn for almost everything. Even when cooking a stew of other ingredients, they often use fresh masa for flavoring and thickening the cooking liquid. Such a corn enriched sauce is called *k'ol*, a lovely aromatic sauce that accompanies a variety of vegetables, meats and tamales.

This recipe comes from the town of Tinum, not far from Valladolid, courtesy of Patricio Najera Mis. Patricio's *k'ol* is flavored with two recados, *Recado Colorado* and *Recado de Puchero*. It is a magnificent feast, heavy in onion, garlic and spices.

Have on Hand:

¼ recipe *Recado Colorado*, Red Spice Paste, page 51
¼ recipe *Recado de Puchero*, page 60

Ingredients:

22 ounces black beans, dried
12 cups water
¼ recipe *Recado Colorado*
¼ recipe Recado de Puchero
1 cup pumpkin seeds, toasted and finely ground
2 cups water
3 cups fresh masa or 1 cup masa harina
2 cups water
2 large tomatoes, chopped

Method:

Rinse the black beans and remove any bits of dirt and stone. Soak the black beans in water overnight. Or, bring the beans to a simmer and allow them to cook for 10 minutes. Turn off the heat and allow them to sit for one hour. Add the two recados to the water and cook the beans for about 2½ hours.

Add the ground pumpkin seeds to 1 cup of water and pour the mixture through a sieve into the cooking pot. Mix the bits of seeds that did not pass through the sieve into the remaining cup of water. Pour them through the sieve and into the cooking pot. Any seeds that remain trapped in the sieve may be thrown away.

174

Mix the masa or masa harina with the water, stirring well with a whisk. Pour the masa and water into the cooking pot and mix the ingredients well. Add the chopped tomatoes and continue to cook the ingredients for another 30 to 45 minutes, until the beans are quite soft and the *k'ol* has thickened to the consistency of a thin pancake batter. The *k'ol* must be frequently stirred to keep it from sticking.

To Serve::
Serve with a stack of hot toasty tortillas to use as a scoop.
Serves 8.
Variation: K'OL BI IB (Lima Beans in a Thickened Corn Sauce)
Follow the directions for K'ol bi Bu'ul, but substitute dried lima beans for the black beans in the preceding recipe.
Variation: K'OL BI CHAY (Chaya in a Thickened Corn Sauce)
Follow the directions for K'ol bi Bu'ul, but substitute a 3 quart bowl of chaya leaves for the black beans (or 2 pounds of spinach). Simmer the chaya or spinach for only 10 minutes before proceding with the remaining instructions.

ONSIKIL BI BU'UL
Toasted Squash Seeds and Beans

If squash seeds are in abundance, this hearthrite is often a dietary mainstay. The Maya garnish their *Onsikil bi Bu'ul* with green *ciruelas*, tiny plums that add flavor and texture to the soup. Olives do not have a similar taste, but the color and flavor both seem to accomplish the same thing—offer a contrast and some zip. If the recado for *onsikil* is prepared ahead of time, this mouthwatering stew is almost effortless to make. A 12 quart stockpot is an appropriate size for this generous meal.

Have on Hand:

Hot freshly made or packaged corn tortillas

Ingredients:

22 ounces dried black beans, washed and sorted
10 cups water
1 large onion, toasted
1 bulb garlic, toasted
16 ounces squash seeds, toasted and finely ground
8 cloves garlic, toasted
1 tablespoon oregano
1 tablespoon black peppercorns
2 cloves
1-inch stick cinnamon
$^1/_3$ cup achiote
4 cups water
3 cups fresh masa or 1¼ cup masa harina
2 cups water
1 cup green *ciruelas* or green olives (not with pimentos)

Method:

Soak the beans overnight or place the beans in the stockpot with the water and bring the pot to a boil. Reduce the heat and simmer for ten minutes. Turn off the heat and let the beans sit for one hour. Bring the beans back up to a simmer and add the toasted onion and garlic. The skins do not need to be removed from the toasted vegetables.

Toast the squash seeds and grind them as finely as possible. Sieve the ground seeds with 4 cups of water. Sieve the remaining seeds (those trapped in the sieve) with 2 cups of water. Repeat once again with 1 cup of water. Any bits of seed that do not come through the sieve on the third try, throw away.

Prepare the recado by toasting the garlic cloves. Throw away the blackened garlic papers and purée the garlic in a blender.

Grind the oregano, black pepper, cloves, and cinnamon in a spice grinder. Add the ground spices to the garlic and process the mixture well.

When the beans have simmered for two hours, add the recado to the pot.

Crush the achiote slightly. Add two cups of water to the achiote, and mix it thoroughly with the fingers, coaxing the red color from the seeds. Pour the mixture through a sieve and into the beanpot. Repeat the process with two more cups of water. Repeat the process a third time with 1 cup of water. Throw the crushed achiote seeds away.

Mix the fresh masa or masa harina with the two cups of water. Pour it through a sieve and into the beanpot. Cook the beans for one more hour, stirring occasionally to keep the masa from sticking. About 20 minutes before the *Onsikil* is finished, add the green *ciruelas* or olives.

To Serve:

Eat with hot floppy tortillas as a soup spoon. Be careful if the olives have pits.

Serves 10.

SOPA DE CALABAZA
Pumpkin or Squash Soup

This is a lovely soup with a delicate flavor and color that is a delight to behold. *Sopa de Calabaza* comes from the recipe files of my friend, Fernando Huertas. It is an excellent choice as a first course for a heavily spiced menu. To serve as an entree for luncheon or dinner enjoyment, add some crusty French bread or a bean-studded *pim* and a bowl of fresh, colorful fruit.

Ingredients:

> 4 pounds pumpkin or winter squash, young and tender, peeled and cut into 2-inch pieces
> Water to cover, as needed
> Salt and freshly ground black pepper to taste
> 2 cups cream
> ¼ cup cilantro or parsley, chopped

Method:

Place the pumpkin or winter squash in a large saucepan with enough water to cover it. Add salt and pepper to taste. Bring the broth to a simmer, cover and cook for 1½ hours.

Transfer the contents of the saucepan to a food processor or blender. Blend until smooth. Return the puréed pumpkin or squash to the saucepan.

Add the cream and bring the soup to a simmer. Cook gently for five minutes and turn off the heat. Check the seasoning. Stir in the cilantro or regular parsley.

To Serve:

Garnish with additional cilantro or parsley.
Serves 8.

CALDILLO DE K'UM
A Light Broth of Pumpkin and Spices

Winter squash and sweet spices go so well hand in hand. This is a versatile dish that may serve as a vegetable or a soup, depending on the needs of the occasion. The Maya love to simmer a large pot of this on their three-stone hearth in late autumn, the season for squash, toasted squash seeds, and brilliant saffron squash blossoms. This *caldillo*, when prepared with other types of Maya squash, changes its name, depending upon the variety used. *Caldillo de K'um* is made with an orange-colored squash that resembles a small pumpkin. *Caldillo de Xka'* uses a green squash with white stripes, the size of a small cantaloupe. *Caldillo de Ts'ol* utilizes an emerald squash with tiny cream-colored speckles.

Have on Hand:
> ½ recipe of *Recado Colorado*, Red Spice Paste, page 51
> Ground dried red chili, chopped green chili, or a favorite chili salsa

Ingredients:
> 4 pounds pumpkin or winter squash, young and tender, cut into
>   2-inch pieces
> 10 cups water
> ½ recipe *Recado Colorado*
> Salt to taste

Method:
Place the pumpkin pieces in a large saucepan with sufficient water to cover.

Add the recado to the pumpkin and water. Stir well. Cover, bring to a simmer, and cook for 1 and ½ hours, or until the pumpkin is very tender. Season with salt, if desired.

To Serve:
Place some of the pumpkin in a bowl. Ladle the seasoned broth on top of it. Garnish with dried red chili or chopped green chili, if desired. The squash in this recipe is not peeled and the skin may be eaten if it is tender enough. Otherwise, it may be eaten with a spoon, leaving the skin behind.

Serves 8.

CALDILLO DE IBES
Lima Beans Cooked in a Light Broth

I adore this soup. It is a meal in itself, so substantial that nothing else is necessary. Some salad or fruit might complement it quite nicely, but I always stuff myself so full of the soup that there is room for nothing else. In spite of my huge appetite, there are always leftovers and *Caldillo de Ibes* improves as it ages.

I owe Lucas and Severiana of Acabchen many thank you's for introducing me to this thick rich stew. Whenever I prepare it I remember the warmth of their hearth and hospitality. Even if I had just finished eating a meal in someone else's home, they would insist on my partaking of at least a small bowl from their daily stewpot. I always shared a few bits of the accompanying tortillas with Mis, the family cat.

Have on Hand:
> ¼ cup or more, *Recado Colorado*, Red Spice Paste, page 51
> Corn tortillas, either freshly made or packaged

Ingredients:
> 1 pound lima beans, dried
> 10 cups water
> 1 large onion, chopped
> 2 tablespoons lard or oil
> ¼ cup *Recado Colorado* or Red Spice Paste
> 2 sweet potatoes, cut into 1-inch pieces
> 6 ounces fideos or spaghetti

Method:
Soak the lima beans and water overnight in a large stockpot. Or, bring lima beans to a boil in the water and let them simmer for ten minutes. Turn off the heat, cover the pot, and allow the beans to steep for an hour.

Sauté the onion in the 2 tablespoons of shortening and add it to the stockpot. Add the *Recado Colorado* to taste and simmer until the limas are tender, about three hours. Add the salt and check the seasoning.

Add the sweet potatoes and cook another half hour.

Add the fideos and cook the pasta al dente.

To Serve:
Serve the soup with a basket of hot tortillas.
Serves 8 to 10.

CALDILLO DE LENTEJAS
A Light Spicy Broth with Lentils

Caldillo de Lentejas is slightly different from the preceding recipes because it does not contain any recado—and it does contain meat. Alberta Chay Uk prepared this wonderful stew for me one evening after the family had made a monthly trip to the market in Valladolid, an excursion that is looked forward to with much excitement and enthusiasm.

We celebrated Alberta and Pablo's return to Acabchen with lentil stew, store bought French bread and avocados. Even the family parrot was invited to join us in the hearty feast.

Ingredients:

> 22 ounces lentils, dried
> 12 cups water
> 2 large onions, chopped
> 1 head garlic, toasted and peeled
> Salt to taste
> 1 tablespoon black pepper, freshly ground
> 2 pounds pork loin, cut into 2-inch pieces
> 6 ounces fideos or spaghetti

Method:

Rinse the lentils and remove any bits of stone and dirt. Soak them overnight in the water. Or, bring the lentils to boil in the water and let them simmer for 10 minutes. Turn off the heat and let them sit for one hour. Add the onions, garlic, salt and black pepper to the stewpot. Simmer for one and one-half hours.

Add the pork to the stewpot and simmer for one more hour. Check to see that the lentils and pork are tender and well seasoned.

Add the fideos or spaghetti to the stewpot and cook according to package directions.

Serves 8 to 10.

POTAGE DE FRIJOL
Bean and Vegetable Stew with Pork and Chorizos

The *potages* of Yucatan are mouth watering. This particular version is filled with pork, rosy pinto beans and a melange of colorful vegetables. One of the lucky bonuses of preparing this meal is leftovers, for it makes plenty. Fortunately, I have a touch of Maya in my soul and enjoy eating whatever is in the stewpot for breakfast, lunch and dinner, until every last morsel has vanished.

Have on Hand:

> Freshly made tortillas or the packaged variety
> Chili or chili salsa of choice
> *Recado Colorado*, Red Spice Paste, page 51

Ingredients:

> 12 ounces dried pinto beans
> 4 quarts water
> 3 pounds pork loin, with some bone
> 1 large onion, toasted
> 1 large bulb garlic, toasted
> 1 green pepper, toasted
> 4 slices bacon, cut into 1-inch pieces
> 2 chorizos, sliced
> 1 large onion, chopped
> 1 large green pepper, chopped
> 2 large tomatoes, chopped
> ¼ recipe *Recado Colorado*, Red Spice Paste
> 2 large potatoes, cut into 1-inch pieces
> ½ small cabbage, thickly sliced
> Salt to taste

Method:

Wash the pinto beans, removing any bits of rock or dirt. Soak them overnight in 4 quarts of water—or, place the beans in a large soup pot with 4 quarts of water. Bring the beans to a boil and cook for 10 minutes. Cover and let the beans steep for one hour.

Toast the onion, garlic, and green pepper. Add these vegetables to the soup pot. Simmer the beans with the vegetables, covered, for one hour.

Add the pork. Simmer for one hour more. Remove the toasted garlic bulb and discard it.

Sauté the bacon in a heavy skillet until most of the fat has been rendered. Pour off the fat and add the bacon, chorizo, onions, green peppers, tomatoes and *Recado Colorado* to the pot. Cook for another ½ hour.

Add the potatoes and cabbage. Cook until all of the vegetables are done, adding more water, if necessary. Add salt to taste.

To Serve:

You may slice the pork, return it to the pot, and serve the entire dish as a stew. Or, serve the pork and other meats and vegetables on a platter with some of the beans. Those left in the broth will add interest to the soup. Fill individual soupbowls with the beans and broth. Pass the chili or chili salsa. Tortillas can be used to scoop up the broth. They may also serve as a taco with meat, beans and vegetables nestled inside.

Serves 10 to 12.

SOPA DE LIMA
Chicken and Lima Soup

Sopa de Lima is usually one of the first soups a visitor discovers in Yucatan. It has a wonderful fresh flavor that can be attributed to the *lima*, a little green citrus fruit with a piquant tang. It is not a lime, although lime may serve as a substitute. The lima is tiny, a little larger than a key lime, and has a small nubbin on one end. This fragrant soup may be offered as a first course or main dish. It is light, though substantial, with chicken slivers, sauteed vegetables, and crispy strips of golden tortilla.

Have on Hand:

   Recado de Salpimentado, page 57

Ingredients:

   2 chicken breasts or other chicken pieces
   8 cups water
   2 tablespoons *Recado de Salpimentado*
   1 large onion, toasted
   1 bulb garlic, toasted
   1 hot green chili, toasted
   3 cups oil
   8 corn tortillas, cut into strips
   ¼ cup oil
   1 green pepper, cut into strips
   1 large onion, sliced
   3 medium tomatoes, cut into eighths
   Salt and freshly ground black pepper to taste
   1 *lima*, sliced, or one lime
   3 hot green chilies, chopped
   3 tablespoons lima or lime juice or vinegar
   5 *lima* or lime halves

Method:

Place the chicken in a large saucepan or Dutch oven and cover with water. Bring to a boil and reduce the heat.

Toast the onion, garlic, and chili. Add them, unpeeled, to the saucepan along with the *Recado de Salpimentado*. Cover and simmer for 30 minutes. Remove the chicken from the pan and allow it to cool. Remove the meat from the bone and tear it into bite-sized pieces. Strain and degrease the broth. Return the meat and broth to the saucepan.

Heat the oil in a heavy skillet. Fry the tortilla strips until a deep golden brown and drain them on paper towels. Set the tortilla strips aside.

Heat ¼ cup of oil in a heavy skillet. Sauté the green pepper and onion until it is soft, about five minutes. Add the tomatoes and and sauté for another five minutes. Add the vegetables to the soup. Season with salt and pepper and simmer for 15 minutes. Add the sliced *lima*. Do not allow it to boil or the broth may become bitter.

Mix the hot green chilies with the *lima* or lime juice (or vinegar) and place them in a small serving dish.

To Serve:

Add a handful of crisp tortilla strips to each serving bowl. Pass the lima or lime halves and the chili salsa to add, if desired.

Serves 6.

CALDO LA SUSANA

This soup is one of my favorite finds, full-bodied and many textured, a specialty of the restaurant La Susana, in Kanasin. Garnished with a bouquet of crispy vegetables, it is somewhat reminiscent of the famous *pozoles* of Jalisco. I am particularly fond of meals where everything goes into one pot, making cooking and cleanup so effortless. Because this soup contains meat, salad, bread, and broth, nothing else is required—except perhaps a bowl of fresh fruit, temptingly chilled ... and an insatiable appetite.

Have on Hand:

K'ut bi Ik, page 72, or chopped hot green chilies (optional)

Ingredients:
1 small (5 to 7 pound) turkey
Water to cover
1 large onion, sliced
1 bulb garlic, toasted
1 or 2 green peppers, sliced
2 bay leaves
1 teaspoon marjoram
1 teaspoon oregano
1 teaspoon thyme
Salt and freshly ground black papper to taste
1 large onion, chopped
2 cucumbers, chopped
2 large tomatoes, chopped
6 corn tortillas, cut into ½-inch strips
Oil, for frying, as needed
6 limes, cut in half

Method:
Place the turkey in a stockpot with water to cover. Add the onion. Toast the garlic and add it to the stockpot along with the green peppers and seasonings. Simmer the turkey until it is tender.

Remove the turkey from the stockpot and separate the meat from the bones. Return the meat to the pot and slowly simmer for another 30 minutes.

In the meantime, heat the oil in a heavy skillet and fry the tortilla strips until crisp and golden brown. Set them aside.

Arrange the chopped onion, cucumber, tomato, tortilla strips and limes in serving bowls.

To Serve:

Ladle the soup into individual bowls and pass all of the garnishes for everyone to be spooned on as desired. *K'ut bi Ik* or chopped green chili is traditionally sprinkled on top.

Serves 8.

PUCHERO YUCATECO

Puchero is a classic Yucatecan meal that requires a huge pot to cook it in. The resulting feast will assuage the hunger pangs of a whole neighborhood. Although *puchero* is a Spanish word for stew, the Maya have borrowed the concept and imprinted it with their own characteristic flavors. It is a savory all-in-one meal that blends pork, beef and chicken with an entire garden of winter vegetables. The contents of the pot are flavored with a sensuous blend of herbs and spices. Served with a hot stack of tortillas, *Puchero* is a total immersion in the Yucatecan culinary tradition. *Puch*, in Maya, means to squash, mash or crush. Sometimes the cooked vegetables are served in a *puch*, all crushed together. I have eaten *puchero* served in this manner, but must admit I prefer an alternate method of its presentation—and perhaps the more prevalent one—with each vegetable decoratively arranged on a platter. There are so many colorful items to choose from, it seems a shame to crush them all into an indistinguishable mass. Nonetheless, whichever way the meal is offered, the results are mouthwatering.

Each family has its own special recipe for *puchero* and prides itself on a precise selection of herbs and spices. I owe a thank you to Agapita Grijalva de Cortez for her generousity in making this *Puchero Yucateco* for me and providing the instructions for its preparation.

Note:

Señora Grijalva advises that the broth will have more flavor if some pork and beef bones are added along with the meats. A pig's cheek is also traditional for adding a little more heft to the broth.

Have on Hand:

Hot freshly made or packaged tortillas

Ingredients:

1 pound beef chuck, cut into 2-inch pieces
1 onion, toasted
1 bulb garlic, toasted
1 onion, toasted
1 bulb garlic, toasted
1 teaspoon oregano
1 tablespoon black pepper, freshly ground

8 cloves
½ teaspoon cumin
½ inch piece cinnamon
1 chicken, cut into serving pieces
1 pound pork loin, cut into 2-inch pieces
3 carrots, cut in half
2 chayotes, cut in half, lengthwise
2 sweet potatoes, cut in half, lengthwise
3 kohlrabi, leaves included
2 potatoes—unpeeled—cut in half, lengthwise
2 very small winter squash, cut in half
½ small cabbage
3 green plantains—unpeeled—cut into thirds
½ cup rice
2 cups water
2 large pinches saffron
6 ounces fideos or spaghetti
1 lima or lime, halved, to flavor the broth
2 cups radishes, chopped
¼ cup cilantro, chopped
½ cup juice from the sour orange or lime juice
4 hot green chilies, chopped
4 cloves garlic, chopped
½ onion, chopped
¼ cup lima or lime juice
1 large avocado, sliced
6 *limas* or limes, halved
1 lima or lime, thinly sliced for a garnish

Method:

Place the beef cubes in a large stockpot with the toasted onion and garlic. Add 12 cups of water. Bring the meat to a simmer, reduce the heat, cover, and cook for one hour.

Prepare the recado by toasting the onion and garlic. Remove the skin from the onion. Cut the onion into quarters and place it in the blender. Separate each clove of garlic from the bulb and place them all in the blender. Purée until smooth. Leave the contents in the blender container.

Place the oregano, black pepper, cloves, cumin, and cinnamon in a spice grinder. Grind to a fine paste. Add the ground herbs and spices to the onion/garlic purée. Process until well blended. Add the spice paste to the stockpot.

Add the chicken and pork to the pot. Simmer for one more hour. Skim off any foam that appears on the surface.

Add the carrots, chayotes, sweet potatoes, kohlrabi, potatoes, and winter squash to the pot. Add more water, if necessary, to cover the vegetables. Cook for 30 minutes. Add the cabbage and plantains. Cook for another 15 minutes.

Meanwhile, make a *salpicón*, a mixture of radishes, cilantro, and sour orange juice. Arrange the *salpicón* on a serving platter.

Mix the chilies, garlic, onion, and *lima* or lime juice. Place them in a serving dish.

Add the rice to the vegetables in the stewpot. Continue to simmer until the rice is tender. Add the fideos or spaghetti and cook until done. Add the 2 *lima* or lime halves and let them add their flavor until the meal is ready to serve. Do not let the limas boil or the broth may become bitter.

Arrange the avocado and *lima* or lime halves on a platter.

To Serve:

Remove the meats and vegetables with a slotted spoon and arrange them on a platter—or mash the vegetables into a puch. Ladle some of the broth with rice and spaghetti into a soup bowl. Garnish the broth with a slice of *lima* or lime. The broth is served as a part of the main meal, rather than as a first course. Each person selects a portion of meats and vegetables, adds a helping of avocado and squeezes on some *lima* or lime. The *salpicón* of radishes may be spooned atop the meats and vegetables—and dropped into the broth. Add a bit of chili wherever desired. The tortillas may be eaten as a bread, on the side, or Yucatecan style, filled with a little bit of everything.

Serves 8 to 10.

SALPIMENTADO

Salpimentado is a famous Yucatecan stew that resembles *Puchero*, but has its own distinctive characteristics. It contains no beef, carrots, cabbage, or potatoes, but features *pepino cat*, a cucumber-like vegetable that dangles profusely from tall full-canopied trees. This particular version is a favorite of Eusebia Mix Pat, of Xanla. The vegetables in this soup may be offered in a *puch*, just as in the *Puchero*.

Note:

If using cucumbers, add them just before serving; they are much more tender and delicate than the pepino cat.

Have on Hand:

> *Recado de Salpimentado*, page 57
> Hot freshly made or packaged tortillas

Ingredients:

> 5-7 pound turkey
> 2 pounds pork, cut into 2-inch pieces
> 12 cups water
> 1 recipe *Recado de Salpimentado*
> 2 pounds winter squash, cut into 2-inch pieces
> 3 *pepino cat*, or cucumbers, cut into thirds
> 2 chayotes, cut in half, lengthwise
> 3 onions, quartered
> 2 mild green chilies
> 2 plantains, green, unpeeled and cut into thirds
> 1 *lima* or lime, halved
> 1 large onion, toasted
> 1 hot green chili, toasted
> ¼ cup cilantro, chopped
> 1 *pepino cat*, chopped, or cucumber
> ½ cup juice from the sour orange or lime juice

Method:

Place the turkey and pork pieces in a large stockpot. Add the water and bring the ingredients to a simmer, skimming off any foam that may form.

Spoon the recado into the water with the turkey and pork. Stir until the spice mixture is well distributed. Partially cover the pan and let it simmer for an hour and a half.

Add the winter squash, *pepino cat*, chayotes, onions, and chilies. Simmer for 30 minutes.

Add the plantains and continue to cook for another 15 minutes.

If using cucumbers, add them to the stockpot along with the *lima* or lime. Allow them to heat through while preparing the *salpicón*.

Toast the onion and chili. Chop the onion and mince the chili. Add the cilantro, chopped *pepino cat* or cucumber and stir in the sour orange or lime juice.

To Serve:

Cut the turkey into serving pieces and place all of the meat on a platter. Remove the cooked vegetables and arrange them on a platter—or crush them into a *puch*. Serve the hot broth in small cups or soup bowls. Each guest spoons some of the *salpicón* over the meat and vegetables and into the broth. Pass the hot tortillas and some onion/chili salsa. The tortillas serve as a little plate on which to put a bit of everything—or as a scoop for the broth.

Serves 10 to 12.

SOPA NOSTALGIA
Winter Vegetable Soup

This is a delicate soup that allows all of the natural flavors of winter's garden to filter through. *Sopa Nostalgia*, another creation from the files of Fernando Huertas, makes a lovely first course or light entree.

Ingredients:

>   8 cups beef or vegetable stock
>   2 chayotes, cut into halves
>   3 pounds pumpkin or winter squash, young and tender, cut into 2-inch pieces
>   2 large potatoes, cut into quarters
>   4 carrots, sliced
>   Salt to taste
>   Black pepper, freshly ground to taste
>   6 eggs, lightly beaten

Method:

Place the beef or vegetable stock in a Dutch oven or stockpot with the vegetables and simmer for one hour, or until very tender.

Remove the chayotes and pumpkin or winter squash from the stock and let them cool. Peel them and return them to the cooking liquid. Add salt and pepper to taste. Bring the vegetables back to a simmer.

Very slowly add the beaten eggs to the hot soup in a thin stream, stirring constantly. Place a cover on the soup and let it rest for five minutes.

Serves 8.

CHILMOLE BI BU'UL
Black Beans in Black Chili Sauce

Chilmole bi Bu'ul is a staple meal in Acabchen that is enjoyed as long as the chili crop holds out. The pungent aroma of this thick bean soup is intoxicating. It provides a lovely contrast to the tortillas used as a soup spoon. Burned chilies, toasted vegetables and perfumed spices result in a rich and hearty meal. Alberta Chay Uk, one of the matriarchs of Acabchen, likes to add a pound or two of pork to this basic recipe.

Have on Hand:

    1 recipe *Recado de Chilmole*, page 52
    Freshly made or packaged hot corn tortillas

Ingredients:

    22 ounces dried black beans
    12 cups water
    1 onion, toasted
    1 bulb garlic, toasted
    1 to 2 pounds pork butt, cut into 2-inch cubes
    4 large tomatoes, chopped
    1 onion, chopped
    3 cups fresh masa or 1 cup masa harina
    2 cups water

Method:

Soak the beans in water overnight with 12 cups of water or bring the beans and water to a boil, simmer for ten minutes and turn off the heat. Cover the pot and let the beans rest for one hour. Bring the beans to a simmer with the toasted onion and garlic. Cover them and cook for 2 hours.

Stir in the *Recado de Chilmole* and add the tomatoes and onions. Add the pork pieces (optional).

Mix the fresh masa or masa harina with the water and strain it through a sieve into the soup pot. Simmer the soup for one more hour, stirring often to keep the masa from sticking. The liquid should have a thin pancake batter consistency. If it is too thick, add a little more water.

To Serve:

Eat the *Chilmole* with hot corn tortillas.
Serves 8 to 10.

FRIJOL CON PUERCO
Pork Cubes Simmered in Black Bean Soup

Frijol Con Puerco is a Yucatecan staple that probably dates back to pre-Conquest times. Pork and black beans simmer contentedly together with a minimum of fuss or embellishment. It is likely that this was their mode of presentation in antiquity. Garnishes became more elaborate with the passage of time and today this rather simple dish makes a grand presentation. Blackened rice, pork, beans and a rainbow of accompaniments make this flavorful meal a gourmet's dream.

Have on Hand:

Hot freshly made or packaged tortillas

Ingredients:

22 ounces black beans, dried—washed, stones and dirt removed
16 cups water
1 large onion, toasted
1 bulb garlic, toasted
4 sprigs epazote (optional)
3 pounds pork, well marbled and cut into 1½-inch cubes; add
    some bones for extra flavor
Salt to taste
¼ cup oil
1 cup long grain rice
2 cloves garlic, chopped
2½ cups broth reserved from the black bean soup
Salt to taste
3 hot green chilies, toasted and chopped
4 large tomatoes, toasted and mashed
2 medium onions, chopped
1 small bunch cilantro, chopped
2 packages red radishes, chopped
4 limes or lemons, cut into wedges
1 large avocado, sliced—if available

Method:

Soak the beans overnight or fill a large stockpot with water, add the beans and bring them to a simmer. Cook for 10 minutes, turn off the heat and let the beans steep for one hour.

Return the beans to a simmer. Toast the onion and garlic. Add the toasted vegetables, skin and all, to the stockpot. Drop in the epazote and simmer, partially covered, for 1½ hours.

Add the pork cubes and bones and cook gently for 1½ more hours. Check to see if any additional water is needed. Add salt to taste. The pork will absorb the color of the beans. Remove the pork bones and the toasted garlic bulb. Reserve 2½ cups of the bean broth.

Prepare the rice. Heat the oil in a heavy skillet and sauté the rice and garlic for five minutes. Add the reserved broth and salt to taste. Cover the rice and simmer until done—about 45 minutes.

Prepare the *chiltomate* by toasting the chili and tomatoes. They are always served together, but if not everyone is a chili lover, crush each of the vegetables separately and place them in separate serving dishes. Otherwise, mix the chili and tomatoes and crush them together.

Prepare the *salpicón* by arranging all of the condiments on a platter: chili and tomatoes, onions, cilantro, radishes, lime wedges, and sliced avocado.

To Serve:

Remove the pork cubes to a separate serving dish. Ladle some soup and beans into a small bowl for each guest. Everyone selects a portion of pork cubes and some black rice, then arranges any desired condiments on top of everything, including the soup. Add a squeeze of lime here and there. If tortillas are served, try a spoonful of rice, pork and condiments as a filling—drizzled with a little soup and a squeeze of lime.

Serves 8 to 10.

Variation: ESPELON GUISADO (Stewed Espelones)

Espelon Guisado is a variation of *Frijol Con Puerco* that can be recreated with black-eyed peas if the *espelon* is not available. Follow the directions for *Frijol Con Puerco*, but substitute *espelones* or black-eyed peas for the black beans in the previous recipe ... then proceed with the following additions:

¼ cup *Recado Colorado*, added with the *espelones* or black-eyed peas

2 pounds winter squash, cut into 1-inch pieces, added 30 minutes before the meal has completed cooking

½ of a medium cabbage, chopped and added 15 minutes before the meal has completed cooking

SOPA DE LA ABUELITA
Grandmother's Rice and Potato Soup

My friend Joaquin Muñoz goes by the name of Guacho. He owns a little silver and arte popular shop just a couple of blocks from the *Zocalo* in Mérida. I never visit the city without giving him a big kiss and an *abrazo* (hug). Much of my jewelry and many of my art treasures are a result of his intrinsic good taste and my many trips to Mérida. Guacho always interrogates me about my newest adventures and the happenings in Acabchen. He is a writer and an artist with a passion for the Maya.

The last time I stopped in to say my "hellos" to Guacho, he was involved in an animated conversation with a friend, Eduardo Lujan. Guacho persuaded Eduardo to do his part in saving their cultural heritage by divulging a family recipe that was a specialty of his grandmother.

Ingredients:

> 2 tablespoons oil
> 1 medium onion, chopped
> 1 small green pepper, thinly sliced
> 3 cloves garlic
> 1 tomato, chopped
> 2 quarts beef, chicken, or vegetable broth
> 3 large potatoes, peeled, sliced and cut into strips
> ¼ cup rice
> 2 sprigs fresh mint
> 2 sprigs cilantro
> 1 large pinch saffron
> Salt to taste
> Black pepper, freshly ground to taste

Method:

Heat the oil in a heavy skillet. Sauté the onion until it is translucent. Add the green pepper, garlic and tomato. Sauté for five more minutes.

Bring the broth to a simmer. Place the potatoes, rice and seasonings in the broth. Simmer for 15 minutes. Add the onion, green pepper and tomato mixture. Continue cooking for another 30 minutes. Check the seasoning and serve.

Serves 6.

BOHBILSIKIL
Pumpkin Seed Stew

Isabel Noh, my friend in Acabchen who lives at the top of a hill overlooking the plaza, remembered an unusual recipe from her childhood days and sent for her mother in Pamba to prepare it for me. Arriving with her shopping tote in hand, Candida Kinil Noh proceeded to make a most interesting stew—a marvelously flavored dish filled with achiote, chaya, and pumpkin-seed balls. We spent the entire morning toasting, grinding, kneading, chopping, and of course, chatting, Isabel and Candida in their soft flowing Maya, and me—trying to talk with them in sign language and Spanish. Thank goodness words are not essential for a conversation and laughter is an international tongue.

This recipe needs a 12 quart stockpot. It makes a LOT of soup.

Ingredients:

> 16 ounces pumpkin seeds, very lightly toasted
> 2 teaspoons oregano
> 2 tablespoons black peppercorns
> 2 large heads garlic, toasted and peeled
> Water, as needed
> ¼ cup achiote seeds
> 1 tablespoon salt
> 6 quarts water, boiling
> 1 bucket whole chaya leaves, washed and trimmed, or 2 pounds
>   whole spinach leaves, washed and trimmed
> 2 cups onion, chopped
> 4 hot green chilies, chopped
> 2 cups juice from the sour orange

Method:

Grind the pumpkin seeds very coarsely in either a hand mill, a blender, or a food processor.

Grind the oregano and black pepper. Add them to the pumpkin seeds. Set the mixture aside.

Make a *k'ut* with the garlic and a small amount of water—mash them together thoroughly in a mortar and pestle or grind them together by machine.

198

Mix the achiote seeds with the salt. Add some water and mash with a pestle until the water turns red. Strain this water into a larger bowl. Repeat this process 5 more times. There should be about 5 cups of liquid. Set aside.

In a large bowl mix the pumpkin seeds with one-half of the garlic mixture and some of the achiote water. Slowly work the ingredients together, working well with the fingers. Add the remaining achiote water, a little at a time, mixing thoroughly after each addition. Grab handfuls of the seeds and squeeze the mixture through the fingers. Continue squeezing for 35 to 40 minutes. This constant kneading will cause the seeds to release their oil.

Form the pumpkin seed mixture into small football shapes about 2½-inches by 1-inch.

Bring the 6 quarts of water to the boiling point. Add the remaining garlic *k'ut*. Drop the pumpkin seed balls one at a time into the boiling water. Cover the stockpot. After five minutes of cooking, add the bucket of whole chaya or spinach leaves and press them down into the liquid. Cover the pot again.

When the pumpkin seeds are cooked, they will sink to the bottom.

Mix the chopped onion, chili and sour orange juice to make the *Mojo*.

To Serve:

Fill bowls with the *Bohbilsikil* and pass the sour orange *Mojo* to add on as desired.

Serves 8 to 10.

SEAFOOD

Fruit from the sea

There are fish not only in the lagoon, but the abundance of fish on the coast is such that the Indians almost do not bother about those of the lagoon, unless it is those who have no apparatus of nets, who are accustomed to kill great numbers of fish with the arrow as there is little water; the others pursue their fisheries on a very large scale, by which they eat and sell fish to all the country. They are accustomed to salt the fish, to roast it and to dry it in the sun without salt and they take into account which of these methods each kind of fish requires, and the roasted keeps for days, and is taken twenty or thirty leagues for sale, and for eating it they cook it again, and it is well flavored and sound.

—Bishop Diego de Landa,
   Landa's Relacion de las Cosas de Yucatan (circa 1566)

$\mathcal{T}$he Yucatan Peninsula is bounded by miles and miles of beautiful white sand beaches and turquoise waters that teem with myriad forms of marine life. The seas are so generous with their bounty that a group of archaeologists doing fieldwork along the coastline were luxuriously provisioned in just one hour by a five-year-old boy with a fishing pole, a bent pin and some string. Even some of the larger inland *cenotes* have certain species of catfish and *mojarra* to enrich the diet of domesticated animals and game. Professional fishermen have traded their sea food for the wild animals, fruit, and produce of the inland regions since ancient times. The old *sacbé* or "white road" that stretched from Cobá to Yaxuna no doubt made the traveling much easier for the merchants who peddled their wares in the markets and cities made accessible by that amazing highway.

Many of these marine animals have found an important niche in Mayan art and architecture, as well as other aspects of their iconography. Archaeologists believe that seafood was of such prime importance to the pre-Conquest Maya that they chose the fish to represent one of the four world quarters. Although there does not seem to be any uniformity in assigning certain animals to specific cardinal directions, most illustrations equate the fish with the South. Fish, not surprisingly, also seem to be associated with water and rain, and are often linked with the rain god. Fish can be found in the manuscripts and on stone carvings with the hieroglyph, *kan*, a maize or bread sign indicating an offering or sacrifice.

The snail (*caracol*) is another marine creature that may be correlated with rain and water but it is also thought to represent the winter solstice and the duality of birth and death. Man rises from the confines of a spirally shell in the Borgia Codex, while God N, who often represents the end of the year, can be seen emerging from a shell in the Dresden Codex. The tortoise is another animal that the Maya revere and honor with symbol and meaning. The House of the Turtles, an elegantly adorned temple in Uxmal, is encircled by a band of these hardshelled reptiles. The glyph for the month of Kayab bears the face of a stylized and rather engaging little turtle. The tortoise also represents the summer solstice, the Venus calendar and rain. According to some early Maya anthropogists,

> The tortoise is bound to man by a curious sympathy. When the woods are wet and the earth is moist, then the tortoise is not seen. But when drought has dried the water-holes and the land is thirsty and the maize may fail, then the tortoise walks abroad. He takes the paths that men take, and the villager meets him on his road to the milpa. All have thus encountered him, pausing in the burning sun, his shell dry and hot, but his eyes filled with tears. The tortoise weeps for men, and it is said that his tears draw the rain.
> —Redfield and Villa Rojas, *Chan Kom, A Maya Village*, 1967

One of the most delicious ways to taste Maya seafood is to head directly for a little fishing village like Chuburna, a short jaunt from the seaport of Progresso. It is possible to find numerous restaurants that are family enterprises, with the men plying the waters in the early morning hours for the daily catch of marine delicacies. The women tend the hearth, prepare the tortillas and mix the sauces. Often a whole washtub will sizzle with oil over an open fire. Fish and other marine life are gently tossed into the roiling pot to bubble and glaze to a crispy deep brown. In order to eat Maya style, it is the custom to order one large fish or a platter of seafood for several people. It arrives at the table accompanied by a potpourri of salsas and a basket of tortillas. Each participant tears off a piece of tortilla and uses it to twist off a juicy bit of meat. Dipped into a bowl of *Xnipek* or other salsa, no seafood could be fresher or taste better than in a house of thatch on the wind-tossed shores of the Gulf or Caribbean Sea.

PESCADO EN TIKIN XIK'
Grilled Fresh Fish with Recado Colorado

The Maya have undoubtedly prepared *Tikin Xik'* for many centuries. *Tikin Xik'* is bathed in *Recado Colorado*, the garlicky red spice paste that imparts an intoxicating flavor to so many Yucatecan banquets. The fish is cooked directly on a charcoal or woodfire grill. An indoor griddle may be substituted, but part of the drama in the presentation of this dish is its lovely smoky flavor. *Tikin Xik'* makes a grand entrance to any gala dinner party when placed upon a bed of soft fragrant banana leaves and adorned with a colorful hibiscus.

Have on Hand:

    Recado Colorado, Red Spice Paste, page 51
    Xnipek or other chili salsa
    Freshly prepared or packaged tortillas
    1 banana leaf, prepared for cooking (optional), page 120

Ingredients:

    3 pounds fish fillets
    ¼ cup *Recado Colorado*, Red Spice Paste
    ¼ cup juice from the sour orange

Method:

Place the fish fillets in a baking dish. Mix the *Recado Colorado* with the sour orange juice. Coat the fillets well on both sides and let them soak in the marinade. Refrigerate for at least one hour.

Cook on a charcoal grill or stovetop griddle for 10 or 15 minutes. The fish should flake with a fork when done.

To Serve:

Place upon a bed of banana leaves or arrange attractively on a serving platter. Offer plenty of salsa and hot tortillas.

    Serves 6.

CERE' DE PESCADO

Snapper performs beautifully in this recipe, a sample of coastal cuisine at its glorious best. *Ceré de Pescado* is a favorite of Lupita Ancona, who shared this island classic with me. An artist from San Pedro, Ambergris Caye, who specializes in Mayan woodcarving, Lupita enjoys preparing meals that blend the generosity of land and sea. She harvests her coconuts from the garland of palm trees that grace San Pedro's reef-protected shores. While the Belizean coast may be more than a dream away, a romantic meal is no further than the nearest seafood market.

Have on Hand:

   Coconut milk, page 276
   Recado Colorado, Red Spice Paste, page 51

Ingredients:

   ¼ cup *Recado Colorado*, Red Spice Paste
   ¼ cup juice from the sour orange juice or lime or lemon juice
   3 pounds fish fillets
   2 cups coconut milk
   3 plaintains, half ripe

Method:

Mix the *Recado Colorado* with the sour orange or lime or lemon juice and brush the fish fillets with the marinade. Allow the fish to marinate for at least one hour.

Preheat the oven to 350 degrees.

Place the fish fillets in a baking dish with the coconut milk. Peel the plaintains, cut them in half and add them to the baking dish. Cover and bake for 25 minutes.

To Serve:

Spoon some of the coconut broth on each serving of fish. Garnish each portion with a plaintain half.

Serves 6.

Variation: CERE' DE LANGOSTO

Prepare a lobster Ceré in exactly the same manner as the preceding recipe, but substitute 8 lobster tails for the fish.

Serves 6 to 8.

PESCADO EN ESCABECHE
Fish in a Piquant Sauce

Ask any Yucatecan to name a favorite method of preparing fish and chances are, *Pescado en Escabeche* will be a frequent answer. Every cook has his/her own variation of this classic recipe that is well-loved throughout the Peninsula. Fish fillets marinate in a tangy vinegared broth, deftly touched with herbs and spices. Adorned with slices of red onion and green chilies, this fish and vegetable medley makes a flavorful and colorful presentation.

Have on Hand:

> *Recado de Escabeche*, page 56
> Hot freshly made or packaged tortillas

Ingredients:

> 3 pounds fish fillets, cleaned & cut into 1-inch slices
> 2 limes
> Salt and pepper to taste
> ½ cup oil
> ¼ cup oil
> 3 red onions, sliced
> 2 cloves garlic, toasted
> 4 chili peppers such as *Xcatic*, Cubanelle, or other mild green
>   pepper, toasted
> ¼ cup *Recado de Escabeche*
> 2 bay leaves
> 1 cup vinegar
> 2 limes, quartered
> 2 hot chilies, chopped

Method:

Place the fish fillets in a shallow glass dish. Squeeze lime juice over the fish and season them well with salt and pepper. Let the fish marinate for 1 hour.

Heat the oil in a heavy skillet. Pat the fish slices dry with paper towels and fry them on both sides in the hot oil until they are a deep golden brown. Drain the fish on paper towels. Carefully pour off all but ¼ cup of the oil. Sauté the sliced onions for 2 minutes and add the garlic, chilies, *Recado de Escabeche*, bay leaves, and vinegar. Stir the mixture and add the fish slices. Simmer for approximately 5 to 8 minutes, or until the fillets are done.

To Serve:

Place a serving of fish in the bottom of a deep soup bowl. Ladle some of the vinegared broth on top of the fish and garnish with plenty of sliced onions and sweet peppers. Top with a squeeze of lime and a touch of chopped chili. Scoop up the fish and broth with a piece of torn tortilla.

Serves 6.

FISH STUFFED WITH CHEESE

This delicious seafood recipe is from San Pedro, Ambergris Caye, where marine life plays a daily role in the diet of the local inhabitants. I first tasted these crispy fillets with melted cheese at Ramon's Village. Enamoured with the flavor, I managed to cajole the directions from Ramon's wife, Mickey Nuñez, the inspiration behind the wonderful meals that emanate from the kitchen of this tropical resort.

Have on Hand:

Wooden toothpicks to secure the stuffed fish

Ingredients:

3 pounds fish fillets, about ¾-inch thick
Salt and freshly ground black pepper to taste
1 lime, the juice
2 cups cheddar cheese, grated
1 cup flour
12 ounces beer
2 eggs, beaten
3 cloves garlic, chopped
2 limes, cut into wedges

Method:

Season the fish fillets with salt and pepper and rub them with the lime juice.

Cut a pocket in the fillets by slicing an opening in one side. Fill the pocket with cheddar cheese and secure with a toothpick.

Heat the oil in a heavy skillet for frying.

Beat the flour, beer, eggs, and garlic together to make a batter. Dip each of the fillets into the mixture and place in the hot oil.

Fry the fish fillets until they are a deep crispy golden brown on the first side. Turn the fish with a spatula and fry on the second side. Carefully remove the fish from the oil and drain them on paper towels.

To Serve:

Serve with a chili or tomato salsa and a lime wedge.
Serves 4 to 6.

POACHED FISH A LA HUT

The following seafood recipe was graciously provided by Shelley Arceo Prevett, San Pedro, Ambergris Caye. Her family owns and operates The Hut, a popular restaurant that specializes in island Maya cuisine. Her recipes make delicious use of coastal seafood, local produce and regional traditions. Fresh fish simmer in a delicately scented coconut broth in this Caribbean specialty. It would be lovely accompanied by *Rice and Beans* and *Ensalada de Aguacate*.

Have on Hand:

Coconut Milk, page 276
Tortillas, freshly made or packaged

Ingredients:

2 cups chicken stock
3 pounds fish such as snapper or hogfish, cleaned and cut into
   fillets
Salt and freshly ground black pepper to taste
3 cloves garlic, minced
½ teaspoon oregano
2 bay leaves
2 tablespoons butter
1 onion, sliced
1 green pepper, cut in half, then sliced
2 tomatoes, chopped
2 cups coconut milk
½ cup white wine

Method:
Preheat the oven to 350 degrees.
Place the chicken stock in a saucepan with the salt, pepper, garlic, oregano, bay leaves, and butter. Simmer for 15 minutes.
Pour the herbed chicken stock into a large flat baking dish. Add the fish fillets. Cover with foil and bake for 15 minutes.
Remove the foil. Spread the onion, green pepper, and tomatoes over the fish. Pour the coconut milk and white wine over the vegetables. Bake for another 15 minutes (covered once again), or until the fish flakes when probed with a fork.

To Serve:

Spoon some of the cooked vegetables and savory stock onto each portion.

Serves 6.

MAKKUM DE PESCADO
Fish Cooked in a Clay Pot

Makkum de Pescado is such an impressive meal when prepared and served in a simple clay pot. *Makkum* means "covered pot" and this recipe is one of the early ones that has survived throughout the centuries. Back in pre-Hispanic times, only tomatoes, achiote, epazote and chili adorned the daily fisherman's catch. With the arrival of the Spaniards, garlic, onion, spices and parsley were available to embellish the family *makkum*.

This is a quick and easy meal to prepare. Everything can be assembled ahead of time and the results will taste even better with a few extra hours for the ingredients to marinate.

Have on Hand:

Tortillas, freshly made or packaged
Chili or chili salsa of choice
¼ recipe *Recado Colorado*, Red Spice Paste, page 51

Ingredients:

3 pounds fish fillets, cut into slices
¼ cup *Recado Colorado*, Red Spice Paste
¼ cup sour orange juice or lime or lemon
1 onion, sliced
1 mild green pepper, such as *Xcatic* or *Cubanelle*, sliced
2 tomatoes, cut into eighths
2 bay leaves
2 sprigs epazote, if available
6 sprigs parsley
2 tablespoons oil

Method:

Place the fish slices in a large baking dish. Mix the *Recado Colorado* and the sour orange juice. Rub it liberally into the fish. Pour any of the remaining mixture over the fish and let it marinate in the refrigerator for at least an hour.

Preheat the oven to 325 degrees.

Place the fish slices with the marinade in a clay pot or casserole. Add the sliced onion, green pepper, tomatoes, and bay leaves. Arrange the epazote and parsley on top. Drizzle the oil over all of the ingredients.

Cover the pot with a lid or aluminum foil and bake for 20 minutes, or until the fish flakes with a fork.

To Serve:

Serve each guest a portion of fish with the vegetables. Pass a basket with hot tortillas. Tuck a little bit of everything into the tortilla and douse with chili salsa.

Serves 6.

CAMARRONES A LA YUCATECA
Shrimp Cocktail, Soberani's Style

The ingredients for this recipe may seem a little strange—and a little too simple and prepackaged to be truly elegant. The results are delicious, however, and are the easiest way to have the taste of Soberani's Yucatecan seafood restaurants without purchasing an airplane ticket to Mexico.

Soberani's is the place to go for a shrimp cocktail served in a soda glass. It is an entire meal that arrives at the table with a bowl brimming with *Xnipek* and a little saucer of limes. Some years ago, as I luxuriated in the thought that I had a whole mountain of shrimp to myself, I tried to imagine what contributed to the delightful flavor. The salsa that drenched the little finger-nail sized shrimp was magnificent, with just a hint of some little something that I could not place. I pleaded with the waiter to divulge the elusive ingredient to me. "The secret," he whispered, "is the croosh, the Orange Croosh." The words did not register immediately, but then the lightning dawned. The secret that he referred to is a brand of orange soda pop.

Have on Hand:

   Xnipek, page 65

Ingredients:

   2½ pounds shrimp
   1½ cups ketchup
   1½ cups orange soda
   8 lime halves
   8 lime wedges

Method:

Clean and cook the shrimp. Set them in the refrigerator to chill. Mix the ketchup and orange soda.

Place the shrimp in cocktail glasses and squeeze a lime half over each serving.

Pour the ketchup-orange sauce over the shrimp. The shrimp should be immersed in the sauce.

Add a lime wedge to garnish.

To Serve:

Serve with *Xnipek* and lime wedges.

Serves 6 to 8.

CELI'S LOBSTER IN THE CAVE

Lobster abounds in the waters surrounding Ambergris Caye and the islanders feast on these delicious little crustaceans throughout the fishing season. The variety found in Belizean water is tiny and delicate. Celi McCorkle developed this succulent way of preparing the lobster for a local recipe contest. She makes her own flour tortillas, nice fat ones that puff when cooked. These little breads can be opened like a pita and stuffed with lobster or whatever tidbits are on the menu. In lieu of fat homemade tortillas, the packaged variety may be used. With the store-bought tortillas, instead of filling a pocket, just place a small amount of cooked lobster and onion in the center and fold the edges over.

Have on Hand:

> *Recado Colorado*, Red Spice Paste, page 51
> Flour tortillas, packaged or homemade
> A favorite salsa, if desired

Ingredients:

> Water, as needed to cover the lobster tails
> 6 lobster tails, 8-ounce
> 2 tablespoons *Recado Colorado*
> 1 tablespoon lime juice
> 2 tablespoons butter or oil
> 1 pound onions, sliced

Method:

Bring the water to a boil in a large saucepan. Add the lobster tails and cook them for 3 minutes. Remove the lobster tails from the water. Set them aside and let them cool.

While the lobster is cooling, mix the *Recado Colorado* with the lime juice.

Remove the lobster meat from the shell. Shred the lobster meat and mix it with the *Recado Colorado*.

Heat the butter or oil in a heavy skillet over a medium flame and add the lobster and onions. Sauté for about 5 minutes, or until the lobster is cooked.

Place a spoonful of the lobster onion mixture on a small flour tortilla and fold the edges over on two sides. They may be enjoyed as is or topped with a favorite salsa.

Serves 6.

POULTRY

A house for Doña Rosita's chickens.

There are many birds of the field, all good to eat .... There are many wild turkeys, which though they do not have as beautiful feathers as those [peacocks] here in Spain, yet have very fine ones and are wonderfully beautiful and are as large as the cocks of the Indians and as good to eat .... The Indians kill all the large ones with arrows in the trees and they steal the eggs of them all and their hens hatch them and they are raised very tame.

—Bishop Diego de Landa,
Landa's Relacion de las Cosas de Yucatan (circa 1566)

*L*iving in the Land of the Turkey and the Deer, the Maya have raised their flocks of turkeys and other birds since the dawn of ancient times. Women tended their animals carefully to ensure an abundant supply of eggs and meat, but they also loved the beautiful feathers used in making and adorning their textile finery. Turkeys were a highly prized commodity that played an important part in both the secular diet and ceremonial rituals. Once the Spaniards introduced the chicken to Mexico, the smaller bird became more common in the Maya stewpot and the turkey was reserved for the more sacred calendar occasions. Such care is bestowed upon both of these feathered creatures today that many of them sleep within their own protected walls of pole and thatch to shield them from the elements and unfriendly marauders.

The contemporary Maya are also fond of pheasants, doves, *curassows* and *chachalakas*. A favorite over the centuries, winged and feathered creatures, no matter the size or species, have long been loved and appreciated, whether steamed in tamales, snuggled into tortillas, simmered in soups and broths, or simply roasted on the embers of a golden fire.

In Acabchen, one of the most curious of the friendly fowl is called *panadera mulix*, a small breed of chicken that looks as if it were sporting a pair of curly britches. For several years, whenever I left Acabchen to return to Mérida, the householders showered me with chickens. I would trek through the jungle with a warm necklace of live hens and arrive at La Carreta with my cackling adornments still draped around my neck. Eventually, it became more and more of a problem to find new homes for these lovely little birds. With diplomacy, I had to convince the villagers of the difficulty of traveling by jeep to Mérida or by plane to Miami with my cache of avian treasure. Nowadays, they graciously dispatch me with presents of honey, dried chili and an assortment of colored beans. Thankfully, the *panadera mulix* remain in Acabchen to personally offer a greeting whenever I return.

PEBRE
Spicy Chicken with Pork Stuffing in a Banana Leaf

Pebre is a spectacularly showy meal, with achiote glazed chicken accompanied by its own banana wrapped stuffing. The salsa literally dances with the flavors of tomatoes, peppers, onions, raisins, capers, and saffron. Sprinkled with crumbly white farmer cheese and vinegared onions, *Pebre* is a delicious example of the marriage of Maya and Spanish cuisines. I owe the discovery of this intriguing meal to Brenda Peraza de Menendez, the proprietress of La Carreta and San Valentin restaurants. The sour orange juice called for in the recipe is sometimes available from Latin markets. The fruit looks like a bumpy wild orange. Lime or lemon juice may be substituted.

Have on Hand:

¼ recipe *Recado de Escabeche*, page 56
Banana leaf, prepared for cooking, page 120, or parchment paper or aluminum foil, 12-inches square
2 tablespoons *Recado Colorado*, Red Spice Paste, page 51
Frijoles Refritos, refried beans, page 159
Tortillas, either freshly made or packaged
Cebollas Encurtidas, pickled onions, page 165

Ingredients:

1 pound ground pork
8 eggs, hardboiled, chopped
¼ cup *Recado de Escabeche*
1 banana leaf or parchment paper
1 chicken, 3-4 pounds
Water to cover
1 teaspoon oregano
1 teaspoon black pepper
1 bulb garlic, toasted
1 large red onion, toasted
2 chili *Xcatic* or other mild green pepper
Salt to taste
2 tablespoons *Recado Colorado*
¼ cup sour orange juice or lime or lemon juice
4 tablespoons oil, divided

222

1 onion, chopped
1 green pepper, chopped
3 large tomatoes, chopped
2 tablespoons capers
2 tablespoons raisins
2 tablespoons black olives, halved
1 pinch saffron
1 cup farmer's cheese, crumbled

Method:

To prepare the *But'* or stuffing, mix the ground pork, chopped hard boiled egg, and *Recado de Escabeche.*

Cut the prepared banana leaf or parchment paper into a 12-inch square. Two pieces of the banana leaf may be overlapped if one piece is too small. Place the meat/egg mixture in the center of the banana leaf and fold over each of the sides, as if tying a package. Secure the package with banana leaf ties or string.

Place the chicken in a Dutch oven or stockpot with the water, oregano, black pepper, toasted garlic, onion, chili and salt. Bring to a simmer and add the *But'* to the cooking pot. Cover and cook for 45 minutes to one hour—the chicken should be completely cooked, but not falling off the bone.

While the chicken is cooking, make the tomato salsa. Heat the two tablespoons of oil in a heavy skillet and sauté the onion and green pepper until the onion is translucent. Add the tomatoes, capers, raisins, black olives, and saffron. Allow the sauce to simmer for 30 minutes, covered. Stir occasionally.

Remove the chicken from the broth and allow it to cool. Mix the *Recado Colorado* with the sour orange or other citrus juice. Coat the chicken with *Recado Colorado.* Cut the chicken into serving pieces. Heat two tablespoons of oil on a griddle or skillet and brown the chicken pieces.

To Serve:

Place each serving of chicken in a bowl with the tomato sauce on top. Sprinkle with some of the farmer's cheese and garnish with *Cebollas Encurtidas.* Open the *But'* and cut it into slices. Accompany each bowl of chicken with a slice of *But'*, some *Frijoles Refritos*, and hot tortillas. Pass the extra salsa.

Serves 4 to 6.

POLLO EN ESCABECHE ROJO
Chicken in Piquant Red Sauce

My friends, Dr. Antonio Cabrera and Melba Menendez de Cabrera, introduced me to this delicious version of *escabeche*. *Escabeche* translates as "pickled" or "soused," but the term "piquant" is more descriptive. It derives its name from the sour orange and onion combination used to bathe the chicken. This is a very simple, easily prepared main dish with a robust flavor. The chicken can be served in the soupbowl, drenched in broth and covered with chopped onions, radishes, and lime juice, or the soup may be offered separately. *Tsah bi Bu'ul (Frijol Colado)* or *Frijoles Refritos* are perfect additions to this meal.

I like to double the recipe and have leftovers for tacos or *Chilaquiles*. The meat may also be drizzled with some of the broth and frozen for later enjoyment.

Have on Hand:

> Hot tortillas, freshly made or packaged
> ¼ recipe *Recado Colorado*, Red Spice Paste, page 51

Ingredients:

> 1 large roasting chicken
> Water to cover
> 1 whole bulb garlic, toasted
> 1 teaspoon oregano
> 4 chilies, mild or slightly hot, such as *Xcatic* or *Cubanelle*, toasted
> 1 large red onion, toasted
> Salt and freshly ground black pepper, to taste
> 3 red onions, sliced
> 1 cup juice from the sour orange or vinegar
> ¼ recipe *Recado Colorado*, Red Spice Paste
> ¼ cup juice from the sour orange or lime or lemon juice
> 2 tablespoons oil, for browning chicken
> 2 hot green chilies, toasted and chopped
> 2 cups sliced radishes
> 2 limes, quartered

Method:

Place the chicken in a large pot and cover it with water. Add the toasted garlic, oregano, chilies, and onion. Add salt and pepper to taste.

Cover the pot and simmer the chicken for about 45 minutes. It should be just underdone.

While the chicken is cooking, slice the red onions. Pour boiling water over them and let them steep for one minute. Drain the onions and place them in a serving bowl. Cover them with the sour orange juice or vinegar and set them aside.

Remove the chicken from the pot and let it cool for a few moments. Mix the *Recado Colorado* and sour orange juice. Coat the chicken well with the mixture. Brown the chicken in the oil, turning it until all sides are a deep amber—or roast the chicken under the broiler until it is brown. Cut the chicken into serving-size pieces.

Place the sliced onions, chilies, radishes, and limes in separate serving bowls.

To Serve:

The chicken may be served in a bowl with some of the broth or the broth may be served separately. I like to add some of the chilies that have been simmering with the chicken to each soupbowl. Offer the sliced onions, toasted green chilies, radishes and limes. To eat Yucatecan style, use a tortilla to pinch off a piece of chicken from the bone. Add some *frijoles*, sliced onion, radishes and a bit of chili, then roll the tortilla up on both sides to keep everything from falling out.

Serves 4.

POLLO EN ESCABECHE DE VALLADOLID

Chicken in a Piquant Sauce, Valladolid Style

This delicious chicken recipe may be an evolved city version of Ts'anchak de Pollo, one of my favorite meals from the countryside. In *Pollo en Escabeche de Valladolid*, a plump juicy chicken simmers in a saucy bath, accompanied by vinegared peppers and onions. I owe this version of *escabeche* to Fernando Polanco Caamal, one of a trio of La Carreta chefs who made me an apprentice in Maya cuisine.

Have on Hand:

> *Recado de Escabeche,* page 56
> Hot freshly made or packaged tortillas

Ingredients:

> 1 roasting chicken, quartered
> 1 large onion, toasted
> 1 bulb garlic, toasted
> 2 bay leaves
> Salt to taste
> 2 quarts water
> ¼ recipe *Recado de Escabeche,* Black Spice Paste
> ¼ cup juice from the sour orange or vinegar or water
> 3 large red onions, sliced
> Boiling water, as needed
> ¼ cup oil
> 1 large green pepper, such as *Xcatik, Cubanelle,* or other type of
>   mild chili, toasted and thinly sliced
> 1 hot green chili, chopped

Method:

Place the chicken quarters in a large saucepan or Dutch oven with the toasted onion, garlic, bay leaves and salt. Mix 2 tablespoons of the *Recado de Escabeche* with 2 tablespoons of sour orange juice or vinegar. Add it to the saucepan and bring the chicken to a simmer. Cover and cook until almost done—about 40 minutes. Remove the chicken from the broth and pat it dry with paper towels. Strain the broth, measure it and return it to the saucepan. Add two tablespoons of vinegar for every quart of broth. Check the broth for correct seasoning.

Put the sliced red onions in a mixing bowl and add enough boiling water to cover them. Let the onions steep for 1 minute, then drain and rinse them in cold water. Set the onions aside.

Mix the 2 remaining tablespoons of *Recado de Escabeche* with 2 table-spoons of sour orange juice or vinegar and rub it onto the chicken quarters. Heat the oil in a heavy skillet and brown the chicken well on both sides. Bring the broth back to a simmer and turn off the heat.

Mix the sliced peppers and onions and stir them into the broth. Be careful that the peppers and onions do not continue to cook—they should have some texture to them.

To Serve:

Place a chicken quarter in a deep soup bowl. Add a ladleful of vinegared broth, making sure that each portion has plenty of sliced peppers and onions. Pass the hot chili and a basket of hot tortillas. To eat Maya style—pinch off a piece of chicken with a section of tortilla, making sure each bite includes a taste of the onion and chili. From time to time, use a piece of tortilla to scoop up some of the tasty broth.

Serves 4.

POLLO PIBIL
Chicken Cooked in an Underground Oven

Traditionally, this exotic meal is cooked in an underground oven or *pib*, but nowadays any kind of oven will suffice. *Pollo Pibil* is a well-loved classic and deservedly so. The little packages are fun to unwrap and the meat is extra juicy, extra tasty, and even extra tender. Many centuries ago, *Pollo Pibil* was prepared as a feast for the gods. Today it is a feast prepared for everyone.

This is a recipe that blends well with almost anything on the menu, but as it is such an ancient meal, something else of great antiquity might add a sense of history. The list of choices is extensive, but *Ton Luch* (Squash and New Corn), *Toksel* (Lima Beans and Pumpkin Seeds) or *Chulibu'ul* (Masa and Young Black Beans) are some delicious options.

Have on Hand:

> Hot freshly made or packaged tortillas
> Chili or favorite chili salsa
> *Recado Colorado*, Red Spice Paste, page 51
> Banana leaves, prepared for cooking, page 120, 4 pieces, 10-
>   inches square—or parchment paper or aluminum foil
> Banana strings or household string

Ingredients:

> ¼ cup *Recado Colorado*, Red Spice Paste
> ¼ cup juice from the sour orange or lime or lemon juice
> 1 large roasting chicken, cut into quarters
> 2 tablespoons oil
> 1 teaspoon achiote seeds
> 2 tomatoes, sliced
> 1 onion, sliced
> Salt and freshly ground black pepper, to taste
> 2 banana leaves, prepared for cooking, or parchment paper or
>   aluminum foil, and banana strings or household string

Method:

Mix the *Recado Colorado* with the sour orange juice or other citrus juices and coat the chicken quarters well with the spice paste. Refrigerate for 1 to 3 hours, if possible.

Preheat the oven to 350 degrees.

Heat the oil in a heavy skillet and add the achiote seeds. When the seeds begin to toast, they will color the oil a shade of lovely saffron. Remove the seeds with a slotted spoon.

Add the tomato and onion slices and sauté them for two or three minutes, until the vegetables have absorbed some of the flavor and color from the achiote. Season them with salt and pepper.

Place a chicken quarter on a portion of banana leaf large enough to easily wrap around the meat. Add a few slices of the onion and tomato. Wrap the chicken in the leaf and tie it securely with banana strings. Continue until all of the chicken quarters have been prepared in this manner. Arrange each of the packages in a baking pan. Cover and bake for one hour.

To Serve:

Each guest unwraps a banana leaf package. Place some of the meat and any accompanying vegetables in a soft tortilla. Add a helping of chopped chili or chili salsa.

Serves 4.

POLLO A LA YUCATECA
Roast Chicken, Yucatan Style

Pollo a la Yucateca is a popular and easy Maya method of preparing chicken. The meat is irresistibly spiced, then simmered to a tender goodness and toasted to a crisp perfection. The chicken is garnished with a handful of vinegary onion slices (*Cebollas Encurtidas*) and a salad of lettuce, tomato and cucumber. Any chicken leftovers can be tossed into *Sopa de Lima, Tacos de Pollo, Chilaquiles,* or any other recipe that requires cooked meat. *Pollo a la Yucateca* would be lovely with some *Tsah bi Bu'ul (Frijol Colado)* or *Frijoles Refritos*. With a side order of hot tortillas, the chicken can be eaten separately or in a taco.

The flavorful chicken broth in this recipe makes a delicious soup. Add a few chopped radishes, cucumbers, some chopped onion and a squeeze of lime for a delicious first course or entree accompaniment.

Have on Hand:

> *Recado Colorado*, Red Spice Paste, page 51
> *Cebollas Encurtidas*, pickled onions, page 165
> Hot freshly made or packaged tortillas
> Chopped hot green chili

Ingredients:

> 1 large roasting chicken
> 8 cups water
> 1 large onion, toasted
> 1 bulb garlic, toasted
> 1 mild green pepper, toasted
> ¼ cup *Recado Colorado*
> ¼ cup juice from the sour orange juice or lime or lemon juice
> 3 tablespoons oil
> *Cebollas Encurtidas*, as needed
> ½ head lettuce, shredded
> 1 tomato, sliced
> 1 small cucumber, sliced

Method:

Place the chicken in a large cooking pot with the water and toasted vegetables. Bring to a boil, cover, and simmer for 45 minutes. The chicken should not be fully cooked. Remove the chicken from the cooking broth and let it cool.

Mix the *Recado Colorado* with the sour orange juice and rub the paste into the chicken. Heat a griddle or heavy skillet and add the oil. Brown the chicken on all sides, reduce the heat and continue to cook until the chicken is done.

To Serve:

Cut the chicken into quarters and garnish each section with the *Cebollas Encurtidas*. Decorate a platter or plate with the shredded lettuce and add some tomato and cucumber slices. Drizzle some of the spiced vinegar from the onions onto the vegetables. Offer a basket of tortillas and some chopped chili to make a splendid taco—or the tortillas may be enjoyed as a bread.

Serves 4.

POLLO MOTULEÑO
Chicken Motul Style

This is a picture-perfect dinner with colorful layers of tortillas, chicken, tomato salsa, ham, peas and crumbled farmer cheese. Its style is reminiscent of Huevos Motuleños, but a plump juicy chicken has been substituted for the morning eggs. This is a substantial meal that needs not a smidge of anything else—but a helping of sticky sweet fried plantains is an ideal addition.

Have on Hand:

> ¼ recipe *Recado Colorado*, Red Spice Paste, page 51
> *Frijoles Refritos*, Refried Beans, page 159

Ingredients:

> ¼ recipe *Recado Colorado*
> 2 tablespoons juice from the sour orange or lime or lemon juice
> 1 chicken, quartered
> 8 cups water
> 2 tablespoons oil
> 1 medium onion, chopped
> 3 tomatoes, chopped
> ½ green pepper, chopped
> 2 cloves garlic, chopped
> Salt to taste
> 3 tablespoons oil, for sauteing chicken
> 3 cups oil
> 8 tortillas
> 2 cups *Frijoles Refritos*
> 6 ounces ham, cooked and cut into ½-inch cubes
> ½ cup peas, cooked
> ½ cup farmer's cheese, crumbled
> Lettuce leaves, as needed

Method:

Mix the *Recado Colorado* with the sour orange or other citrus juice and rub it on the chicken quarters. Place the water in a large saucepan or Dutch oven and bring it to a boil. Add the chicken quarters, partially cover, and reduce the heat to a simmer. Cook for 45 minutes, until the chicken is almost done.

Meanwhile, prepare the tomato salsa. Heat the oil in a heavy skillet and sauté the onion until it is translucent. Add the tomatoes, green pepper, garlic, and salt. Simmer, covered, for 30 minutes.

Remove the chicken from the water. When the chicken is cool enough to handle, pat it dry. Heat the oil in a heavy skillet and brown the chicken well on all sides. Drain the chicken on paper towels.

Heat the three cups of oil and fry the tortillas until they are golden brown. Drain them on paper towels. Have the lettuce leaves, *Frijoles Refritos*, tortillas, chicken, tomato salsa, peas, ham and crumbled farmer's cheese at hand.

To Serve:

Line a serving plate with the lettuce leaves. Place 2 heaping tablespoons of *Frijoles Refritos* in the center of the lettuce leaves. Top with a fried tortilla and one of the chicken quarters (the chicken bones may be removed before serving, but the presentation is more spectacular with an entire chicken quarter). Drizzle some tomato salsa on top of the chicken and top with another fried tortilla. Add more tomato salsa and garnish with the peas, ham, and crumbled cheese.

Serves 4.

PAVO MECHADO
Stuck Turkey

Pavo Mechado is a favorite holiday recipe. The aroma wafting from the kitchen is so delicious and inviting that it can attract a whole blockful of neighbors. If the *Recado Mechado* has been ground up ahead of time, this is an easy meal to prepare, for the turkey roasts quite simply, with spices, some sherry and a potful of tipsy vegetables. The bird may be stuffed or not, but I consider the stuffing the most delicious part of all. Such a showpiece deserves a tamale such as *Bu'uliwah* or *Tutiwah* to share the spotlight, but a quickly patted *pim* or deftly pressed tortilla will do almost as well.

Have on Hand:

½ recipe *Recado Mechado*, page 58

Ingredients:

1 turkey, 5-7 pounds
2 tablespoons oil
¼ recipe *Recado Mechado*
1 tablespoon juice from the sour orange or lime juice or lemon
   juice
2 pounds ground pork
2 tablespoons oil
1 onion, chopped
1 small green pepper, chopped
4 cloves garlic, chopped
2 tomatoes, chopped
¼ cup raisins
1 tablespoon capers
10 green olives, chopped
4 eggs, beaten
¼ recipe *Recado Mechado*
1 tablespoon juice from the sour orange or lime juice or lemon
   juice
Cloves, as needed
Cinnamon sticks, slivered, as needed
1 bottle sherry
2 large onions, toasted and quartered

2 green peppers, mild ones such as *Xcatic* or *Cubanelle*, toasted
 and quartered
3 bulbs garlic, toasted

Method:

Rub the turkey with the oil and brown it on all sides in a heavy skillet or griddle.

Prepare the *picadillo* by measuring ¼ cup of the *Recado Mechado* and mixing it with the sour orange juice. Blend the *Recado Mechado* into the ground pork. Heat the oil in a heavy skillet. Add the spiced pork and cook gently until it begins to turn gray. Add the onion, green pepper, garlic, tomatoes, raisins, capers, and green olives and simmer for about 10 minutes—until most of the liquid has been absorbed. Let the mixture cool and add the beaten egg.

Stuff the turkey with the picadillo and truss it well. Any leftover stuffing can bake in a separate baking pan. Because the separate pan of stuffing will only take about one hour to cook, allow the turkey to have a head start.

Preheat the oven to 325 degrees.

Measure another ¼ cup of the *Recado Mechado* and add a tablespoon of sour orange juice. Coat the turkey with the seasoning paste.

With a toothpick, prick a hole in the turkey and insert a clove and a sliver of cinnamon stick in the opening. Repeat with the spice inserts every 2 or 3 inches.

Place the turkey in a large baking pan and add the bottle of sherry. Toast the onions, green peppers, and garlic bulbs and arrange them around the turkey. Bake the bird for 2½ hours, or until done, basting frequently. Cover the pan with aluminum foil if the turkey browns too rapidly. Be careful to not overcook the turkey.

To Serve::

Slice the turkey into serving pieces. Spoon some of the turkey juices onto the stuffing.

Serves 8 to 10.

RELLENO BLANCO
Turkey in a Thickened White Broth with Saffron/Tomato Salsa

One tropical Thanksgiving, Brenda Peraza de Menendez spent a week with me in Miami. She graciously offered to prepare one of her specialties for the holiday. Brenda chose to make an elegant *Relleno Blanco*. This is not one of those effortless endeavors that emerges in jiffy time, but is a creation to consider for that special occasion or holiday when a grand celebration is in order.

As in many Maya hearthrites, the turkey simmers on top of the stove, surrounded with sherried spices and a maize-thickened broth. Accompanied by a spicy pork stuffing wrapped up in a banana leaf package, the *Relleno* is topped with a saffron-tomato salsa.

The pork stuffing may be prepared solo—without the turkey. This recipe calls for making the filling in a double package, one to eat with the turkey, one to save for later. When there is no turkey to keep the pork-in-a-banana-leaf company, the recipe is humorously referred to as *Pavo Oido*, Escaped Turkey.

Do not let the long list of ingredients seem intimidating. When the recado, banana leaf package, saffron/tomato salsa, turkey/k'ol and vegetable medley are tackled one task at a time (and in the order just mentioned), meal preparations flow easily. Preparing the banana leaves and making the recado ahead of time can be a big time-saver.

Have on Hand:

1 or 2 prepared banana leaves, page 120.
Depending upon the size, two 14-inch squares should be sufficient. Parchment paper or aluminum foil may be substituted. This recipe makes two small banana leaf packages. If one single package is preferred, use a slightly larger banana leaf, piece of aluminum foil, or parchment paper.
Banana leaf string or household string to tie the tamale packages
Hot freshly made or packaged tortillas
Hot green chili, chopped

Ingredients:

Recado: The following ingredients are for Brenda's version of *Recado de Puchero*, the "white" seasoning paste that is also known as *Recado de Adobo Blanco* (Please see the chapter on

Recados). There is no saffron in her recado; she adds saffron to the tomato salsa and vegetable medley, instead.

    5 cloves garlic, toasted
    1 onion, toasted
    2 tablespoons black pepper, freshly ground
    ½ teaspoon cumin
    1 tablespoon oregano
    6 cloves
    1½-inch cinnamon stick
    4 allspice berries
    ¼ cup sherry

Stuffing—Banana Leaf Package
    2½ pounds pork, ground
    1 onion, chopped
    1 mild red pepper, chopped
    1 tomato, chopped
    1 tablespoon capers
    6 large sliced olives
    1 cup slivered almonds
    1½ tablespoons black pepper, freshly ground
    1 teaspoon salt
    1 egg, beaten
    6 hard boiled eggs
    1 or 2 banana leaves, prepared for cooking

Tomato Salsa
    ¼ cup lard or shortening
    1 large onion, chopped
    6 large tomatoes, chopped
    2 mild green chilies, chopped
    1 hot green chili, whole
    2 pinches saffron
    $^1/_3$ cup raisins
    2 tablespoons capers

Turkey/K'ol
    1 turkey, 5 to 7 pounds
    12 cups water
    1 bulb garlic, toasted
    1 large onion, toasted

2 mild green or red chilies, toasted
2 teaspoons oregano
4 allspice
½ teaspoon cumin
1 1-inch piece cinnamon
2 bay leaves
1 cup flour
1 cup water

Vegetable Medley to Add to the K'ol
¼ cup lard or shortening
1 medium onion, chopped
2 cloves garlic, chopped
1 mild green chili, toasted, chopped
4 tomatoes, chopped
2 pinches saffron
1 sprig epazote
1 tablespoon vinegar

Method:

To make the recado, toast the garlic and onion. Remove the skin from each of the garlic cloves and place them in a blender. Remove the skin from the onion. Cut the onion into quarters and place it in the blender. Purée the garlic and onion until they are smooth. Do not empty the blender.

Place the black pepper, cumin, oregano, cloves, cinnamon, and allspice in a spice grinder. Grind the spices to a fine powder. Add the ground spice mixture to the blender and mix well. Pour the spice paste into a small container. Add the sherry and stir well to blend. Divide the mixture into two parts and set them each aside.

Place the pork, onion, mild red pepper, tomato, capers, olives, almonds, black pepper, salt, and beaten egg in a large mixing bowl.

Separate the egg yolks from the whites and set them aside. Chop the egg whites and add them to the pork mixture. Add one half of the prepared spice paste to the pork and blend the ingredients well.

Preheat the oven to 325 degrees.

Arrange the two halves of a banana leaf on a work surface. The leaves should overlap about 2 inches. Place half of the pork on a banana leaf and pat it into a rectangle about ½-inch thick. Arrange three of the egg yolks on top. Fold the banana leaf over on all four sides and tie like a package with the banana strings or household string. Repeat this procedure with the remaining banana leaf halves and pork mixture.

Place the banana packages on the rack of a broiler pan or other large baking pan. Fill the bottom pan halfway up the sides with water. Bake the packages for 1½ hours. When they have cooked, set them aside.

Meanwhile, prepare the saffron-tomato salsa. Heat the lard or shortening in a heavy skillet. Sauté the onion until it is translucent. Add the tomatoes, mild and hot green chilies, saffron, raisins, and capers. Simmer for five more minutes. Set the salsa aside.

Place the turkey in a large cooking pot with the 12 cups of water. The water should cover about half of the turkey. Add the garlic, onion, peppers, herbs, and spices. Bring the turkey to a simmer and cook it, covered, for about 1½ hours. The meat should not fall off of the bone. Remove the turkey from the broth and let both broth and meat cool slightly.

Preheat the oven to 350 degrees.

When the turkey is cool enough to handle, rub it with the remaining seasoning paste. Place the turkey in a large baking pan and set it aside for a few moments. Strain the broth in which the turkey has been cooking. Discard the vegetables and seasonings. Return the filtered broth to the pot. Mix the flour and water together and make a smooth paste. Strain the flour paste through a sieve and into the broth. This thickened broth is known as *K'ol.*

Place the turkey in the oven and bake, without a cover, until golden brown (about 30 to 40 minutes). While the turkey is browning, return the saffron-tomato salsa to the burner and let it simmer, very slowly.

Heat the lard or shortening in a heavy skillet. Sauté the onion until it is translucent. Add the garlic, chili, tomatoes, saffron, and epazote. Simmer the vegetables for five more minutes, then add them to the strained broth or *k'ol*. Add the tablespoon of vinegar and carefully simmer for 30 minutes. Pay careful attention to the broth during this time, for it must be stirred frequently or it will stick and burn.

To Serve:

This is a meal that deserves to be presented in large soup bowls. Flat plates look pretty, but don't hold enough of the delicious sauces. Open up the banana leaf packages and cut the spiced pork into slices. Spoon some of the *k'ol*, the thickened turkey broth, into the bottom of each bowl. Add a piece or two of the turkey and a slice of the spiced pork. Top everything with a ladle full of the saffron-tomato salsa. Pass the tortillas and chili.

Serves 8 to 10.

BAMBOO CHICKEN
Iguana

In the month of Muan, the ancient Maya celebrated a festival dedicated to Ek Chuah, the god of merchants and cacao plantations. The iguanas offered in sacrifice for this special occasion were painted a bright blue. The pre-Conquest *nacom* or warlord was forbidden to eat meat during a three-year period, but loyal subjects kept his pantry filled with plenty of iguana and fish. The Spaniards also appreciated this strange-looking lizard during the season of Lent, when only iguana or fish could provide the animal protein in their diet.

An iguana is a fascinating creature to watch as it stealthily creeps among the rocks and crevices of the northern Yucatan plain. It has delicate flesh much loved by all who try it. Some say that the flavor reminds them of a wonderful juicy chicken. Serve with *Rice and Beans* (page 161) and *Fried Plaintains* (as explained in the recipe for *Huevos Motuleños*, page 259).

Ingredients:
>   4 pound iguana, cleaned and cut into serving-size pieces
>   Water to cover
>   Juice of one sour orange or lime
>   ¼ cup lard or vegetable oil
>   1 onion, chopped
>   3 cloves garlic, chopped
>   Salt and freshly ground black pepper,to taste
>   1 teaspoon thyme
>   ½ cup chicken stock or water
>   1 cup coconut cream
>   2 tablespoons bread crumbs

Method:

Soak the iguana in warm water for 1 hour. Rub the iguana pieces with the sour orange or lime juice.

Heat the lard or oil in a heavy skillet and sauté the iguana until it is well browned.

Add the onion and sauté until the onion is translucent. Add the garlic, salt, pepper, thyme, and the chicken stock or water. Cook until the iguana is tender.

Stir in the coconut cream and breadcrumbs and turn off the heat.
Serves 6 to 8.

PORK, BEEF, AND GAME

Don Luis home from the hunt.

The Indians have been without many animals and especially have they lacked those which are most necessary for the service of man; but they had others, most of which they made use of for their sustenance and none of them was domesticated .... There are hogs—small animals and very different from ours, for they have their naval on their backs .... There are wonderfully many deer, and they are small and their flesh is good to eat.
—Diego de Landa, *Landa's Relación de las Cosas de Yucatan*

*T*he pre-Conquest Maya relied upon hunting to a much greater extent than the Maya of today. Many of the men were professional hunters who never planted a grain of corn, but traded wild game from the forests for cultivated vegetables from the fields. Hunting was of such importance that ceremonies were held twice a year during the months of Zip and Zac to honor the gods who were the protectors of the animals. During the month of Zip, a plea was made to the gods for a successful hunt, while in the month of Zac, forgiveness was requested for taking an animal's life.

Yucatan is known as the Land of the Turkey and the Deer. Before the arrival of the Spaniards, deer was perhaps the most important animal to the ancient Maya, both as a food source and as an offering to the deities. According to the Dresden Codex, a deer was chosen to represent the cardinal direction East. This graceful animal was associated with god M, the god of the hunt and war.

In order to kill a deer, a Maya hunter needs to circumvent the effects of the *zip*, a supernatural being who guards and cares for these animals. The *zip* actually looks like a deer, but is much smaller. These ethereal creatures can only be seen by the oldest and most experienced of all the hunters. Because the zip does not have a corporeal body, it cannot be captured unless one resorts to magical tactics. A hunter must use a cross-marked bullet and stuff the gun barrel with leaves from the *zipche* (Bunchosia glandulosa {Cav.} DC, a pretty little shrub with bright yellow flowers).

The ancient Maya had two types of wild pig to choose from in supplementing their diet, the collared peccary or *citam* and the wild boar or *keken*. Today the term *keken* is usually used when referring to the domesticated pig. These animals were of considerable importance in their agricultural ceremonies, as well as a food source. They were thought to represent both sky and water and along with the deer served as a symbol of the hunt.

Although the cow is a relative newcomer to the Mayan menu, it has been adopted with alacrity and enthusiasm. There are numerous ranches in the peninsula and *tasajo*, a form of dried beef, has become the *vaquero's* specialty. Cattle have become important enough to have their own deity, X-Juan-Thul, a kindly protector who is generously propitiated for keeping evil winds away from the corral. In larger villages the bullfight has become an integral part of the local fiesta. Even the dances that traditionally accompany these ceremonies are closely associated with the bulls, as the girl takes the part of the *toro* and the boy vanquishes her in his role as the *vaquero*.

Various small animals found in the milpa often supplement the daily vegetable diet. The Maya are particularly fond of the armadillo, agouti, gopher and *pisote*. Because wild animals are no longer as plentiful as they were centuries ago, the forest inhabitants have been replaced to a large extent by domesticated pig and fowl. Consequently, bi-yearly ceremonies offered to Zip and Zac have disappeared. These deities are now honored only once as a part of the Cha'a chak rituals, when a village makes its yearly plea for rain (please see Fiestas and Ceremonies, page 289).

COCHINITA PIBIL
Pork Cooked in an Underground Oven

Visitors touring Mérida and the surrounding countryside may still find *Cochinita Pibil* prepared in the traditional manner, particularly when the weekend looms near. An any-day visit to one of the local markets may also result in a culinary bonanza. Just peek into one of the glass enclosed stalls piled high with juicy roast meats and crispy condiments—one of them is certain to contain some cochinita. The pork is most often sold as a taco. The vendor carves the meat into thin slices, pops it into a tortilla, then garnishes the purchase with some pickled red onions and a chili. It is good and easy eating, a treasure to savor at a makeshift table, to munch while standing, or even to gulp on the run.

Cochinita Pibil is so picture perfect, it suggests the cook has been slaving away in the kitchen. What a joy to discover that the preparations are deceptively simple. A tenderloin of pork, bathed in *Recado Colorado*, Red Spice Paste, slowly roasts on a bed of banana leaves. A Maya *pib* is the ultimate cooking device, but an ordinary household oven makes an adequate substitute.

Have on Hand:

> *Recado Colorado*, Red Spice Paste, page 51
> Hot freshly made or packaged tortillas
> *Cebollas Encurtidas*, pickled onions, to serve as a garnish, page 165
> Banana leaf, prepared for cooking, page 120, enough to make a 24-inch square will be sufficient; aluminum foil or parchment paper may be substituted
> Banana leaf strings or household string
> Broiler pan or large baking dish with a rack

Ingredients:

> ¼ cup *Recado Colorado*, Red Spice Paste
> 2 tablespoons juice from the sour orange or lime or lemon juice
> 1 banana leaf, prepared for cooking
> 5 pounds pork tenderloin, boneless
> 5 large cloves garlic, chopped
> 3 hot green chilies, chopped
> *Cebollas Encurtidas*, pickled onions, as needed

Method:

Take ¼ cup of the *Recado Colorado* and mix it with the sour orange juice. With a sharp knife, make ½-inch slices in the pork so that the recado may penetrate it for better flavor.

Preheat the oven to 325 degrees.

Arrange the banana leaf halves on a work surface so that they make a square of approximately 24-inches. Place the pork tenderloin in the center of the square. Gently rub the recado into all surfaces of the pork. Distribute the garlic cloves on top of the pork. Wrap the banana leaves around the tenderloin like a package and tie it securely with banana leaf ties or household string.

Place the banana leaf package on the top grid of a broiler pan. Fill the bottom pan about halfway with water. Cover the entire top of the pan with aluminum foil and carefully seal the edges so that the package will not dry out. Bake for 3½ hours, or until the pork is done.

To Serve:

Place the banana leaf package on a serving dish and untie it at the table. Slice the pork and pass it with the tortillas and *Cebollas Encurtidas*. Spoon a little of everything into the tortilla and add a touch of chili.

Serves 8.

CHANCLETAS DE LOS ALUXES
Stuffed Chayote

Chancletas mean sandals and these little "shoes" may be prepared with either eggplant or chayote. Stuffed with *picadillo* and adorned with hard-boiled egg slices, they do resemble the Maya *alpargartas* (thick soled, two-strap sandals). I am partial to this recipe because it tastes wonderful, looks great and can be prepared ahead of time, but I love it most of all because it represents an adventure.

Many years before my first journey to Yucatan, I had read stories about the mysterious *alux*, diminutive denizens of the jungle who can either help or harm, depending upon their mood or whim. If propitiated with the proper offerings, it is said that they will show a friendly nature. If a traveler wanders off the familiar path in the dark of night, the *alux* will put the wayfarer back on the appropriate trail. When feeling mischievous, they might move objects around so that one cannot find anything. They play games, sing, whistle and are famous for hiding shoes. If vexed, events can take a more serious bent, for the *alux* may steal or cause bodily harm. To ensure a measure of good fortune, the Maya are careful to prepare special offerings for these capricious little creatures.

Some years back, an Englishman traveling through the Puuc (the rolling hill area near Uxmal) decided to spend the night in the palace of Sayil. He kept hearing strange music and throughout the evening someone or something continually untied his hammock. The caretaker of the site was able to illuminate the cause of the problem. These ruins were haunted and the hapless traveler had fallen victim to those pesky *alux*. After reading the story of the Englishman's perplexing journey, my curiosity got the best of me. I vowed to one day hang my hammock in the palace of Sayil, spend the night and find out for myself if the palace were truly haunted.

After several trips to Uxmal, I found it was not easy to locate a guide who would assist me in such a quest. Many of the Maya have a healthy respect for abandoned ruins and refuse to visit the deserted temples at night. I asked the staff at the Hacienda Uxmal if they would please do me a favor and prepare some nourishment for my nocturnal search. They did.

The ruins at Sayil were closed and the night was dark, but I visited the caretaker's hut and explained the nature of my search. The caretaker and his wife just laughed and shook their heads and said there was no such thing as an *alux*. They kindly humored me, however, and helped hang my hammock. They even offered the use of a handy gas lantern. I removed my hiking boots and placed them under the hammock before retiring for the night. With a little luck, it was possible those boots might disappear by morning. I settled in for a night of sleuthing, happily munching on the Hacienda's delicately sauced chicken and sipping a bottle of red wine.

The moon was full and the jungle was alive with its cacaphony of raucous noises. I watched and waited and listened—and watched and waited and listened some more. Eventually I fell asleep. I did not awaken until morning. The caretaker and his wife were already up and about, attending to the immediacy of a new day and its demanding chores. I peered under my hammock. My boots were still there, in exactly the same position that I had left them. What a disappointment, for I had counted so much on an evening of pranks. Glancing across the horizon, I gazed into the tangled bush where the tiny *alux* were thought to dwell. All of a sudden, I realized what had happened—those elusive little people had cooked up a perfect trick to foil my search. They simply played hooky and stayed away.

Upon returning to the Hacienda Uxmal that morning, I met a most interesting gentleman. When informed of my passion for recipes and folklore, he offered to share a family favorite. I told him his recipe for the *chancletas* would make a perfect *alux*'s sandal. Unfortunately, he vanished from the dining room before I was able to learn his name. His identity remains to this day as mysterious as the tiny little men who inspired my nocturnal journey. Thanks to the unknown visitor, *Chancletas de los Aluxes* have always been a delicious reminder of the Puuc, Uxmal and a night of adventure.

Note: The recipe calls for a little more pork than is needed. Any leftover pork may be used for another meal in tacos. Another alternative, if lack of time is a factor, is to substitute 2 cups of ground pork for the pork loin in the recipe. Cooking the pork loin in onion, chili, garlic and oregano, however, gives it additional flavor.

Have on Hand:
    Chopped chili or favorite chili salsa

Ingredients:

1½ pounds pork loin—or 2 cups ground pork
6 cups water
1 onion, toasted
1 mild green chili, toasted
1 bulb garlic, toasted
1 teaspoon pregano
6 chayotes
12 cups water
3 tablespoons oil
1 medium onion, chopped
3 cloves garlic, chopped
1 hot green chili, chopped
1 large tomato, chopped
8 green olives, chopped
¼ cup raisins
2 tablespoons capers
$^1/_3$ cup chopped almonds
¼ cup sherry
4 eggs, hard boiled and sliced
½ cup bread crumbs

Method:

Place the pork loin in the water with the onion, chili, garlic, and oregano. Bring the pork to a simmer, add a cover and cook for 1½ hours. While the meat is cooking, prepare the chayotes. When the meat has cooled, shred it finely with a fork or grind it in the food processor.

Note: If ground pork is being used, it may be browned in the oil before adding the onion, garlic, chili, and tomato.

Place the chayotes in a large saucepan with the water. Bring the water to a boil, reduce the heat, cover the vegetables, and simmer them for 1 hour. Remove the chayotes from the water and let them cool. When they are cool enough to handle, cut them in half and scoop out the pulp, leaving a shell about $^1/_3$ -inch thick. Chop the pulp and set it aside.

Preheat the oven to 325 degrees.

Heat the oil in a heavy skillet. Sauté the onions until they are translucent. Add the garlic, chili, and tomatoes. Sauté them for five more minutes.

Mix the ground pork, chayote pulp, sautéed vegetables, olives, raisins, capers, almonds, and sherry. Fill the reserved chayote shells with this mixture. Sprinkle each shell with bread crumbs and arrange the sliced hard boiled eggs on top. If a strip of egg slices is arranged at the broader part of each chayote shell, it really does look like an *alux's* tiny sandal.

Bake the *chancletas* for 30 minutes at 325 degrees.

To Serve:

Add a favorite chili salsa or chopped chili to each *chancleta*.

Serves 6.

CHULETAS A LA YUCATECA
Pork Chops, Yucatan Style

Whenever my parents are in Mérida, they dine every evening at San Valentin's, an outdoor cafe on the Paseo de Montejo, Mérida's broad tree-lined boulevard. Without fail, my dad orders his *Chuletas a la Yucateca.* Chef Julio begins to stoke up his grill the moment he spies the Hammans' on their evening stroll. At San Valentin's, these marvelous pork chops are served with *Frijol Colado,* an order of french fries and a vinegared lettuce, tomato, and cucumber garnish.

Have on Hand:

> *Recado Colorado,* Red Spice Paste, page 51
> Tortillas, freshly made or packaged, if desired
> *Tsah bi Bu'ul (Frijol Colado),* Enriched Black Bean Purée, page 172
> Chili or tomato salsa

Ingredients:

> $^1/_3$ cup *Recado Colorado*
> 2 tablespoons juice from the sour orange or lime or lemon juice
> 6 pork chops, loin cut, about ¾-inch thick
> 1 tablespoon oil or lard

Method:

Mix the *Recado Colorado* and the sour orange or other citrus juice. Rub the mixture into the pork chops and set them aside to marinate several hours or overnight.

Heat the oil in a heavy skillet. Sear the meat on both sides, then slowly cook until done. Do not overcook; unless the pork chops are extra thick, 6 or 7 minutes should be plenty of cooking time.

To Serve:

Chuletas a la Yucateca may be served with *Tsah bi Bu'ul (Frijol Colado),* a chili or tomato salsa and a vegetable garnish on the side. The entire meal can also make a beautiful taco by slicing a few bites of the pork chop into a tortilla and adding some *Tsah bi Bu'ul (Frijol Colado)* and chili or tomato salsa.

Serves 4 to 6.

MAKKUM DE CARNE
Meat Simmered in a Pot

This is a delicious and easy way to slow-cook meat. The words, *mak*, "to close" and *kum*, "cooking pot," explain the title of this ancient hearthrite. A clay pot is the traditional cooking vessel, but any covered pan or casserole may be substituted. I like to line the pot with banana leaves and tuck in an extra one under the lid, but I am always looking for an excuse to make use of my backyard supply of leaves.

Have on Hand:

> Hot fresh or packaged tortillas
> Chili or chili salsa of choice
> *Recado Colorado*, Red Spice Paste, page 51

Ingredients:

> 3 pounds pork or beef, from the loin, cut into 2-inch chunks
> ¼ cup *Recado Colorado*, Red Spice Paste
> ¼ cup sour orange juice or lime or lemon
> 1 onion, sliced
> 2 green peppers, sliced
> 2 large tomatoes, cut into eighths
> 2 bay leaves
> 2 sprigs epazote, if available
> 6 sprigs parsley
> 2 tablespoons oil

Method:

Place the meat cubes in a large baking dish. Mix the *Recado Colorado* and the sour orange juice. Rub it liberally into the meat. Add all of the remaining spice paste and allow the mixture to marinate in the refrigerator for least an hour.

Place the meat cubes with the marinade in a clay pot or casserole. Add the sliced onion, green pepper, tomatoes, and bay leaves. Arrange the epazote and parsley on top. Drizzle the oil over all of the ingredients. Cover the pot with a lid or foil and bake at 350 degrees for 1 hour or until done.

To Serve:

Serve each guest a portion of the meat with some of the vegetables and cooking liquid. Pass a basket with hot tortillas. A little bit of everything can be spooned into the tortilla and doused with chili salsa.
Serves 6.

TASAJO
Dried Salted Beef

Tasajo is a beef fillet that has been heavily salted and allowed to dry in the sun for a couple of days. It is then charred on a woodfire or charcoal grill or tossed into a *puchero* or other kind of stew. A favorite with the *vaqueros* or cowhands, this recipe was given to me by Wilbert Diaz Pell, who was born in Dzoncauich, a region located in the heart of Yucatan's cattle country. He explained that it is a typical Sunday dinner in his hometown. Wilbert cautions that *Tasajo* should be well rinsed so that the meat will not taste too salty. He suggests serving the grilled steak with *Tsah bi Bu'ul (Frijol Colado)*, Enriched Black Bean Purée, page 172—or *Ts'anchak bi Bu'ul*, Yucatecan Black Beans, page 171.

Have on Hand:

Freshly made or packaged tortillas to make a taco, if desired

Ingredients:

3 pounds beef loin fillets
1 cup salt
3 large tomatoes
1 large onion, cut into sixths
3 hot green chilies
2 sour oranges or limes

Method:

Pour the salt over the beef and hang it outside in the sun to dry for two days. The meat should be brought back into the house at night to protect it from the dew. When the meat is dry enough it should look black and dry.

Rinse the beef very well.

Grill the beef, tomatoes, onion, and chilies on a woodfire or charcoal grill until the meat is cooked to taste and the vegetables are charred and tender.

To Serve:

Slice the beef and arrange it on a platter with the vegetables. Pass the sour orange or lime to squeeze onto the steak and vegetables. The meal can be enjoyed as is, on a plate, or the steak and vegetables may be placed on a tortilla and folded to make a taco.

Serves 6.

ONSIKIL BI CEH
Squash Seeds with Venison

Onsikil bi Ceh or *Pipian de Venado* might well have been considered the national hearthrite of the ancient Maya. Once plentiful, this beautiful animal is now a rarity and the government has begun to prohibit its use as a meat source.

Los Almendros, with restaurants in both Mérida and Ticul, used to be one of the few places where one could sample this extraordinary meal. Traditionally roasted in an underground *pib*, the meat emerged tender and juicy from its smoky cavern.

Because deer meat is unavailable unless one has a friend who is a hunter, I suggest the use of pork as a substitute.

Have on Hand:

Hot freshly made or packaged corn tortillas

Ingredients:

3 pounds venison (or pork), cut into 1-inch cubes, and cooked
for 15 minutes on a charcoal grill
6 cups water
1 large onion, toasted
1 bulb garlic, toasted
16 ounces squash seeds, toasted and ground
8 cloves garlic, toasted
1 tablespoon oregano
1 tablespoon black peppercorns
2 cloves
1-inch stick cinnamon
$1/3$ cup achiote
4 large tomatoes, quartered
2 sprigs epazote
4 cups water
3 cups fresh masa or 1 cup masa harina
1 cup water

Method:

Place the venison (or pork) cubes in a Dutch oven, add the water and toasted onion and garlic. The skins do not need to be removed from the vegetables.

Toast the squash seeds and grind them as finely as possible. Sieve the ground seeds with 4 cups of water. Sieve the remaining seeds (those trapped in the sieve) with 2 cups of water. Repeat once again with 1 cup of water. Any bits of seed not able to pass through the sieve on the third try, throw away.

Prepare the recado by toasting the garlic cloves. Throw away the blackened papers and purée the garlic in a blender.

Grind the oregano, black pepper, cloves, and cinnamon in a spice grinder. Add the ground spices to the garlic and process the mixture well.

Add the recado to the pot.

Crush the achiote slightly. Add two cups of water to the achiote and mix it thoroughly with the fingers, coaxing the red color from the seeds. Pour the mixture through a sieve and into the stewpot. Repeat the process with two more cups of water. Repeat the process a third time with 1 cup of water. Throw the crushed achiote seeds away.

Add the tomatoes and epazote sprigs to the venison broth.

Mix the fresh masa or masa harina and water together thoroughly. Pour it through a sieve and into the stewpot. Simmer the meat for 30 minutes, stirring occasionally to keep the masa from sticking.

To Serve:

Serve with plenty of hot tortillas.

Serves 6 to 8.

TSIK DE VENADO
Deer with a Vegetable Medley

As in the preceeding recipe, *Salpicón de Venado* is traditionally prepared with deer that has been cooked in a *pib*. Pork may be substituted for the venison in this recipe. A charcoal grill adds extra flavor, but the meat may be braised or stewed with delicious results.

Have on Hand:

Freshly made hot tortillas or the packaged variety
Favorite chili salsa, if desired

Ingredients:

1½ pounds Venison or pork (and water, onion, and toasted garlic bulb if the meat is cooked in a Dutch oven)
2 cups chopped radishes
1 large onion, chopped
¼ cup chopped cilantro
½ cup juice from the sour orange or lime or lemon juice
1 or 2 hot green chilies, chopped

Method:

Cook the venison (or pork) on a charcoal grill for about 20 or 25 minutes, or until tender and fully cooked—or place the meat in a Dutch oven with enough water to cover. Add 1 whole toasted onion and 1 bulb of toasted garlic. Simmer for about 1 hour, or until tender.

Shred the meat with a fork.

Mix the cooked meat with the radishes, onion, cilantro, and sour orange juice. The chilies may also be mixed in or served on the side.

To Serve:

Spoon into a tortilla and enjoy unadorned or with chopped chilies or a salsa.

Serves 6.

EGGS

A jícara of eggs from Doña Rosita's chickens.

*A*lthough the Maya did not have access to the domestic chicken and their tasty eggs until the Spaniards introduced them from the Old World, they have been partial to other types of eggs for many centuries. Evidence suggests that this delicious commodity was once considered an important gift to the gods. Landa noted in his informative manuscript that "... they offered the image bread made with the yolks of eggs ..." Incense burners have been excavated from ancient sites that show figures holding offerings of bird eggs in their hands. Archaeologists have also unearthed watering troughs comparable to the ones still used for domestic fowl.

Rural Maya continue to rely heavily upon eggs in their daily diet. Almost every household has at least a few chickens to provide a delicious *torta* to accompany the morning tortillas. I doubt that any eggs will ever taste as delicious as the ones I consumed with such relish and enthusiasm in Acabchen. Freshly laid by the village hens and cooked to perfection over a smoky wood fire, a bowl of eggs often serves as a warm welcome to a new day. There was always a huge stack of hot tortillas to provide an edible scoop for the repast. Chili always accompanied this feast, either a scorching jabanero, split down the middle and presented enticingly on a small leaf, or a bowl of crushed chilies. Usually the species was of a rich red variety, such as the much loved *chili seco*, but often the prize was a deep vibrant green. The jabanero, sometimes difficult to cultivate and always guarded with care, often sits in a favored spot by the kitchen door. When the jabaneros are scarce, a single chili can be shared by several individuals, each gently pressing a tortilla onto the cut surface of the pepper. The jabanero is so hot that just a touch of the skin and seeds can provide plenty of flavor and fire.

The village Maya often enjoy eggs as their evening meal, sometimes prepared as a simple *torta*, sometimes mixed with a bit of onion, tomato, or chaya. As one gravitates toward the city, preparations can become more elaborate and such delicious concoctions as *Huevos Motuleños* or *Huevos Rancheros* appear on the menu.

Whether offered unadorned or dressed in fancy clothing, the egg is always consumed with a side of chili. Don Luis, my friend from Acabchen, always says, "If we have no chili, we don't feel as if we are eating."

HUEVOS MOTULEÑOS
Eggs Motul Style

Eggs Motul Style are named after the town that was once the capital of an ancient Maya province called Ceh Pech. A province often bore the name of the family that ruled the region. Pech, a name still fairly common in Yucatan, was the surname of the most powerful nobles within the region. Motul, the ruling capital for this regal family, was the site of an important religious center called Uquí or Ucí long before the Franciscans built a church and monastery where the city now stands.

Whenever friends announce a forthcoming visit to Mérida, I always make them promise to have *Huevos Motuleños* at least once. It's the sort of thing that they might not try on their own, particularly if they are likely to stick to the familiar old standbys that everyone recognizes and loves. It's a hearty way to begin the day, providing plenty of energy for pyramid climbing, jungle trekking, or simply market browsing.

Note: Please read the recipe carefully before beginning. Several principal steps need to be completed at about the same time for everything to end up hot and ready to serve at the proper moment.

Have on Hand:

> Corn tortillas, prepared on a griddle in advance, or the pack-
>   aged variety
> *Tsah bi Bu'ul (Frijol Colado)*, Enriched Black Bean Purée, page
>   172, or canned black beans, puréed in a blender
> *Xnipek* or other salsa

Ingredients:

> 1 medium onion, chopped
> 1 jalapeño or other hot chili, toasted and chopped
> 1 or 2 cloves garlic, toasted and chopped
> 4 large tomatoes, toasted and chopped
> 3 tablespoons oil
> 12 corn tortillas
> 2 cups oil for frying tortillas
> 2 cups *Tsah bi Bu'ul (Frijol Colado)*, black bean purée
> 12 eggs
> Butter, margarine, or oil for frying eggs
> 8 ounces ham, cooked and cut into one-half inch cubes

8 ounces monterey jack, shredded

1 cup peas (in Yucatan, these peas are always of the canned variety), frozen or fresh ones, though not traditional, taste better

3 very ripe platanos, peeled and cut in half lengthwise, then each piece halved

1 cup oil

Xnipek, as needed

Method:

Toast and chop the onion, chili, garlic, and tomatoes. Heat the oil and sauté the onion until it is translucent. Add the chili, garlic, and tomatoes. Simmer the salsa for 30 minutes and keep it warm.

Meanwhile, heat the *Tsah bi Bu'ul (Frijol Colado)*.

Heat the oil in a heavy skillet. Fry the tortillas until golden but not too crisp. Drain them on paper towels. Arrange two tortillas on each plate, overlapping them slightly.

Have the ham, cheese, peas,and sauce ready to assemble.

Fry the platanos in oil until they are a deep golden brown and crispy. While they're cooking, prepare the eggs.

Fry the eggs sunny side up. While the eggs are cooking, spoon $1/3$ cup of *Tsah bi Bu'ul (Frijol Colado)* on each pair of tortillas. Arrange the two eggs on top of the beans.

Add the ham, cheese, and peas to each serving and spoon a generous portion of *Xnipek* or other tomato salsa. Garnish the *Huevos Motuleños* with slices of fried platano.

To Serve:

Serve with some extra *Xnipek* or other chili to add a touch of fire.

Serves 6.

CHAY HE
Eggs with Chaya or Spinach

This egg/chaya scramble makes an ideal breakfast, lunch, or light supper. Isabel, one of my mentors from Acabchen, prepared this meal for me with all of the ingredients only a half dozen steps from her back door. The chili she collected was *chili max*, a tiny little thing no bigger than a rice grain. For such a tiny little chili, it really packs a whollop.

Have on Hand:

> Hot freshly made or packaged tortillas
> Chili, either dried red chili, coarsely ground, chopped green
> chili, or one of the chili salsas

Ingredients:

> 8 eggs, lightly beaten
> 12 chaya leaves or 2 cups of spinach leaves
> ¼ cup water
> 2 tablespons lard, butter, or oil
> 3 slices onion, chopped
> 2 small tomatoes, chopped
> 1 tablespoon lime juice

Method:

Cook the chaya in ¼ cup of water for 20 minutes. Set it aside. (If using spinach, cook it in the water left on the leaves after washing them. Cook the spinach for a minute or so, only until limp and wilted.) Let the chaya/spinach cool. Chop the leaves into ½-inch pieces.

Beat the eggs and set them aside.

Heat the oil in a heavy skillet. Sauté the onion until it is translucent. Mix in the tomato and lime juice. Add the tomato mixture and cook for one minute longer. Add the chaya or spinach and stir well.

Add the beaten eggs. Stir and cook until done.

To Serve:

Serve with hot tortillas and chili or a chili salsa.
Serves 4.

FRITO DE TOMATE
Eggs with Tomatoes

When I first saw the tomatoes that grew in the milpas of Acabchen, I was somewhat disappointed. They were nothing like the tomatoes I had grown accustomed to in Miami. In the first place, they were quite small. In the second place, they were misshapen. In the third place, they were not even red. Orangish, perhaps, but certainly not red. I was not impressed. At least I was not impressed until I had my first taste of these little tomatoes one early September morning. The usual scrambled eggs were lightly flecked with pumpkin-colored bits. Nestled in a wrapping of corn tortillas, *Frito de Tomate* has the tart piquant taste of an almost "wild" tomato. *Xkolipak'*, milpa tomatoes, do not bear well when given the attention and care of a family garden. They thrive on independence and glory in neglect. There is truly no substitute for their sweet/tart essence.

In lieu of a Maya tomato, substitute one of a more ordinary variety and add a tablespoon of lime juice. It is really not possible to contrive a substitute for their elusive flavor, for these unique tomatoes are available only in the land of the Maya. When autumn nears and the new harvest beckons, it is time to return to Acabchen.

Have on Hand:

Freshly made corn tortillas or the packaged variety
Chili to use as a seasoning, dried red chili, coarsely ground or chopped green chili or *K'ut bi ik*

Ingredients:

2 or 3 eggs, lightly beaten
1 small tomato, chopped
1 tablespoon lime or lemon juice
1 tablespoon lard, butter, or oil

Method:

Beat the eggs and set them aside.
Chopped the tomato and mix in the lime juice.
Heat the oil and sauté the tomato for 2 minutes. Add the beaten eggs and cook until done, stirring occasionally.

To Serve:

Use a bit of soft tortilla to use as a pincer to pick up a bit of egg. Dip the egg into some chili with each bite or add a bit of sauce to it.

Serves 1.

TORTA DE HUEVO
Fried Egg Torta

While living in Acabchen, a crusty Fried Egg Torta was my breakfast mainstay, as well as an occasional dinner treat. Rosita would sit at the hearthfire and pour a rather large amount of lard into a small frying pan. After the oil was hot, she added a few well-beaten eggs and allowed them to cook, unattended, until well set. The *torta* emerges from the skillet with a beautifully browned crust, yet the center is firm and moist. Accompanied by a hot stack of her fragrant tortillas, a small bowl of ground *chili seco*, and a large bowl of steaming coffee (coffee was traditionally served in a jícara, but the jícara over time has given way to the modern bowl), this wonderful egg recipe is quite heavenly. To eat Maya style, one takes a torn piece of tortilla and uses it to pick up a bite of egg. This morsel is then dipped into a small bowl of ground chili and popped into the mouth.

I have adapted Rosita's recipe to a more low-fat variety, by changing the fat from lard to oil and reducing the quantity used. The taste is not quite the same, but delicious, nonetheless. A small nonstick skillet is perfect for this recipe.

Have on Hand:

> Ground dried red chili
> Hot homemade tortillas or the packaged variety

Ingredients:

> 3 large eggs
> 1 tablespoon oil

Method:

Beat the eggs with a fork or whisk in a small bowl.

Heat the oil over medium heat and tip the skillet to coat it well with oil. Add the eggs and reduce the heat to low. Continue to cook until the eggs have set. Slide the *torta* onto a serving plate.

To Serve:

Provide plenty of hot tortillas and dried red chili.

Serves 1.

BEVERAGES

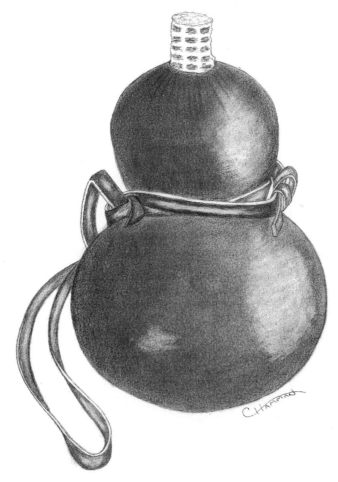

A Maya thermos.

*T*he weather in the Yucatan Peninsula is warm. It never takes long for visitors to get in the habit of frequent pauses for something cold and refreshing to drink. One must first decide how to quench a thirst, for there is a dizzying array of liquids from which to choose.

Vendors stock their push carts with glass jars brimming with blocks of ice and intriguing juices. These *aguas frescas*—cool waters—come in luscious flavors such as tamarind and *jamaica*, shimmering liquids that glide easily over a parched tongue. I became so intrigued with the flavor of tamarind in my Mexican travels that I planted a beautiful tree in the middle of the front yard. It keeps me well provided with fruit and exquisite little orchid-like flowers.

Licuados are luscious concoctions of water, fruit and sugar, blended or mashed into a pastel froth. Milk, or even yogurt, may be used instead of the water for a heavier, richer combination. A bewildering selection of strange jeweled-color fruits makes it difficult to decide what kind of *licuado* to try. Creamy white *guanabana*, burnt orange *mamey* and seed studded *pitaya* are just an example of the many delicious offerings. Another popular refreshment is *horchata*, an appealing, barely sweet rice drink. It has a light milky appearance and cool soothing taste.

Unfortunately, some of the more unusual beverages are not usually available in the restaurants or even the market. Refrescos made from achiote and chaya can be difficult to find and a sampling of *pinole* is an even rarer experience. Village markets are the best places to indulge in a quest for the unusual, but it is not always a good idea to trust the quality of rural water. Because some of these refreshments are an acquired taste, it is best to sample them in small amounts.

As the Sun God, Kinich Ahau, begins his descent in the West, the hands of the clock indicate it might be time for a cocktail. Mexico's marvelous *cervezas* and mixed drinks offer a respite from the heat and frenzy of an action-filled day. Anyone who wants to extend their culinary repetoire beyond the well-loved margarita, may want to try a taste of *Xtabentun*, the honeyed anise-flavored liquor featured in some of area's more unusual cocktails. This regional drink is steeped from a beautiful white-flowered plant that bears the same name as the beverage.

Some of Mexico's cocktails are not classic recipes, but have been invented or adapted by enterprising individuals to meet the needs and tastes of modern times. This evolution is not surprising since the invention of the cocktail itself can be traced to an enterprising individual. According to the legend ... there were many English pirates bombarding the coastline of Mexico. They loved the potent liquors in the local cantinas and kept the bar business hopping. It is said that on the Isla del Carmen off the coast of Campeche the buccaneers had imbibed such huge quantities of rum that supplies were dwindling. To keep his burly clients happy, the tavern keeper consolidated his odds and ends of wines, fruit juices and liquors. His hodge podge larder was soon transformed into a liquid rainbow of color. Surveying his own ingenuity, the tabernero declared that his potable palette was as vivid as a *cola de gallo*, "the tail of a cock." As the story goes, this ingenious invention was carried around the world when swashbucklers demanded their cocktails in every port.

LICUADOS

Almost every city block in Mérida has a little cubby hole that dispenses these delicious fruit drinks. They are thirst quenching, light, and oh so refreshing. *Licuados* can be made with any fruit, but my favorites are banana, melon, mamey and pitaya. *Pitaya* is difficult fruit to find, but well worth the search. Offspring of the night-blooming *cereus*, it looks somewhat like a rosy-red artichoke on the outside. The inside is creamy white, a soft delicate pulp studded with a bunch of crunchy little seeds—the seeds look like poppy seeds.

Some people mash or chop the fruit to make a *licuado*. Others use a machine to blend it into a purée. Both methods yield a delicious beverage. *Licuados* prepared with water are lighter and not quite as rich as those made with milk or yogurt.

Ingredients:

½ cup fresh fruit
1 cup milk, yogurt or water
6 ice cubes
Sugar to taste, about 2 tablespoons

Method:

Place all of the ingredients in a blender and purée.
Serves 1.

HORCHATA DE ARROZ Y ALMENDRA
Rice and Almond Drink

This delicious cooler is as popular in Yucatan as the *licuados*. *Horchata* takes a little planning to prepare because the condiments must be steeped 12 hours ahead of time. It is a wonderful soothing drink.

Ingredients:

> 2 cups rice
> 4 cups water
> 1/3 cup almonds
> 1 cup water
> Sugar to taste
> Rose water to taste

Method:

Place the rice and water in a glass or ceramic container with a cover and let the mixture soak overnight.

Place the almonds and water in a separate covered container and let them soak, also.

Drain the rice and grind it as finely as possible. Mix the rice with 2 quarts of water and pass it through a fine sieve into a 1 gallon container.

Peel the almonds and process them to a fine grind. Mix the almonds with 1 quart of water and pass them through a fine sieve into the same container as the rice.

Add the sugar, water and rose water to taste.

To Serve:

Pour into tall glasses and serve with plenty of ice.
Makes about 3 quarts of horchata.

PINOLE — K'A
Toasted Corn Beverage

Pinole is a mixture of finely ground toasted corn and spices. The Maya use this "instant" mix to prepare both an iced drink and a hot *atole*. They love a hot bowlful of it in the morning, as an alternative to coffee. Later in the day, *Pinole* emerges as a cool refreshing beverage. *Pinole* is also utilized for the Hetzmek ceremony when a young infant is introduced symbolically to the work that is considered appropriate to its sex (household work for little girls, fieldwork for little boys). A bowl of *K'a* is offered to ensure that the young child has a good memory, for *kahal* is the Maya word for "to remember."

Ingredients:

　　1 pound dried corn
　　1-inch stick cinnamon
　　5 allspice berries
　　Sugar to taste

Method:

Toast the dried corn in a heavy skillet until it is a medium golden brown. This process will have to be done in batches; pour in just enough corn each time to barely cover the bottom of the pan.

Grind the corn as finely as possible in a hand grinder. A food processor or blender may be used if a hand grinder is not available. Pulverize the cinnamon and allspice and mix it with the ground corn.

Stir in some sugar to taste.

A cold beverage: REFRESCO DE PINOLE

Add a spoonful or two of *pinole* to a glass of water, whisk the mixture thoroughly and pour it over a tall glass of ice cubes. I like to add a squeeze of lime or lemon.

A hot beverage: ATOLE DE PINOLE

Pinole can be made into a hot beverage called *Atole de Pinole*. Mix ½ cup of *Pinole* with ½ cup of water. Bring 1 quart of water to a boil in a saucepan. Slowly add the *Pinole* to the boiling water, stirring all the while. Turn down the heat and simmer, stirring occasionally, until the liquid begins to thicken.

Makes about 4 cups.

DESSERTS

Fernando and his watermelon.

*T*here is no doubt that the Yucatecans have a sweet tooth and some of the most delicious confections to be found in Mexico are from the peninsula. The most traditional of all of the desserts in the Maya region make use of the prolific array of tropical fruits and nuts that thrive in this lush temperate zone. The fruits in some of them, such as *Dulce de Papaya*, shimmer in a light delicate syrup that is slightly sweet and ever so delicious. Others, such as the *pastas* and *atropellados*, are wonderful thick pastes of vegetables or fruits, slow cooked to a rich concentrated flavor. They may be intended for a heavenly sweet snack or destined to add the crowning glory to a meal.

Because miles of feathery coconut palms span the sandy beaches that fringe Yucatecan shores, it is not surprising to find this crunchy nutmeat in an assortment of candies, pastes and puddings. In fact, the Maya have a passion for nuts and seeds of all kinds. Squash and sesame seeds are swirled into honey, almonds are whipped into candies and pies, and walnuts provide texture and flavor in cakes and ice cream.

Frozen tropical ices may well have been Mexico's gift to the world. According to the Spanish chroniclers, Moctezuma dispatched his swift runners into the high snowy mountains to fetch a frosty treasure—ice. Ices and ice creams are still a national passion and can be found on almost every street corner. The flavors from which to choose are endless and imaginative, for even corn is usually listed with the usual tropical fruits and assorted nuts. According to many surveys, those old stand-bys chocolate and vanilla are still the world's favorite choices. Mesoamerican enthusiasts are quick to point out that the flavoring ingredients for both of these delicacies were first cultivated in the moist jungles of Mexico's hinterland.

According to legend, chocolate was a gift from the god, Quetzalcoatl, to the people of Tollan. Some of the cacao was grown within the Yucatan Peninsula, but most of it was imported from Tabasco and Honduras. The Maya traditionally used this precious commodity as a festal libation, but today its enticing flavor may be found in an array of tempting desserts.

Many sweet concoctions would not be as delicious without the flavor of vanilla, that fragrant brown pod that grows from the vine of an orchid (see Glossary for legends about chocolate and vanilla). Vanilla

272

beans are expensive, but will hold their intense aroma for many years. I purchased a small vanilla bird about 20 years ago in Papantla, a beautifully woven little creature that still emits its rare perfume. The natives of Papantla, Veracruz, are famous for their artistry in creating small flowers, animals, and other decorative objects from the waxy vanilla pod. Covered with brandy or cognac, these beautiful works of art provide a constant supply of vanilla whenever called upon—and my little vanilla bird is always being called upon to flavor one of my favorite addictions—flan.

Flan may well be the Yucatecans most famous dessert. The best-known version is redolent with vanilla, but coconut is also a popular flavor. *Queso Napolitano*, an extra heavy flan, is made with sweetened condensed milk, rather than whole milk. As its name implies, this dessert is similar in taste and texture to a thick cream cheese. Every cookbook and restaurant features its own particular rendition of flan; the only way to pick a favorite is to try them all.

XKA BI KU'UM
Sweet Pumpkin Dessert

If the rains fall abunduntly in Yucatan, fields will be filled with soft yellow pumpkins (*Ku'um*), pale green and white calabazas (*Xka'al*) and dark green squash (*Ts'ol*). The vegetables will keep well for several months in the milpa, but as they mature, these winter squash serve mainly as food for the pigs and as a source of pumpkin seeds.

There is a method of preserving this autumn harvest that is fascinating to watch. The making of *Xka bi ku'um* is usually shared with neighbors, for a tub filled with pumpkins, water, and honey occupies a hearthfire for three days at a stretch. A family thus needs to borrow another hearth to cook the daily meals. During this long slow cooking process, the pumpkins turn a rich mahogany hue and develop a heavy glossy glaze.

Severiana Tamay, who provided this recipe from Acabchen, cuts her pumpkins in half and cooks them in a huge washtub. I have adapted her instructions to fit urban needs.

Ingredients:
>8 pounds pumpkin or other winter squash, cut into 2-inch pieces
>Water, as needed
>16 ounces honey

Method:
Place the pumpkin or other winter squash in a large stockpot. Add double the water needed to cover the vegetables. Pour in the honey and stir. Cover the pan and slowly bring the mixture to a simmer. Turn the heat to its very lowest setting.

Cook the squash until the syrup is thick and sweet. Stovetops differ, but six to eight hours should be enough to condense the syrup sufficiently. Turn off the heat and let the squash steep overnight. If the syrup needs to be a little thicker, return the pot to a slow simmer the following morning. The pumpkins should be a deep mahogany color when they have finished cooking.

To Serve:
In the rural areas, nothing is needed to enjoy these thick sticky candied pumpkins but a sweet tooth. I like the addition of some homemade sour cream, *Crema Agria*, a citified Latin custom—and the recipe follows. Sour cream cuts the sweetness and provides a contrast in color as well as flavor.

CREMA AGRIA
Homemade Sour Cream

A beautiful thick cream is often called for in both main dishes and desserts in Yucatan. The Yucatecans sometimes resort to using a canned cream, but I prefer to make my own. This recipe is basically a creme fraiche. I try to save ¼ cup of it to use in preparing cream the next time, but usually it all disappears before I can salvage any leftovers.

Note:

If the sour cream is being made the same day it is needed, begin at least 12 hours ahead of time. If the day is warm, 8 hours should be sufficient. Setting the bowl outside in the sun can accelerate the coagulating process, but be sure to keep an eye out for hungry cats.

Ingredients:

2 cups whipping cream
¼ cup buttermilk—or leftover *crema agria*

Method:

Place the whipping cream and buttermilk in a mixing bowl. Stir the mixture well and cover the surface of the liquid with a piece of plastic wrap to keep a skin from forming.

Keep the cream in a warm spot overnight. Stir and refrigerate until ready to serve.

This cream should keep for about a week.

Makes about 2 cups.

COCONUT
To Prepare a Coconut for Cooking

Preheat the oven to 425 degrees.

Ingredients:

1 Coconut

Method:

With an ice pick, poke holes in two of the three eyes of the coconut and allow the milk to drain out. Reserve the milk. Place the coconut on a baking pan and bake it for 15 minutes.

When the coconut is cool enough to handle, crack it open with a hammer.

Some recipes do not require that the brown skin be cut from the coconut. If the coconut needs to be skinned, simply cut away the thin brown outer layer from the white coconut meat with a sharp knife.

To Grate the Coconut:

Cut the meat into 1½ inch pieces and place them in the blender with the reserved milk. Process the coconut until it is finely grated. Drain the coconut.

Or, do not cut the coconut into small pieces. Grate the large pieces by hand with a hand grater.

The coconut meat is now ready to make coconut milk.

To Make Coconut Milk:

Heat 1 cup of water in a saucepan until it boils. Place the grated coconut in a sieve and set the sieve over a mixing bowl. Pour the hot water over the grated coconut, pressing with the back of a spoon to extract all of the rich milk.

If more milk is needed for a recipe, the procedure may be repeated with the same grated coconut, but the second processing will not result in milk with as full and rich a flavor as the first pressing. If still more milk is needed, repeat the process with another coconut.

Refrigerate until ready to use.

Makes approximately 1 or 2 cups of coconut milk.

COCTEL DE FRUTAS CON XTABENTUN
Fruit Cocktail with Xtabentun

Coctel de Frutas con Xtabentun is not just an ordinary fruit cocktail. It is a light and lovely dessert that I first tasted at Los Aluxes in Mérida and adds just the right touch to any meal. I like to select a kaleidoscope of brightly colored fruits and display them seductively in a bowl of transparent glass or crystal. If possible, allow at least an hour or two for the flavors to marry with the *Xtabentun*. A small amount of sugar may added to the fruit, if desired, but I prefer the natural sweetness of the fruit and liqueur.

Ingredients:

> 4 cups fresh fruit, such as mango, papaya, melon, oranges, strawberries, grapes, bananas (peel and slice just before serving)
> ½ cup *Xtabentun*
> 6 to 8 maraschino cherries with stems

Method:

Wash and peel the fruits as necessary and cut the larger ones into bite-sized pieces. Mix the fruits with the *Xtabentun* and place them in the refrigerator to marinate. Stir them very gently from time to time to make sure that the liqueur is exposed to all of the fruits before serving time.

To Serve:

Garnish with a maraschino cherry.
Serves 6 to 8.

JAVIER LUNA'S FLAN BUDÍN
Flan Pudding

Flan Budín is a variation of the traditional flan. It requires, of all things—French bread. Javier Luna, manager of La Carreta, gave me this recipe that has long been a favorite in his family. Yucatecans are quite continental in their culinary tastes and have eagerly adopted many aspects of French cuisine. Years of geographic isolation caused these peninsula dwellers to look to Europe, rather than Mexico, for imports, styles and ideas.

This love of French bread is not limited to the city. During my first month in Acabchen, my translator, Amelia Cime, returned to Chan Kom to finalize plans for her wedding. She returned a few days later, heavily laden with long skinny loaves of French bread and an assortment of sweet sugary rolls—all gifts from the family's own beehive oven. Strange. I hunger for "real" tortillas. She hungers for "real" bread.

Have on Hand:

>　8-inch square baking dish
>　pan large enough to hold the 8-inch baking dish

Ingredients:

>　½ stick butter
>　½ loaf—8 inches French bread, stale
>　Water to cover
>　1 can sweetened condensed milk
>　1 can evaporated milk
>　4 eggs
>　1 teaspoon vanilla
>　$^2/_3$ cup sugar, to caramelize
>　2 tablespoons raisins
>　¼ cup hot water
>　2 tablespoons almonds, lightly toasted

Method:

Melt the butter and set it aside.

Cut the bread into slices and place them in a saucepan. Add just enough water to cover the bread. Bring the liquid to a simmer and cook for just a few minutes. The bread slices should be very soft. Gently squeeze the liquid from the bread and place the slices in a blender or food processor.

Add the sweetened condensed milk, evaporated milk, eggs, and vanilla to the bread. Pour in the melted butter and process the mixture until it is well blended.

Preheat the oven to 325 degrees.

Caramelize the sugar, $1/3$ cup at a time. Heat a heavy skillet over a medium-low flame. Add $1/3$ cup of sugar. Gently stir with a wooden spoon until the sugar has melted and turned a golden brown. Pour the melted sugar into an 8-inch square pan. Repeat the process with the second $1/3$ cup of sugar. Do not be concerned if the caramel does not cover the entire bottom of the baking dish.

Pour the milk and egg mixture over the caramelized sugar. Place the 8-inch pan inside the larger one. Carefully add enough water to reach halfway up the sides of the smaller pan. Bake for 1 hour, or until a knife inserted in the center of the custard comes out clean.

Meanwhile, place the raisins in a small bowl and plump them for 15 minutes in the hot water.

Garnish the *budín* with raisins and almonds. Chill in the refrigerator.

To Serve:

The flan may be unmolded, or cut the flan into serving pieces. Remove each piece with a spatula and spoon on plenty of the caramelized sugar.

Serves 8.

QUESO NAPOLITANO

I always make a double recipe of this dessert, one for me and one for everyone else. Amazingly, I don't consider myself a dessert lover, but this is one of those things that I cannot leave alone. A spoonful disappears every time I open the refrigerator door. The best *Queso Napolitano* I have ever tasted comes from Mérida's La Carreta and this is their recipe.

Have on Hand:

> 8-inch square pan or one with an equivalent area
> Pan large enough to hold the 8-inch baking dish

Ingredients:

> 2 cans sweetened condensed milk
> 10 eggs
> 2 teaspoons vanilla
> 2/3 cup sugar, to caramelize

Method:

Mix the sweetened condensed milk, eggs, and vanilla with a whisk or in a blender.

In a very heavy skillet, caramelize the sugar, $1/3$ cup at a time. Place the sugar in the bottom of the skillet and cook on medium-low heat until the sugar has melted and turned a golden caramel color. Pour the melted sugar into an 8-inch square baking dish. Repeat with the second $1/3$ cup of melted sugar. Do not worry if there are empty spaces in the baking dish that the caramel does not cover. Be very careful not to touch the hot caramel to test its temperature. It clings like glue and can give a frightful burn.

Pour the milk, egg and vanilla mixture over the caramel. Preheat the oven to 325 degrees.

Place the 8-inch square dish inside the larger baking pan. Add water to the larger pan until it reaches halfway up the sides.

Bake the *Queso* for 1 hour, or until a knife inserted in the center comes out clean. Let the dessert cool, then refrigerate it.

To Serve:

The *Queso* may be unmolded, or carefully cut the *Queso Napolitano* into serving pieces. Remove each piece with a spatula and spoon some of the caramelized sugar on top.

Serves 8.

PIE DE COCO A LA ALBERTO'S CONTINENTAL PATIO
Alberto's Coconut Pie

Everyone visiting Mérida deserves an evening at Alberto's Continental Patio, either for cocktails or dinner or both. The setting is heavenly ... an elegant eighteenth century mansion turned restaurant with the dining room built around a garden patio. Alberto's could just as well be a museum, for the owners have amassed such a lovely collection of old Maya pottery, colonial paintings and contemporary art that one could spend hours, just strolling and looking. The ambiance is lovely and the cuisine is an unlikely combination of Maya and Lebanese. Guests dine in the company of proud and ever-vigilant sentinels, stately old trees that may well have been witness to Montejo and the Spanish invasion.

The coconut pie served at Alberto's is exceptional. Once the fresh coconut is removed from its shell, the recipe is extremely easy to prepare.

Have on Hand:

> Coconut, prepared for cooking and cut into 2-inch pieces, page 276. Thin brown skin may be left on the coconut.

Ingredients:

> 1 large or 2 small coconuts, cut into pieces; save a piece to grate or curl for garnish
> 2 cups graham crackers, crushed
> 1 stick butter, melted
> 2 large eggs
> 2 cans sweetened condensed milk

Method:

Cut the prepared coconut meat into 2-inch pieces.

Preheat the oven to 250 degrees. Mix the graham crackers and melted butter. Press the mixture into a 10-inch pie pan.

Place the coconut pieces in a blender with 2 eggs and 2 cans of sweetened condensed milk. Blend the ingredients well. Pour the coconut mixture into the crust and bake for about 90 minutes or until a knife inserted in the center comes out clean. The pie is baked at a very low temperature so that the filling will not bubble. Allow the pie to cool, then refrigerate it.

To Serve:

Garnish with grated coconut or coconut curls.

Serves 6 to 8.

Variation: PIE DE ALMENDRAS A LA ALBERTO'S CONTINENTAL PATIO (Alberto's Almond Pie)

Prepare this delicious almond pie in the same manner as the preceding recipe, but substitute 1½ cups whole shelled almonds and ½ cup raisins for the coconut in the preceding recipe.

Pour enough boiling water over the almonds to cover them and let them steep for 2 minutes. Drain the almonds and let them cool. Peel off the skins and sliver the almonds with a sharp knife.

Mix the almonds and raisins in the pie crust shell.

Blend the eggs and sweetened condensed milk in a blender and pour the mixture over the almonds and raisins.

Serves 6 to 8.

CABALLEROS POBRES
Poor Cowboys

This recipe is rather time-comsuming, but the results are truly worth it. Luckily, everything can be fussed with ahead of time. Joaquin (Guacho) Muñoz, my friend with the jewelry shop in Mérida, declared that my book would not be complete without his favorite dessert recipe.

Ingredients:

>1 small loaf french bread, cut into 1-inch slices (8 pieces)
>1 cup milk
>1 tablespoon sugar
>1 teaspoon vanilla
>4 egg whites
>1 egg yolk
>2 cups oil
>1 cup water
>2 cups sugar
>2 cloves
>1 inch stick cinnamon
>¼ cup raisins
>¼ cup almonds

Method:

Cut the French bread into 1-inch slices. Mix the milk, sugar, and vanilla. Dip each slice of bread into the milk mixture and place it in a colander.

Beat the egg whites until they are stiff but not dry, to make a soft, but firm meringue. Beat the egg yolk. Fold it very carefully into the egg whites, making sure that the whites do not deflate.

Heat the oil in a heavy skillet. Dip each bread slice into the meringue and drop it into the hot oil. Cook until golden brown. Turn each bread slice over and cook on the remaining side. Drain the bread on paper towels.

Heat the water in a heavy saucepan and add the sugar and spices. Cook until the sugar dissolves and the liquid thickens into a syrup. Add the raisins and almonds. Dip each piece of bread into the sugar syrup and place it in a serving dish. When all of the bread has been dipped, spoon any remaining sauce on top. Refrigerate until ready to serve.

Serves 8.

HA TSIKIL KAB
Squash Seed Candies

The name of this recipe translates literally as, Squash Seed Honey Water. Both honey and squash seeds are frequent Maya offerings to the agricultural deities. These little golden candies have a more mundane purpose, for vendors sell them in the streets of Mérida and throughout the countryside.

Ingredients:

> 2 cups pumpkin or squash seeds
> 1 cup honey

Method:

Toast the pumpkin seeds until they are golden. Place the seeds in a heavy saucepan.

Add the honey and blend the mixture well. Bring the honey to a simmer and cook over medium heat for about 10 minutes, or until the liquid foams and bubbles.

Drop the candy by tablespoon onto some wax paper and let it cool. Store in an airtight container.

Makes about 3 dozen candies.

COCO BRUT
Celi Jean's Recipe for Mama Blake's Wonderful
Coconut Candy (San Pedro, Ambergris Caye, Belize)

One of my first remembrances of sunny San Pedro was the old Blake House where I stayed as a teenager. There was not a single hotel on the island at the time and Mama and Papa Blake had graciously offered my family the third floor of their island home. I was a 16 year-old dreamer and enthralled with the amenities of the place—or the lack of them, for there was no electricity, running water, telephone, or newspaper to interrupt my reverie. Tropical bedding was a gauzy sling that hung from the rafters, summoning me to sleep with Caribbean breezes.

Several times daily, one of the local inhabitants would wield a machete and do battle with the nearest coconut palm. The victory trophy was a moist green coconut filled with a lovely thirst-quenching balm. After an afternoon of sampling green coconuts, exploring and beachcombing, I found Mama Blake in the kitchen cooking coconut candy. As a coconut addict I was in heaven, but unfortunately, never learned the name of that delicious island treat.

The years have changed the face of San Pedro. The once sleepy fishing village is now a tourist mecca with hotels, telephones, electricity and a continuous supply of running water. It even has its own newspaper, the Coconut Wireless. Alas, Ambergris Caye is no longer my private paradise, for the rest of the world has discovered it, too. Yet, some things remain the same. On a recent visit I tracked down Celi Jean Grief, at her family's Holiday Hotel. I needed an informant's help in clarifying some local history. When I launched into a nostalgic description of Mama Blake's delectable coconut candy, she not only identified it for me, but supplied a recipe. *Coco Brut*, it seems, is a San Pedro specialty.

Have on Hand:

2 fresh coconuts, prepared for cooking, page 276

Ingredients:

2 coconuts, brown skins removed and coarsely
chopped
1½ pounds sugar
½ cup water

Method:

Mix the chopped coconut meat, sugar, and water. Transfer the mixture to a saucepan and cook over medium heat for about 25 minutes or until the syrup forms strings when dripped from a spoon. Drop by the teaspoonful onto a sheet of waxed paper and let it cool. Store the *Coco Brut* in an airtight container.

FIESTAS AND CEREMONIES

Don Lucas offering a Jícara of squash and tortillas to the gods.

*A*s the first iridescent rays of dawn filter through the morning haze, a sign that the gods of earth, sky, and water are now awake and ready to receive their offerings, Don Casellano tips a gourd of sacred wine to the heavens and scatters several drops of its contents to the north, east, south, and west in a prayer of thanksgiving. Newly harvested ears of golden corn had been tied in pairs and strung from branches of towering trees. Small gourds of corn porridge were ceremoniously placed atop a narrow altar. With a recital of chants that spanned many millenia, Don Casellano, wise man, sacred priest, and custodian of ancestral ways, invited all the spirits of field and bush to partake of the festive display and join in thankful celebration. Traditional Maya still honor an ancient pact entered into with the gods of their ancestors; they will take from the land no more than they need and give solemn promise to share with the deities a portion of their yearly bounty.

According to the 16th century Bishop Diego de Landa, there were two types of ceremonies in which the Maya celebrated their feasts. The first type was associated with the yearly calendrical cycles: the solar calendar of 365 days and the sacred calendar of 280 days. The second type was associated with the Maya life cycle.

With the passage of time, holy traditions have become more relaxed and families elect to eat special sacred foods on ordinary occasions. As casual preparation of ambrosial dishes has become more commonplace, banquet feasts once destined to honor the gods are found on tables for the pleasure of man. Now, when the festive mood inspires, culinary treasures gathered from the depths of ages past can be enjoyed on a holy day, holiday or simply any day.

MENUS FROM THE ANCIENT MAYA CALENDAR CYCLE
The 260 Day Sacred Calendar and the 365 Day Solar Calendar

The New Year

Ancient New Year festivities took place around the stones that marked the entrance to each Maya village. Everyone celebrated the beginning of each year by refurbishing their houses and temples. This fiesta was a homemaker's delight, as the replacement of all furniture, accessories and clay vessels had a vital role in this yearly ritual. Floors were carefully swept clean and any debris deposited beyond the limits of each settlement. Last year's garments ended up in a trash heap along with all of the other household debris. No one, on pain of death, could take any of the discarded paraphenalia. Old fires had to be extinguished and a new one rekindled during the New Fire ceremony. The embers were carefully tended and not allowed to die out through the following year.

Some conscientious individuals prepared for the occasion by fasting for a period of up to three months. It was the time for a thorough cleansing of home, temple, village and soul, a time of purification and renovation to assure the promise of good fortune for another year.

At the turn of the century, the Lacandon Maya of Chiapas were still paying homage to their new year when they gave thanks each autumn for a plentiful harvest (in the sixteenth century, the Maya new year began in the month of July). All of their old clay idols and incense burners were replaced with new ones, each carefully decorated with red paint made from crushed achiote seeds. While the men worked with pottery, the women were occupied preparing a new wardrobe of white cotton garments for the family. This multi-purpose new year/harvest celebration required many days of feasting and ritual with X-*tanchucua*, a porridge of chocolate and corn, great quantities of sacred wine, bean tamales and *jícaras* of roasted wild game—monkey was said to be a well-loved favorite.

My interpretation of their New Year's banquet substitutes super market cow for the usual jungle beasts, such as the Lacandon monkey. It provides an easy introduction to the exotic flavors of a ceremonial stewpot.

MENU:

BALCHÉ, Honeyed Bark Liquor, page 310
X-TANCHUCUA, Porridge of Chocolate and Corn, page 300
BU'ULIWAH, Black Bean Tamales, page 137
CHOCOLOMO, Maya Jungle Stew, page 293

CHOCOLOMO
Maya Jungle Stew

Chocolomo translates literally as "hot loin" and refers to meat that has been recently sacrificed. Now associated with the bullfight, *Chocolomo* is prepared with the meat and various organs of a cow. I have tamed the recipe somewhat and reduced the necessary animal parts to a single cut of beef.

Ingredients:

3 pounds beef chuck, cut into 2-inch cubes
2 cups water
4 large tomatoes, toasted
3 medium onions, toasted
2 bulbs garlic, toasted
1 pinch cumin
1 teaspoon oregano
1 teaspoon black pepper, freshly ground
2 sprigs fresh mint
2 cups radishes, chopped
1 large onion, chopped
¼ cup cilantro, chopped
½ cup juice from the sour orange or lime or lemon juice
1 large onion, toasted
2 hot green chilies, toasted

Method:

Place the beef cubes in a large saucepan or Dutch oven with the water, toasted vegetables, herbs and spices. Slowly bring the ingredients to a simmer, cover and cook until the beef is tender, approximately 1½ hours.

While the meat is cooking, prepare a *salpicón* of radish, onion, cilantro and sour orange juice. Mix all of the ingredients together and let them marinate in the refrigerator.

Toast the onion and chilies. Cut the onion into quarters and place them with the chilies in a *molcajete* or mortar. Crush the ingredients together and spoon them into a serving bowl. Set the mixture aside.

To Serve:

Offer some of the *salpicón* and crushed onion/chili salsa to season the *Chocolomo.*

Serves 4 to 6.

THE VILLAGE FIESTA and THE FIESTA OF THE HOLY CROSS

Most traditional societies participate in a festival honoring the rites of spring, a celebration of new vegetation and rebirth. Manuscripts indicate that this was a season of continuous feasting and holiday rituals for the Maya. When the Spaniards forbid the observance of these heathen ceremonies, the natives became more creative in their worship. The Fiesta of the Holy Cross, on May third, and the village fiesta in honor of a local or individual patron saint, often had many rites in common. This is an exceptionally colorful and fascinating time to witness the native world with a profusion of bullfights, parades, passion plays and fireworks scheduled in villages and tiny pueblos throughout the countryside.

A number of the picturesque activities that continue in modern celebrations can be traced to pre-Hispanic New Year festivities. According to Robert Redfield, the *cuch*, or burden of a fiesta that was once a life or death undertaking, is now represented by a *ramillete*, a small decorated pole that dangles colored streamers, cigarettes, a doll and a bird. The *cargador*, who has accepted the burden and expense for the current fiesta, passes the decorated ramillete (*cuch*) to the cargador who has agreed to take on the burden and expense for the following year.

This diminutive *ramillete* has evolved from an archaic rite called "the bringing in of the ceiba" (a sacred Maya tree). The towering *ceiba* has dwindled over the years to a symbolic ramillete. Ceremonies at one time involved cutting down the *ceiba* and carrying it to the central plaza where the tree became a focal point during several days of festivities. Fruits and vegetables were hung from its lofty branches and a series of agricultural ceremonies involving a *pisote* and a pig were carried out with much eating, drinking and enthusiasm.

The modern *ramillete* is usually delivered to the new cargador along with a pig's head, some rum, cornhusk cigarettes and a potpourri of fruits and vegetables from the milpa. If a real pig is not available, one is fashioned from corn dough, honey and squash seeds. The pig's head is danced around a table, nine times in a clockwise direction, then the steps are retraced in a counter-clockwise pattern. A man follows be-

295

hind, calling the pig and shaking a rattle filled with kernels of corn. The pig, the milpa and agriculture are still closely associated for the Maya.

MENU:

KEKEN RELLENO NEGRO, Pig in Toasted Black Chili Sauce, page 297

TS'ANCHAK BI CHAY, Chaya Simmered in a Light Broth, page 149

WAHI-SIKIL, Squash Seed Bread, page 90

KEKEN EN RELLENO NEGRO
Pig in Toasted Black Chili Sauce

Alberta and Pablo of Acabchen offer a pig to their patron saint, Fatima, during a yearly ritual each May. Although the celebration ostensibly pays homage to a Catholic saint, the activities associated with the occasion focus upon a pig and ancestral forest deities. The burden or *cuch* of the fiesta is not passed on to anyone else, but remains within the family.

Pablo was in charge of killing the pig and cutting the meat into manageable pieces. On the morning of the feast, he strung the carcass from the rafters and proceeded to dig the *pib*. Alberta prepared the recado while other family members made two kinds of sausage, *Longaniza* and *Morcia*. Nothing was allowed to go to waste, for all of the pork fat went into a big cookpot. Slow-simmered for an afternoon, it yielded a quantity of creamy white lard.

In a reenactment of pre-Hispanic rites, Pablo and his sons began a parade through the family compound with the head of the pig balanced high overhead. They kept step to a lively cadence, a rhythm carefully punctuated by chants and rattles. The happy troup returned to the house and circled the banquet table nine times before reversing their direction. This procession is called the Okostah-pol, the Dance of the Head and is a preliminary "thank you" to the deities of the milpa. Planting season lay only a few weeks ahead.

All of the men lent a hand at *pib* digging, for three ovens were necessary to hold the washtubs of pork and black chili. At last the pits were ready, the ovens fired and all of the ingredients assembled. Both men and women gathered around to help tend the stewpots, for by now the sun had set and the hour was late. We each took our turn swirling and churning the thick broth by candlelight. The stirring sticks were so long and sturdy they felt more like broomsticks than mixing spoons. The intoxicating aroma of *Relleno Negro*, heavy with garlic and spices, permeated the warm summer evening. When Alberta was finally satisfied that the spices were balanced and the sauce was of the proper consistency, the men covered the cooking vessels with banana leaves, a layer of rock, then earth, and left them to simmer throughout the night.

I needed no reminder to awaken the following morning. When the children arrived to summon me for breakfast, I was dressed and ready.

Alberta had the table set and a pile of hot tortillas waiting. She hustled in with a steaming bowl of the most succulent pork I have ever tasted. It was the kind of meal that makes one want to moan in ecstacy.

The recado Alberta used in making this famous hearthrite for Fatima is the *Recado de Relleno Negro*, Fiesta Version. Usually only Yucatecan travellers will have access to such large amounts of chili. With this thought in mind, I have suggested a lighter toasted chili paste for this meal, one that calls for a lesser amount of the fiery fruit. Anyone wishing to make Alberta's Fiesta Version will find that it is well worth the time and trouble—even a trip to Mexico—to buy the chilies to prepare it. The paste keeps beautifully in the refrigerator for many months and is delicious on pork, chicken, beef and vegetables.

Have on Hand:

> 1 recipe, *Recado de Chilmole*, toasted chili spice paste, page 52
> Hot freshly made or packaged tortillas

Ingredients:

> 7 cups masa, or 4 cups masa harina
> 5 quarts water
> 8 large tomatoes, diced
> Salt to taste
> 1 recipe *Recado de Chilmole*
> 7 pound pork loin roast, boneless

Method:

Preheat the oven to 325 degrees.

In a large mixing bowl blend the masa harina with the water. Stir with a whisk until all of the lumps have disappeared.

Add the chopped tomatoes and salt. Stir in the *Recado de Chilmole* and blend well.

Place the pork roast in a roasting pan and pour the the recado/masa mixture on top of it. Cover the pan with foil and place it in the oven.

Bake for about 2½ to 3 hours. Occasionally stir the recado/masa and turn the roast.

To Serve:

Slice the pork. Fill a soft hot tortilla with some of the pork and plenty of sauce.

Serves 8 to 10.

ALL SAINTS' DAY, HANAL PIXAN
(Dinner of the Souls)

One of the most interesting of all Yucatecan celebrations occurs around the time of Halloween. The date for the current celebration corresponds to All Saints' Day in the Catholic Church calendar, but origins of this time-honored festival can be traced much further back in time to a month the Maya called Xul (Shool). The hieroglyph for Xul is the figure of a dog, the faithful animal that the pre-Conquest Maya believed accompanied their soul on a journey through the underworld.

The Maya call this holiday Hanal Pixan and believe the spirits of departed ancestors come back for a weekly sojourn on earth at this time of year. If the spirits are propitiated, they will then find their way to the "other side" and leave the earthbound alone. Ceremonies begin on October 31st with the Dinner of the Child Souls. Altars are decorated with a profusion of flowers, gourds of chocolate, tamales and flickering candles. Favorite tidbits and possessions once enjoyed by the deceased child might also be placed on an altar.

The following day, November 1st, is set aside as the Dinner of the Adult Souls. Each family places a candle and gourd of bread and chocolate in the doorway for those who have no one to honor them. Usually the stockpot is filled with *Ts'anchak bi Kax*, Chicken in a Peppery Broth. The Maya believe that only female chickens may be cooked during Hanal Pixan, for roosters are too likely to crow and scare away the departed spirits. The *octave* of this dinner occurs eight days later, and various types of tamales—*Pibiwahes*, *Chachakwahes*, or *Muk-bipollo*—are prepared for this occasion when the spirits will begin their leavetaking. Apparently, the type of tamale is not crucial to the celebration, but the type of oven is vital. Only a *pib* (underground oven) will suffice for the *octave* of the festival.

MENU:

> PIBIWAH—BU'ULIWAH, Bean Tamales (any type of bean may be used), page 306
> TSAH BI YAX IK, Enriched Green Chili Salsa, page 74
> X-TANCHUCUA, Porridge of Chocolate and Corn, page 300

X-TANCHUCUA
Porridge of Chocolate and Corn

In Mexico, the native population does not usually mix their chocolate with milk. They use water instead and whip it to a froth with a wooden chocolate beater known as a *molinillo*. The beverage is prepared over an open fire in a clay pitcher that adds its own wonderful earthy flavor to the brew. No other type of container will give the same results, but it will be delicious nonetheless.

Ingredients:

>2 heaping tablespoons cocoa
>4 heaping tablespoons sugar
>1 heaping tablespoon masa harina
>6 cups water
>½ teaspoon cinnamon
>¼ teaspoon vanilla

Method:

Mix the cocoa, sugar and masa together in a clay pitcher or heavy saucepan. Stir in ½ cup of the water and whip the mixture with a whisk until all of the lumps have dissolved. Cook on medium-high heat while adding the remaining water, a little at a time. When the porridge is steaming and has thickened somewhat, turn off the heat, strain the chocolate and serve.

Serves 6.

CHRISTMAS (OK NA)

The inhabitants of pre-Conquest Mexico had a celebration corresponding quite closely to Christmas. The ancient Maya celebrated with a festival called Ok Na on a day set aside by their priest in the month of Chen or Yax, sometime after the 23rd of December. It was a time for renovation, rejuvenation and prayers for rain. Their temples were refurbished and new idols and braziers of clay were offered to the gods of the forest and field. No occasion was overlooked, it seems, for addressing the deities who provide moisture to the burdgeoning crops. Ok Na seems very much like a second New Year's celebration.

The Maya of Chiapas believe the birth of the sun god occurred on December 26th. The Aztecs, who often shared a similar belief system with the Maya, paid homage to their god, Huitzilopotchli, at this time of year. Huitzilopotchli was said to return to earth on December 26th when his people celebrated the "coming down of the waters." This fierce god in infant form was given the name "water." It was an annual custom for the priests to make a tamale, set it aside and keep an all-night vigil on that date. Every person in the temple tried to stay awake so that when the child descended to earth, some lucky individual might catch a glimpse of him leaving a footprint on the soft corn dough of the tamale. This holiday celebration seems to be a wintertime plea for springtime rain, a just-to-be-sure insurance policy for next year's harvest.

With all of these rain ceremonies in mind, it is not surprising to learn from the natives of Yucatan that a favorite holiday food during this joyous season is a tamale seasoned with achiote, a condiment that is synonymous with rain.

MENU:

CHA'CHAKWAHES, Chicken Tamales Flavored with Achiote, page 41
X-TANCHUCUA, Porridge of Chocolate and Corn, page 300

MENUS FROM THE ANCIENT MAYA AGRICULTURAL CYCLE and MENUS FOR PROTECTION AND SANCTIFICATION

Agricultural offerings are prepared by village households at carefully specified times in the harvest cycle. Hallowed foods and sacred dishes associated with the agricultural calendar are few in number, consisting only of a golden wine, corn porridge with honey, special *pib* roasted breads and meat simmered in a corn-thickened broth. The type of ritual and its importance in the cycle determine which recipes are prepared as offerings and set upon the altar. Several rites of the hearth may be traced to the first ceremonial centers of the Maya, revealing an association with the sacred menu that may go back at least 5,000 years.

The appropriateness of an ingredient as an offering depends on whether it is thought of as "hot" or "cold." Mayan deities are finicky eaters and will consume only foods they consider cold. Some anthropologists trace the Mesoamerican notion of hot versus cold to Greek humoral pathology. Others feel that the Maya refer to actual temperatures because plants are better able to survive in cool wet places like *cenotes*, but tend to shrivel and die in the heat. It is also possible that cool and wet may have an association with rain. For whatever reason, a limited number of specified foods are thought to be cold and therefore appropriate for ceremonies. Foods cooked on the comal or griddle are hot. Those prepared in the *pib* or earth oven are cold. When broth for the bird or beast is cooked on a hearth, rather than a *pib*, Balché or rum must be added to raise the meal to the level of sacred and make it fit for a hallowed offering.

A sacred gift must also be virgin or *suhuy*, something kept apart and holy. Wild forest animals fit this part, for they are thought to be under the care of supernatural guardians who keep close contact with the gods of field and bush. If a wild animal is unavailable for sacrifice, a domesticated one will do—after it has been offered a sip of *balché*, thus transforming it from secular to sacred. If no animal is available for the ceremony, adding some animal fat to a vegetable offering will elevate the gift to an animal category.

Some portion of the foods for most of these sacred festivities is cooked underground in the earthen *pib*. After the gods have consumed the "essence" of each dish, all invited mortals may eat the remainder of the sacred banquet. Because Maya gods are fast and sparing eaters, village inhabitants may almost immediately continue their celebration and consume the fruits of their ceremonial endeavors.

Women must remain within the confines of their own house compound during agricultural festivities. It is believed that if a woman is present at a ceremony, the gods will be displeased and show their pique by witholding rain. Women may shell, grind and cook the corn, but men are in charge of preparing the ceremonial breads. The men sacrifice the animals, but return them to the domestic hut for women to cook on a specially constructed hearth.

With the exception of *balché*, all of the ingredients needed for these rituals are easily available in urban markets. A lovely red or white wine should provide an alternative to this traditional elixir—and an oven, range top, or charcoal grill offer adequate substitutions for native cooking methods. Indeed, over the centuries Maya deities have needed to be flexible, patient and adapt to whatever is at hand.

U HANLI KOL (Dinner of the Cornfield)

The Maya celebrate their agricultural calendar with two Thanksgivings, although the first and most important of these ceremonies is celebrated only once every four years. Known as U Hanli Kol, this grand celebration may be offered during any month, but is most often observed in early spring when permission is asked of forest deities to fell the trees and plant new fields. Such a request is accompanied by gifts of *balché*, corn porridge, sacred breads and sacred fowl. It represents a "thank you" for a harvest that is yet to be collected and implies a solemn contract with the gods. No man will fell more forest than is needed to feed the family; man will "borrow" from the gods only what is vitally necessary.

MENU:

> BALCHÉ, Honeyed Bark Liquor, page 310
> PAVO EN K'OL INDIO, Turkey Simmered in a Sacred Broth,
>   page 311
> TUTIWAH, Pumpkin Seed Tamale, page 313
> SAKA', Dried Corn Porridge, page 309

BURNING THE FIELDS

Once the trees have been felled from the forest, the dry brush must be burned to ready the fields for planting. There must be a strong wind to carry the flames quickly across the field, for the wood must burn thoroughly or the planting will not be a good one. If flames are to burn forcefully, bowls of corn porridge must be offered to the ancient gods of fire. Choosing the proper date for this burning is critical, for the field must be dry. If the farmer waits too long, the spring rains may come and make a good fire impossible. The Maya offer *Saka'* to the Moson-ikob — the whirlwinds, to ensure their aid in fanning the flames. The offering needed for this ceremony is 13 *jícaras* of *Saká*.

MENU:

> SAKA', Dried Corn Porridge, 13 jícaras, page 309

SOWING THE FIELDS

Elaborate festivities at one time accompanied the rites of sowing the new fields. J. Eric S. Thompson, an early twentieth century anthropologist, witnessed a ceremony among the Maya in which an all-night vigil was kept on the evening before the crops were to be planted. The inner spirit of the corn called Santo Ixim was thought to hide in the last ears of the harvest brought in from the previous milpa. Those last ears to be gathered were drizzled with the blood from a sacrificed chicken and set aside for sowing. Cacao and ground corn were then offered to the gods in small gourds. Such practices, unfortunately, no longer take place in Yucatan, for only the "grandfathers" remember the ceremony. Nowadays the typical offering is 13 *jícaras* of *Saká*.

MENU:

> SAKA', Dried Corn Porridge, 13 jícaras, page 309

AN INDIVIDUAL PLEA FOR RAIN

In Mamita, a ceremony is still being offered to the Four Winds in a ritual plea for rain. Four chicken heads and four chicken feet are buried at each of the four corners of a farmer's cornfield during the ceremony. A *Pibiwah* (corn tamale) and a gourd of *Saka'* (corn porridge) are then set out for each of the Four Winds. Each bread requires four tortillas or *pimes*. The number of tortillas in each offering is an indication of the deity—in this case, one of the Four Winds—for whom it is being prepared.

MENU:

PIBIWAH, Bread Cooked in a Pib, 4 breads, page 306
SAKA', Dried Corn Porridge, 4 jícaras, page 309

Pibiwah is a general term used to describe the sacred tamales that are slowly roasted in a *pib* or underground oven. These ceremonial breads may be further distinguished by their contents. A *Bu'uliwah*, for instance, includes black beans, *Ibewah* includes lima beans and *Tutiwah* indicates the presence of pumpkin or squash seeds. Out of necessity, a regular oven may be substituted for a *pib* in the following recipe.

PIBIWAH—BU'ULIWAH
Black Bean Tamale

Have on Hand:

2 recipes Masa for Tamales, page 116
Tsah bi Bu'ul (Frijol Colado), Enriched Black Bean Purée, page 172
8 ten-inch pieces of banana leaves, prepared for cooking, page
    120, or parchment paper, or aluminum foil
Banana leaf ties or household string
Favorite chili salsa

Ingredients:

2 recipes masa
¾ cup pumpkin or squash seeds, toasted
Water as needed
½ cup honey
1 recipe *Tsah bi Bu'ul (Frijol Colado)*, Black Bean Purée
8 10-inch pieces banana leaves, aluminum foil, or parchment
    papers
Banana strings or household string to use as ties

Method:

Line up the 8 banana leaf pieces, side by side.

Pat out 8 fat tortillas using ¼ cup of masa for each one. Place each of the tortillas on a banana leaf.

Mix the pumpkin seeds with enough water to make a thin paste (about $1/3$ cup of water). Spread a layer of pumpkin seed paste over the top of each of the tortilla.

Pat out 8 more fat tortillas and place them on top of the first layer. Spread on a spoonful of honey.

Add a third layer of tortillas. Spread on a heavy layer of *Tsah bi Bu'ul (Frijol Colado)*.

Add the fourth layer of tortillas. Make four indentations in the top of each tortilla, one for each of the Four Winds. Spread on another layer of pumpkin seeds, adding extra in each of the indentations.

Fold over the edges of a banana leaf and wrap it as if it were a package. Tie the Pibiwah with string to secure the contents. Prepare the remaining tortillas in the same manner. Place them in a steamer and steam for 1 to 1½ hours—or place the tamales on the rack of a large roasting pan. Pour in about an inch of water (but don't let the water reach the level of the tamales). Cover the whole roasting pan with foil and bake at 325 degrees for 1½ hours. The masa should flake with a fork when it is done.

To Serve:

Unwrap the tamale and spoon some salsa on top. Serve with extra beans and salsa.

Serves 6 to 8.

CH'A'CHAAK
A Village Plea for Rain

A Ch'a'chaak is of crucial importance because it combines the efforts of all the villagers in a collective plea for rain. Each family contributes some corn, live fowl and squash seeds for the raingods' dinner. In some towns, the Ch'a'chaak is only offered in case of drought. In other areas, the ceremony is performed annually in July, even if the supply of rain is plentiful. This is a three-day celebration for both agriculture and the hunt, as both activities are thought to be under the jurisdiction of the same deities. The men offer gourds of *Saká* to San Marcelino, San Cecilio and San Gabriel, protectors of the deer and other wild animals and ask for success in finding a good supply of game. The *xmen* consults his *zaztun* (divining crystal) to determine the best place for the men to hunt.

As a woman, I was not invited to the Ch'a'chaak, for females must remain cloistered in their homes during these crucial days, tending to their regular household chores and grinding extra corn and squash seeds for the ceremony. It is of particular importance to avoid any area near the sacred well, lest the men who are performing rituals for the gods of thunder and lightning be contaminated by a woman. It is said that when the raingods fill their calabashes to water the fields, they fill them with this virgin water. All of the village men spend two nights in the jungle, offering *Balché* and *Saká* to the gods. When they return, there is a joyous celebration and fabulous feast for everyone.

The following menu is offered for all of the most important agricultural and protection ceremonies. Only a few minor substitutions are allowed by the deities. A deer or pig from the hunt or several domestic chickens may be substituted for the turkey. Because *Balché* is difficult to find, rum or *agardiente* is a more common liquid offering. No other changes may be made.

MENU:

> SAKA', Dried Corn Porridge, page 309
> BALCHÉ, Honeyed Bark Liquor, or Rum, or Agardiente, page 310
> PAVO EN K'OL INDIO, Turkey Simmered in a Sacred Broth, page 311
> TUTIWAH, Pumpkin Seed Tamale, page 313

SAKA'
Dried Corn Porridge

Saká is not a part of the secular hearth, but is cooked only on ceremonial occasions. When dried corn is cooked for *Saká*, it is prepared without the usual builder's lime that is necessary for softening the tough outer covering. *Saká* is therefore considered sacred or "cold," an appropriate food for the gods. It may be served with honey or chili; the deities seem to prefer the honeyed version.

Have on Hand:

Chili liquid from *K'ut bi Ik* (optional), page 72

Ingredients:

1 pound dried corn
Water as needed
$^1/_3$ cup or more honey, or chili liquid from *K'ut bi Ik* (optional)

Method:

Place the dried corn in a large saucepan and add three times as much water as corn. Bring the corn to a simmer, cover it and cook for 1½ hours. Let the mixture cool.

Purée the mixture in a blender.

Pass the purée through a sieve and into a cooking pot. Bring the mixture to a simmer and cook until it has the consistency of creamed soup. Add a little more liquid, if needed. Sweeten with honey or add chili to taste.

To Serve:

Serve at room temperature.
Serves 12 or more.

BALCHÉ
Sacred Wine of the Gods

Balché is prepared with bark from the *balché* tree, a tree that is so rare it is even difficult to find in Yucatan. When the Spaniards arrived in the peninsula, they were appalled at the drunken condition of the natives. It seemed as if the Maya were always celebrating a fiesta, recovering from a fiesta, or planning the next fiesta. To make matters worse, the Mayan gods demanded inebriation as a show of piety, so copius amounts of *balché* were constantly being consumed. Spanish officials quickly issued a decree forbidding the usage of this wicked beverage. Not unlike Prohibition, this hasty edict caused more problems than it solved, so within a few years the decree was appealed. Nonetheless, the cultivation of *balché* went into a decline from which it never recovered. This is a tragedy for both man and the gods, as *balché* is a delicious elixir that tastes a little like bubbly pineapple juice.

Now available only in the most isolated parts of the peninsula, most *balché* trees are known only to the *xmen* who harvest its bark for the most sacred of the yearly ceremonies. The holy beverage is thought to provide protection from evil spirits and propitiate the gods of rain.

One cannot help but hope that the Maya gods will accept an offering of fine wine or a bottle of bubbling champagne, in lieu of the elusive *balché*.

Ingredients:

> 4 large pieces of *balché* bark
> 2 quarts water
> 1 cup honey
> 2 inch piece cinnamon
> 6 allspice berries

Method:

Place all of the ingredients in a clay pot and allow them to steep for three days.

Strain the liquid and serve at room temperature.

Serves 8.

PAVO EN K'OL INDIO
Turkey Simmered in a Sacred Broth

This is the most delicious turkey I have ever eaten. It is wonderful hot or cold. No wonder the gods are partial to this hearthrite and have requested it for the most important of their agricultural and purification ceremonies.

Have on Hand:

> 1 recipe of *Recado Colorado*, Red Spice Paste, page 51
> Hot chili, toasted and chopped, or a favorite salsa

Ingredients:

> 1 turkey, about 12 pounds
> 5 quarts water
> 1 or 2 hot green chilies, whole, toasted
> 2 onions, toasted
> 2 bulbs garlic, toasted
> 1 recipe *Recado Colorado*
> Salt to taste
> 6 cups masa or 2½ cups masa harina

Method:

Place the turkey in a large stockpot with the water. If the turkey is not covered with water, add some more.

Add the *Recado Colorado* and bring the turkey to a simmer. Cover and cook for 3 hours, or until tender. Check the broth for salt. Add more, if necessary.

Remove the turkey from the stockpot and place it on a large platter until it has cooled. Debone the turkey and set the meat aside.

Strain the broth from the stockpot. If a *Tutiwa* (tamale) will be accompanying the turkey, set aside 3½ cups of the broth to mix with it. Return the remaining broth to the stockpot; there should be at least 10 cups of liquid. If not, add additional water.

Remove 1 quart of liquid from the pot to prepare a thickened broth or *K'ol*. Set it aside to cool.

Add the 6 cups of masa or 2½ cups of masa harina to the cooled liquid and stir with a whisk until all of the lumps disappear. Add the *K'ol* to the stockpot and simmer over medium heat, stirring frequently, until it begins to resemble a thin pancake batter. Return the turkey meat to the pot and simmer the *K'ol* for 30 more minutes. Stir frequently, for the mixture has a tendency to stick. Check the seasoning.

To Serve:

Because this hearthrite is always offered in gourds during a ceremony, a bowl would make a similar serving dish. Place a portion of *Tutiwah* on the bottom of the bowl and add plenty of turkey and thickened broth. Some toasted chili or salsa makes a lovely topping.

Serves 12.

TUTIWAH
Pumpkin Seed Tamale

Have on Hand:

> 1 recipe Masa for Tamales, page 116
> 1 banana leaf, prepared for cooking, page 120, or parchment paper or aluminum foil
> Banana strings or household string for wrapping
> *Salsa Ranchera, Xnipek,* or other salsa

Ingredients:

> 1 large banana leaf
> 1 recipe Masa for Tamales
> ½ cup pumpkin or squash seeds, toasted and ground
> ¼ cup water

Method:

Toast the pumpkin or squash seeds until they are golden brown. Be careful to keep the heat low, for the seeds burn quickly and easily. While the seeds are still warm, place them in a blender and grind them to a fine powder.

Add ¼ cup of water to the pumpkin seeds and blend the mixture well.

Place the banana leaf sections lengthwise, ribbed side down, on a work surface, leaving a 2 inch overlap in the center. Position the sections so that the outside edges are still on the outside and the ribbed edges are still at the center.

Place half of the masa mixture in the center of the banana leaf and shape it into a circle. Sprinkle with all but 2 tablespoons of the toasted pumpkin seeds. Press the remaining masa dough onto the first layer, taking care to not distort the shape. Make 13 indentations in the masa, starting with an indentation in the center; the design will represent the shape of a Maya cross. Deposit a scant ½ teaspoon of the pumpkin seeds into each indentation.

Preheat the oven to 325 degrees.

Fold the banana leaves around the masa, as though wrapping a package. Tie the package with string and place it on the rack of a baking pan. Fill the baking pan about half full with water. Place the tamale on the rack, cover the entire pan with foil, and bake it for 1½ hours.

To Serve:

Open the tamale at the table and cut it into serving pieces. Add some *Salsa Ranchera, Xnipek*, or other salsa.

If serving with *Pavo en K'ol Indio*, place a slice of *Tutiwah* in the bottom of a bowl and add the turkey, broth and salsa on top.

314

LA PRIMICIA (The Promise)

The *Primicia* is a Thanksgiving that marks the culmination of the agricultural cycle, a time when the harvest is first brought in from the fields. Deities and honored spirits look forward with anticipation to this feast as a "thank you" for the largesse received. If the weather has been good and crops are plentiful, a *pib* is prepared to roast several hundred pounds of freshly picked corn. The usual dried corn tortillas are replaced with *Is-wahes*, fresh corn tortillas and *Saká*, dried corn porridge, is supplanted by *Ak'sa'*—made with young tender corn. Corn is often the beverage, main dish and bread during these joyous early days of the harvest. It is a festive time with everyone enjoying a gluttony of new corn.

Corn is the only crop that is considered vital to the Maya. As other fruits and vegetables begin to ripen in the milpa, a portion is cooked and offered to the gods, but the Maya do not usually build a *pib*. Because the ceremonies for other foods are not thought to be crucial to their well-being, there is no need for a *xmen* and women are allowed to participate in the abbreviated ritual. To prepare the offering, the woman of the house simmers the first fruits of beans, squash, or other vegetable in a *ts'anchak*—with water—and makes a stack of nine tortillas. She fills a gourd with some of the *ts'anchak* and places two sticks on top of the gourd to make a sign of the cross. The cross forms a sturdy base that holds the nine tortillas. The gourd and its contents are secured with string and carefully hung from the branches of a nearby tree. The number nine in the tortilla stack signifies that the offering is intended for Diós Padre Terno (the Father in the Holy Triad).

MENU:

> PIBILNALES, Corn Cooked in an Earthen Oven, page 316
> AK'SA', Fresh Corn Porridge, page 318, or any vegetables
>   cooked in Ts'anchak
> TORTILLAS or IS-WAHES

PIBILNALES
Corn Cooked in an Earthen Oven

Pibilnales may sometimes be found in Yucatecan markets. Still enveloped by their protective shucks, they have a deep beige color and firm chewy texture that differentiates them from regular field corn. They will last for three or four days before developing a soft orange fungus that villagers consider a special delicacy. This fungus is quite beautiful—a soft pumpkin color. Once the corn develops this *kuxum*, it is toasted on the coals, as indicated in the the recipe following this one.

It is impossible to duplicate the flavor and texture of corn cooked underground. Luckily, a covered grill lends a smoky flavor to the still husked ears. The Maya eat their *Pibilnales* without any condiments and so do I. They are good with lime and chili—or even butter, for the nontraditionalists.

Ingredients:
Ears of corn, husks intact
Lime wedges
Dried red chili, ground, or butter

Method:
Leave each ear of corn in its husk. Wash it thoroughly, wrap it in foil and place it directly on some barely smoldering coals. Turn frequently and cook for about 15 to 20 minutes, or until done.

To Serve:
Remove the husk from each ear. Squeeze with lime and sprinkle with dried red chili.

POKBILNALES
Toasted Corn

Pok refers to something that has been cooked over a fire. *Pokbilnales* are *Pibilnales* that have developed an orange fluff or *kuxum*. Once this *kuxum* appears, corn is no longer eaten "as is," but is given a toasting directly on the coals of a hearthfire. The orange *kuxum* disappears after a few minutes of cooking and the kernels char and toughen a bit.

To prepare *Pokbilnales*, simply remove the husks from any cooked corn and reheat it directly over the coals on a grill.

AK'SA'
Fresh Corn Porridge

Ak'sa' may be prepared with either chili or honey. The honeyed version is the one that is offered to the gods, but I prefer it with chili.

Have on Hand:

Chili liquid from K'ut bi Ik, page (optional), page 72

Ingredients:

2 pounds fresh corn kernels, cut from the cob
Water as needed
Salt to taste
Honey, or chili liquid from *K'ut bi Ik* (optional)

Method:

Place the corn in a large pot with enough water to cover it, plus 4 cups.

Cover the pot and simmer the corn for 1 hour. Let the mixture cool.

Purée the corn and water in a blender. Pass the mixture through a sieve and into a cooking pot. Cook for another 30 minutes until slightly thickened. Season with salt, if desired. Add a little more water if necessary to make the porridge like a very thin cream soup.

Stir in honey to taste or drizzle some liquid chili on top.

To Serve:

Serve in small bowls or jícaras.
Serves 12 or more.

IS-WAHES
Fresh Corn Tortillas

This is an unusual once a year treat, rarely encountered beyond village environs. Typically prepared in early autumn when burgeoning fields burst with their harvest of young corn, *Is-wahes* have a flavor similar to cornbread. They are usually enjoyed at a very special October breakfast, accompanied by new ears of toasted corn *Pibilnales* and gourds of the fresh corn porridge called *Ak'sa'* or *Atole Nuevo*. Basic *Is-uahes* contain only freshly ground corn, a little water and a little salt. Preparations are lengthy, for the Maya grind the corn, sun-dry the masa for several days and then grind it once again. The masa is dried one more day and put through a strainer. This delicate dough is then formed into tortillas. Some cooks add sugar, flour, or lard to the basic recipe. Depending upon the additions, *Is-wahes* can taste like a dry naturally sweet cornbread—or a crisp short cookie. All versions of this harvest delicacy are delicious.

Is-wahes are more difficult to make than a regular tortilla, for they have a tendency to stick. Any leftover Is-wahes can be dried in the sun for a day or two, then perforated in the middle. The Maya string them into long garlands and hang them from the rafters for extended storage, but they are at their very best freshly made.

Have on hand:

Cloth-lined basket for *Is-wahes*
Griddle or heavy skillet

Ingredients:

Corn, freshly cut from the cob
Salt
Water to mix with the corn and form a thick paste
Vegetable oil

Method:

Grind the corn and set it in the sun to dry from 1 to 3 days.

Grind the corn once again and set it in the sun to dry for 1 more day. Force the masa through a sieve.

Add just a bit of water to the mixture—barely enough for it to hold together. Form a walnut-sized bit of masa into a tortilla. Follow the instructions for using a tortilla press in Basic Corn Flour Tortillas.

Heat a griddle or large heavy skillet. Pour about ½ teaspoon of oil onto the griddle: spread it evenly over the surface with a paper towel. Cook the *Is-wahes* like a cracker over low heat until they are golden brown, about 5 minutes on each side.

To Serve:

Place the cooked cornbreads in a cloth-lined basket. They may be eaten like a cracker or a bread, with meals or as a snack.

IS-WAHES DULCE
Sweet Is-wahes

This sweet variation is more typical of large villages or urban areas.

Ingredients:

2 pounds corn, freshly cut from the cob
1 egg, beaten
1 cup flour
¼ cup sugar (or to taste)
1 cup lard, butter, or other shortening

Method:

Grind the corn and dry it for one day in the sun.

Mix the ground corn with egg, flour, sugar, and lard, butter, or other shortening.

Form tortillas and cook them in the same manner as for basic *Is-wahes*.

Serves 6 to 8.

THE LOH (Redemption of the Priest)

A Purification and Sanctification Ceremony

Casellano's principal occupation is caring for his milpa, but he also serves as the caretaker of Acabchen. As the local *xmen*, he needs to take some very serious precautions. Every two years he offers rites to the gods and spirits that inhabit the bush and asks for their blessing and protection from evil winds. Because of the importance of this offering, there must be no cutting corners on any of the ingredients. The menu for a Loh is the same as for a Cha'a'chak, when an entire village pools its resources in a plea for rain.

Preparations for these rites begin the morning before the ceremony, when Casellano heads into the bush and collects enough *hol* and *bob* leaves for the tamales. The night before the rituals, Casellano and his invited guests dig a *pib* and construct an altar. In the meantime, Rosita grinds and cooks the 45 pounds of corn needed for making the masa and Casellano's sacred breads. By 4:30 A. M., Casellano is ready to initiate the ceremony by placing a small cross in the middle of a leaf-covered altar. He dips a small leaf into a *jícara* and sprinkles *Saká* in each of the four cardinal directions. Chanting to both the Maya deities and Catholic saints, he invites them to the feast and asks for their help, cooperation and blessing.

To make the breads, the men spread a sheet of plastic on the ground and set a bucket of masa in the center. Casellano takes a ball of masa, flattens it a bit with the palm of his hand, and sprinkles an offering of ground squash seeds into the middle of the dough. He then presses the masa into a *pim*, a fat tortilla. As Casellano prepares each *pim*, Lucas brushes it with a pumpkin-seed liquid. The process continues until there are thirteen *pimes* in the pile. Casellano decorates the top *pim* with thirteen indentations to make the sign of the cross and fills each indentation with squash seeds. He then flattens the entire tamale and wraps it securely.

The men continue to work with the masa, creating several piles of bread with a specific quantity of *pimes* in each pile. The number of squash seed indentations on the top of each *pim* must correspond with the number of *pimes* in each pile. This number is a symbol for the recipient of the offering. The number 13, for instance, is a gift for the god of rain, El Diós de la Lluvia. The number four represents the *balamoob* who guard the entrances to the village. The tiniest one, with three flattened breads in a bundle, is offered to the *alux*, El Señor Sansifuriano, who guards the deer and other wild animals in the forest.

Five chickens are to be offered for Casellano's protection ceremony. As he holds each one up to the gods, he tips a bit of rum into each beak before the sacrifice. This tiny sip of rum is needed to transform Rosita's domestic hens into the sacred variety. Copius sips of rum for all human participants accompany the offerings. Now the breads have finished baking and it is time to unearth the sacred oven. The holy banquet is now ready.

To serve his offering to the deities, Casellano places the chickens and their broth into four metal buckets. He unwraps the four largest *pimes*, coarsely crumbles the breads, and stirs them into the broth. There were now four buckets of chicken to decorate the altar, but the savory display lacked an important finishing touch. Casellano picked up the chickens' feet and arranged them so that their toes stuck out from the top of each pail. He set the buckets on the altar, arranged the breads in their proper positions and lit two candles. Dropping to his knees, Casellano placed the tiniest bundle on the ground in honor of the *alux*.

I was entranced, for the bush was alive with Casellano's gods. The altar, lush with jungle leaves and aglow with flickering candles seemed to emit an electrical charge. I could feel the proximity of the ancient Maya spirits, felt warmed by their energy and comforted by their presence. To begin the feast, Casellano wrapped a piece of chicken in a *bob* leaf and placed it in a jícara with a generous helping of *K'ol* on top. It did not take long for the deities to consume the essence of the carefully prepared offerings. As Casellano's mortal guests gathered around the altar to share in the ambrosial feast, I had no doubt that each of us relished the banquet with as much gusto and enthusiasm as the gods.

THE MAYA LIFE CYCLE

The four most important life cycle ceremonies are the Handwashing Ceremony, Hetzmek, Wedding and Death. The Handwashing Ceremony and Hetzmek are usually small private family gatherings. The wedding, as one might imagine, can be a rather grand affair. Rural Maya do not pay any attention to birthdays, but the yearly anniversary of a death is a time of fond remembrance and celebration.

THE HANDWASHING CEREMONY

When a child is born, the parents solemnly ask a trusted man and his wife to serve as the *compadres* who will carry the little one through the baptism ceremony. With the acceptance of such a favor, a close and significant union is established between the two families. After the baptism, when the child nears its first birthday, the parents provide a dinner and ceremony for the godparents of their baby. It is a solemn occasion with decorations of candles, frangipani and chili leaves. A small gourd of flower-filled water is provided for washing the hands of the compadres and all invited guests. The parents provide a feast for their compadres and a gift of four candles and some cigarettes.

MENU:

> PAVO MECHADO, Stuck Turkey, page 234
> Tortillas

HETZMEK

When a baby is tiny and needs to have its head supported, it is carried in its mama's arms. When the child reaches three or four months of age, it is old enough to be held on a mama's hip and such an occasion is considered to be a rather momentous one. When Robert Redfield was doing studies in Chan Kom during the 1930's, he found that the exact timing of the Hetzmek was often three months for a girl, since the hearth that she will learn to use has three stones and four months for a boy, because the milpa he will learn to word has four corners. Redfield explained that the nine objects placed on the table for this ceremony will vary with the sex of the child.

The godmother and godfather take turns setting the child upon her/his hip and walking around the table nine times. Each time, they pick up one of the objects, place it in the baby's hand, and give instructions as to its significance and usage. The following list of objects and their meaning was compiled by Redfield while he lived among the Maya in Chan Kom.

A pencil, so that the child may learn how to write

A book, so that a child may learn how to read

A hammer—or needle and thread, so that a child may learn how to work

A hatchet, so that a child may learn to clear a milpa

A catechism, so that a child may learn how to pray

Some coins, so that a child may learn to earn money

Some bread, so that a child may learn to eat anything, no matter how humble

Some cooked chicken, so that a child may learn to eat rich and delicious food

Some eggs, so that a child may have an awakening of understanding

Some Kah or Pinole, so that a child may have a good memory [ka-hal, to remember]

Each time a turn is taken around the table, a large squash seed is opened and consumed, to represent the opening and blossoming of the little one's intelligence.

MENU:

CHAY-WAH, Chaya or Spinach Bread, page 136
TS'ANCHAK BI KAX, Chicken in a Peppery Broth, page 29
PINOLE, Toasted Corn Beverage, page 270
HE, Eggs, Hard Boiled
TOPP, Toasted Large Squash Seeds

A MAYA WEDDING

While researching ceremonial cuisine for my thesis, I found that wedding information was rather sketchy. Then, miraculously, there it was—a seventeenth century manuscript on the Lacandon Maya that

Tozzer ferreted from the Archives of the Indies at Seville. The manuscript reads:

> Marriages are made in this fashion: ... the women guests paint themselves and paint the bride and decorate her hair and neck with as many beads, *tistines*, and copper bells as can be procured. And the men paint the bridegroom like themselves, black like devils. The form of the marriage is [as follows]:—the bride gives the bridegroom a small stool painted in colours and also gives him five grains of cacao and says to him, "This I give thee as a sign that I accept thee as my husband." And he also gives her some new skirts and another set of five grains of cacao, saying the same thing. The *cacique*, who is the priest on all these occasions, joins their hands, places for them a *petate* in the middle of the house, and there the newly-wedded couple take their seats.

THE PAINT:

The Lacandones use two colors of ceremonial paint—black, a result of smoke collected from burning sacred copal, the fragrant pine resin found in Chiapas—and red, a dye made from achiote seed. Both of these dyes are considered representations of rain. When the copal is burned, it emits a thick black smoke that represents man—a few pine needles sprinkled on top create a white smoke, representing woman.

THE STOOL AND NEW SKIRTS:

The traditional seat or stool in a Maya home is called a *kanche*. Hollowed from a single piece of wood, it measures about 18"x 10"x 8". As the jaguar seat or throne of a Maya noble was indicative of authority, the same symbolism may apply to the male in the wedding ceremony. A Maya woman's gift of a seat or stool to her husband could be interpreted as her assent to his power and the acknowledgement of his right to rule from the throne within his own home. The woman's gift of new skirts is called a *muhul*. Fragrant pink and white frangipani blossoms called *chacnicte* and *zacnicte* are often used as floral decorations. Thought to ensure fertility, the Lacandon Maya considered these beautiful flowers the mother and father of the gods.

THE CACAO:

Cacao was the pre-Columbian Indian's principal form of currency. It is rather disheartening to note the supposed value of a wife. The cost of a slave has been recorded at 100 beans of cacao. A woman of the evening could be secured for 10. Yet, the allotment for the services of a wife had been set aside at only 5.

The marital exchange of chocolate is in essence a contract, with the man acknowledging that he will provide for his woman and she, in turn, acknowledging that she will manage wisely the affairs of the home and hearth. Nowadays the same contract is a part of the ceremony, but silver coins have replaced the chocolate.

THE BALCHÉ:

Balché, the primary offering for any ancient Maya ceremony, is also a prerequisite for the nuptial festivities.

MENU:

> TSIK DE VENADO, Deer with a Vegetable Medley, page 255
> PAVO EN RELLENO NEGRO, Turkey in Blackened Chili Sauce
>   (see *Chilmole de Pollo*, Chicken in Black Chili Sauce, page 328)
> TORTILLAS
> BALCHE', page 310

DEATH

A Maya village will collectively honor all of its dead during the eight days of Hanal Pixan and the *octave*, but individual families pay homage to their own loved ones on the anniversary of the actual day of death. It is a time of fond remembrance and festivity, a time to think of the dear one and all they represented.

On the first anniversary of a death, something simple like *Caldillo de Ibes*, Lima Beans Cooked in a Light Broth, is offered, for the soul is vulnerable at such an early date and is unable to handle anything too spicy. By the second anniversary, the soul is more stable, understanding and accepting of its situation. An elaborate meal of toasted chili can at this point be tolerated and *Keken Relleno Negro*, Pig in Toasted Black Chili Sauce, is the traditional offering of remembrance from this time onward.

MENU:

> CALDILLO DE IBES, Lima Beans Cooked in a Light Broth,
>   page 180
> KEKEN EN RELLENO NEGRO, Pig in Toasted Black Chili
>   Sauce, page 297
> X-TANCHUCUA, Porridge of Chocolate and Corn, page 300

CHILMOLE DE POLLO
Chicken Cooked in Black Chili Sauce

The name of this meal is part Nahuatl and part Spanish, which gives some indication as to the nature of its origin. *Chilmole* may have been on the Maya menu for centuries, but chicken is a decided newcomer to its polyglot cuisine. Whether new, old, or in-between, anything cooked in *Recado de Chilmole* is delicious. Add a brightly colored vegetable, such as *Chocho* or *Elote Indio* to complete the portrait of a perfect feast. A turkey (*pavo*) may be substituted for the two chickens in this recipe.

Have on Hand:

     1 recipe *Recado de Chilmole*, page 52
     Hot freshly made or packaged tortillas

Ingredients

     2 chickens
     10 cups water
     1 recipe *Recado de Chilmole*
     1 onion, chopped
     4 tomatoes, chopped
     3 cups fresh *masa* or 1 cup *masa harina* and 2 cups water

Method:

Brown the 2 whole chickens on a charcoal grill, griddle or heavy skillet. Continue cooking until the meat is nicely browned and partially cooked.

Place the chickens in a large stockpot filled with water and add the *Recado de Chilmole*. Add the chopped onion and tomatoes. Bring the mixture to a simmer.

Mix the fresh *masa* or *masa harina* and water; strain it through a sieve into the stockpot. Stir frequently so that the mixture does not stick. Cook until the chicken is done, 30 to 40 minutes.

To Serve:

Remove the chicken to a cutting board and cut it into serving-size pieces. Place a portion of chicken in a large soup bowl and drench it with several ladles of chilied broth. Take a torn piece of tortilla, pull some of the meat from the bone, and dip it into the sauce. Provide plenty of napkins.

Serves 8

A GLOSSARY OF MAYA CULINARY INGREDIENTS
Both Ancient And Modern

"Utensils for making chocolate."

$\mathcal{T}$he names of the flora and fauna that make up this selection of Maya ingredients are listed in English, Spanish and Maya, whenever possible. Occasionally, there is no counterpart for the Spanish or Maya word in English, usually because the item is not encountered beyond its provincial locality. In a few cases, the Spanish word is so well known and accepted that English is not even necessary. A number of these culinary foodstuffs are commonplace throughout the world and have been included only to introduce the Spanish or Maya nomenclature. In such cases, no comment or explanation is needed. A number of the more exotic ingredients are not necessary for the recipes in this book, but have been included because they might be encountered in the city and village markets or an extended trip into the countryside.

The use of many of these plants and animals is not restricted to the culinary realm. They often play a dual role, serving as sustenance for daily living, as well as the basis of remedies for the *yerbatero*, or healer in the village. Many of the medicinal recipes are quite ancient and no longer used, but a few are still employed, in spite of access to modern medicine. Anyone interested in learning more about the healing properties of native plants may want to refer to Ralph L. Roys, *The Ethno-Botany of the Maya* and *The Ritual of the Bacabs*. Two very informative treatises in Spanish are *Nomenclatura Etnobotanica Maya*, by Alfredo Barrera Marin, Alfredo Barrera Vazquez, and Rosa Maria Lopez Franco, and *Plantas Medicinales del Estado de Yucatan*, by Rosa Ma. Mendieta and Silvia del Amo R. Other interesting sources are Bishop Diego de Landa and other clerics who wrote extensively about the plants and animals they encountered during the sixteenth and seventeenth centuries. Their comments are included whenever possible. Additional references are listed in the Bibliography.

ACHIOTE, ANOTTO, KUXUB, Bixa orellana, Linnaeus:
Landa noted, "There is a little tree which the Indians are accustomed to grow by their houses, which bears some prickly husks like chestnuts, although not so large nor so hard. These open when ripe and contain little seeds, which they employ, as do the Spaniards also, to color their stews. It gives a color like saffron, so fine a color that it gives it a deep stain."

Achiote is an important ceremonial offering to the gods and serves as one of the most important condiments in Yucatecan cuisine. Because the ancient Maya associated the tiny seeds with rain, they used them in most of their agricultural rites, not only to season the stews offered to the gods, but to adorn their bodies and paint their clothing. Achiote was also used as currency during the pre-Hispanic era.

Medicine: Tender leaf tips were employed for the treatment of hives. The seeds were crushed and used as a poultice for hemorrhoids.

AGOUTI, ZUB or TZUB, Dasyprocta punctata yucatanica, Goldman:
According to Landa, "There is a little animal, very sad by nature, which always goes in caverns and hiding places ... and for hunting it the Indians set a certain trap in which they catch it. It is like a hare and goes by leaps and is timid. It has very long and thin front teeth, and a little tail even smaller than a hare's, and is of a dark greenish color. It is wonderfully tame and amiable and is called *zub*." The *agouti* was an important food source for the ancient Maya. Although game in the bush is no longer abundant, this little animal still provides an occasional dinner when the hunt has been a fruitful one.

Medicine: The claws were crushed and utilized in a beverage to alleviate bleeding in women.

ALLSPICE, PIMIENTA GORDA, PIMIENTA DE TABASCO, Pimienta dioica:
Allspice comes from a tree with pale peeling bark and luxuriant foliage. The berries are harvested during the summer months and dried in the sun. The leaves of this tree make a delicious tea, while the berries are used to flavor recados and *pinole* (a parched-corn beverage). The ancient Maya used its berries to embalm the bodies of their priests and nobles.

Both Jamaica and Guatemala claim to have grown the first allspice. A Spanish expedition led by a priest named Fray Diego Delgado led to the founding of a mission at a site called La Concepción de la Pimienta. The exact location of this mission was not noted, but the journal states that it was in a region of allspice trees. Although there does not appear to be a Maya name for this important condiment, the pre-Columbian usage of the berries and the allspice forest mentioned in 1622 indicate that the Maya have been utilizing these aromatic trees for many centuries.

AMARANTH, UELITE CHINO or BLEDO, X-TEZ, Amaranthus dubius, Mart.:

The name for this wild amaranth comes from the word *Tez-cuntah*, which means to salute. According to the *Motul Dictionary*, *Tezcuntech ix ahau* was a phrase the Maya used to salute their important lords.

ARMADILLO, UECH, Dasypus novemcinctus mexicanus, Peters:

Landa observed, "There is another little animal like a very small pig lately born, especially in its forefeet and snout, and it is a great rooter. This animal is all covered with pretty shells so that it looks very like a horse covered with armor, with only its ears and fore and hind feet showing and with its neck and forehead covered with the shells. It is very tender and good to eat." An armadillo can be somewhat gamey in flavor, but provides interesting variety during a village hunt.

ARROWROOT, CHA'AK, Maranta arundinacea, Linneaus.

AVOCADO, AGUACATE, ON, Persea gratissima, Gaertn., Persea americana, Miller:

Landa states, "There is a large fresh tree which the Indians call *on*. It bears a fruit like large gourds, which is very delicate, and has a taste like butter; it is mellow and buttery. This is very nourishing. It has a large pit and a delicate rind. It is eaten, cut up like a melon and with salt." The name is derived from the Nahuatl word *aguacatl*. This delicious fruit is one of the oldest in Mexico; the remains of avocados have turned up in the El Riego phase in the Tehuacan Valley, approximately 7200-5200 B.C.

Medicine: The toasted seed provided relief from diarrhea. The boiled seed was utilized for urinary problems.

BALCHÉ: Lonchocarpus longistylus, Pittier.

The *Chilam Balam of Chumayel* states that *Balché* was the first meal of their Creator. When offered to the gods, this drink is called *ha*. If some ground cacao is added to the libation, the mixture is called *uyonin*. The tree and the drink made from the bark both bear the same name. The Maya ferment the bark in honey, water and spices and offer the fragrant elixir to their agricultural deities during the most important ceremonies. Maya gods demanded that their devotees show them the proper respect by becoming inebriated. Because the alcoholic content of *Balché* is rather low, copius amounts of this beverage were needed to produce the desired state of drunkenness.

BALSAM-PEAR, CUNDEAMOR, YACUNAH-AK, Momordica charantia, Linnaeus:

A member of the squash family, this trailing garden beauty is called the "love vine." It bears little yellow flowers and sweet orange fruit with many seeds.

BEAN, FRIJOL, BU'UL: Phaseolus vulgaris, Linnaeus.

Bu'ul is the general term for the kidney bean. Landa described two varieties of small beans, one black and another that came in different colors. *X-kolibu'ul* (a small bean grown in the milpa with the corn and other vegetables) and *tsama* (a large bean grown separately) are two varieties of black beans that may be found today.

Beans were said to have been crushed with limas and squash seeds to make the first *Bolon Tsacab* (God K, according to Seler), a god that has close associations with the rain god. Beans were also used by the *xmen* in divination rituals. The sowing of beans was at one time accompanied by an all-night vigil, but this practice has not been observed for several decades. The Maya feel that beans have a spirit dwelling within, but this spirit can only be found during the early period of a harvest. If the harvest is plentiful, the first gathering of beans is offered to the deities in the form of tamales or *Bu'uliwah*. During times of scarcity, a bowl of cooked black beans and some tortillas are hung from a tree as a gesture of thanksgiving.

Some of the different varieties of beans found in Yucatan today may be identified as follows: New Bean, *Frijol Nuevo, Ak'bu'ul*; Green Bean, *Ejote, Cachibache; Espelon, X-pelon, Frijol Bayo*; White Bean, *Frijol Blanco; Black Bean, Frijol Negro, Tsama*; Milpa Bean, *Frijol De Milpa, X-kolibu'ul*.

Medicine: Mashed beans were prescribed as a remedy for sore eyes, dysentery, hiccoughs caused by drunkenness, and pain caused by sorcery. Beans were also offered to women when they failed to menstruate.

BEETS, REMOLACHA or BETABEL, Beta vulgaris, Linnaeus, var. rapacea.

BLACK PEPPER, PIMIENTA CASTILLA, Piper nigrum:

Black pepper is used extensively in many of the recados or seasoning pastes.

BOBCHE, or BOB: Cocoloba Schiedeana, Lindau:

The *bobche* is a tree with sturdy green leaves used in making tamales for agricultural ceremonies. According to the *Motul Dictionary*, the leaves also provided handy packets for transporting dried chili from distant fields to home pantry.

BONETE, KUM-CHE, Leucopremna mexicana, Standl.:

The *Relación de Yucatan* says, "There is another fruit which the Indians and Spaniards call *cunche {kum-che}*. It bears a large fruit with a thick rind, so that they make a very good conserve like diacitron (lemon-peel preserved in sugar). The interior is soft like that of an early fig, yellow and very similar to it in taste. The seeds are like coriander seeds, which taste of common-cress. It is a thick tall tree, and the interior of the trunk is spongy and white like that of a green gourd. It is useful to the natives, because in years of scarcity they make a food and drink of it with which they sustain themselves."

Medicine: The *kum-che* was used as a remedy for jaundice, tumors and kidney problems.

BREADNUT, RAMON, OX, Brosimum alicastrum, Swartz:

Landa has written, "There is another very beautiful and fresh tree which never loses its leaves and bears small savory figs, which they call *ox*." Maler noted, "This foliage is the principal green fodder of the country from June to March and the boiled fruit is eaten alone or with honey or corn meal. The small hard pits of the fruit were placed formerly in a gourd to form the *topp-ox-kab*, or diviner's rattle." The pits can be ground and used as flour when corn is not available.

Medicine: *Ramon* has been utilized for asthma, all kinds of coughs, laryngitis and chest pains.

BRUSSELS SPROUTS, COL DE BRUSELAS, Brassica oleracea var. gemifera.

CABBAGE, REPOLLO or COL, Brassica oleracea, Linneaus.

CALABAZA, K'UM—MEHEN-K'UM—KA—TS'OL:
There are numerous varieties of winter squash in Yucatan. The most popular ones are:

Cucurbita maxima, Duchesne is called *k'um*, a lovely pale gold squash that is cultivated for its seeds as much as for its use as a vegetable. When mature, it is about eight inches across. The Maya consume the flesh when the vegetable is young and tender. When the squash has hardened and matured over a period of several months, the seeds—*tsikil* or *pepita menuda*—are scraped from the orange flesh, then toasted and sprinkled on almost everything. They form the basis of one of Yucatan's famous stews, *Onsikil* or *Pipian*.

This species is identified by its rounded stem and leathery skin.

Curcurbita pepo, Linnaeus, called *kaal*, is rather round, green in color, and decorated with a white stripe. *Kaal (Ka* or *XKa')*) is prized for its large white seeds known as *top*, or *pepita gruesa*. Both *top* and *tsikil* were ground and mixed with beans to create the body of an important deity associated with rain, according to the *Chilam Balam of Chumayel*.

This species may be identified by a stem that has five sides: the stem expands as it extends from the vine toward the fruit.

Cucurbita moschata, Duchesne, *ts'ol*, is a beautiful squash with an exquisite delicate flavor. It is about 8 inches in diameter and somewhat flattened on top. The color is a deep emerald speckled with cream or ochre. The inner flesh is pale gold and of a very fine texture.

This species is also five sided, but the stem is more slender and expands just as it reaches the fruit.

Medicine: Gum from the *ts'ol* was utilized for burns. Flesh from the *kaal* was used to treat ringworm.

CARROTS, ZANAHORIA, Daucus carota, Linnaeus.

CAULIFLOWER, COLIFLOR, Brassica oleracea var. botrytis, de Candolle.

CHARD, ACELGA, Beta Vulgaris, Linnaeus, var. cicla.

CHAYA, CHAY, Jatropha acontifolia, Mill.:
Chaya is a little bush that grows prolifically and is easily transplanted in the tropical regions of Northamerica. It has deep emerald green leaves that have been likened to spinach, although the flavor is not the same. Almost every Maya house has an abundant planting of chaya that provides a plentiful harvest all year round. The leaves are used in beverages and as a vegetable. It has been utilized over the centuries as a famine food when nothing else could be harvested. According to Kekchi legend, Lord Xulub turned to the chaya plant to save his people from starvation.

To plant chaya, cut a small stalk from the mother plant, let it dry for a few days, then set it into the earth. Water on a daily basis until the roots are established.

Medicine: Chaya served as a remedy for jaundice, infected gums, hemorrhoids—and to expel a retarded placenta after childbirth.

CHAYOTE, KIIX-PACH-KUUM, Sechium edule (Jac.) Swartz:
This pale green squash is often utilized in village and city cooking, but is not grown in all of the rural areas. It bears a Nahuatl name.

CHESTNUTS, CASTAÑO DE MALABAR or CASTAÑAS, Artocarpus incisa, Linnaeus.

CHICKEN, POLLO, KAX.

CHILACAYOTE, Cucurbita ficifolia, Bouche':
The fruit of this member of the squash family is large and has white pulp with black seeds. Quite versatile, it is cooked like a vegetable, made into beverages and desserts, or eaten in salads.

CHILI, CHILE, IK:
More that 90 different kinds of chilies fall under the heading of Capsicum. Each variety of chili has its own characteristic flavor and depth of bite. Chilies that are not native to the area are shipped to the

Yucatan from all parts of Mexico. *Chili poblano* (*ancho*, when dried), *chili pasilla*, *chili mulato*, and *chili cascabel* are examples of imported varieties. Chilies are rich in vitamins: the red ones are an abundant source of vitamin A, while green chilies are rich in vitamin C.

Chilies are employed symbolically in ritual and play a vital part in sanctification and purification ceremonies because they chase away any "evil winds" that may cause illness or death. Sorcerers have been known to cast spells with chili. The spells are thought to harm only the guilty, not the innocent. An *hechicero* works his black magic by rubbing chili on a clay figure, then burying it in the earth. Chili has even been utilized as a weapon, for it is said that the Maya were able to keep swashbuckling pirates at bay in the Gulf of Mexico by filling the air with acrid chili smoke. Thus chased back into the sea, the marauders ventured on to more hospitable ports.

The following list of Yucatecan chilies are some of the more widely cultivated varieties.

Capsicum annuum Linnaeus: *yax-ik, chili verde*, a small green chili that becomes *chili seco* or *chak ik* when dried; *sucure ik*, a tiny green, red, or white chili; and *x-kat-ik*, a long slender pale green or yellow chili that is rather mild in flavor. *Capsicum annuum* is an annual or biannual plant.

Capsicum frutescens Linnaeus: *chile del monte* is about the size of a grain of wheat but its fire really packs a whollop. *Capsicum frutescens* is a perrenial plant.

Capsicum chinense var. jabanero, is the jabanero chili—sometimes called chili bravo or *Ts'its'ik-ik*—a little lantern-shaped chili that must be handled with care because of its exceptional bite. The jabanero is so hot that when chilies are in short supply they are sometimes cut in half and placed on the table. Each person touches a bit of tortilla on the cut chili surface. Just this simple "touch" will give the tortilla plenty of fire.

Medicine: Chilies have long been noted for their medicinal value—sore gums, aching bones, convulsions, asthma, pneumonia, colds, stomach pains, dysentery, and even ulcers are said to benefit from their potent oils. In the case of the latter ailment, chili is said to be so hot it scares the ulcer away.

CHIPILIN, Crotalaria vitellina, Ker.:
The leaves of this herb are used to season tamales in Guatemala and the southeastern part of Yucatan.

CHOCOLATE, CACAO, CACAO, Theobroma cacao, Linnaeus:

According to legend, only the gods were permitted to feast upon chocolate. Quetzalcoatl, a beneficent deity, decided he wanted to take on an earthly form so that he might teach the people of Tollan about the calendar, art and science. He also wished to make them a gift of chocolate, even though the other gods would have forbidden such a loving gesture. When Quetzalcoatl descended from Venus and came to earth, an adoring populace bestowed him with the name, Lord of the Evening Star. Quetzalcoatl planted many cacao trees and with the help of his subjects built the magnificent city of Tula. The citizens of Tollan were so happy and prosperous that the gods became jealous. The deities were particularly enraged to see how much everyone was enjoying the many benefits of chocolate, a beverage that, in their opinion, should have remained only with the divine.

The gods decided to have a conference; the concensus was that Tezcatlipoca, Quetzalcoatl's archrival, was the perfect choice for wreaking heavenly vengence. Poor Qetzalcoatl had a premonition in one of his dreams that this idyllic kingdom would soon come to an end. Just as he feared, serious problems began to develop. The cagey Tezcatlipoca made an appearance before him one evening. Offering a cup of fermented maguey juice, the scoundrel promised that if Quetzalcoatl consumed this beverage, all would be well and everyone in his kingdom would live happily ever after. Gullible Quetzalcoatl drank the potent liquid and immediately became so drunk that he disgraced himself in a night of wanton debauchery. The people of Tollan were thoroughly disgusted.

A heartbroken Quetzalcoatl surveyed his kingdom and noticed with sad eyes that not only had he disappointed his people, but all of the cacao trees had wilted and died. The situation was more than he could bear. Dejected and forlorn, he decided to leave this earthly world, but promised to return once again when the timing was right. Before setting out for his homeland—the beautiful evening star known as Venus—Quetzalcoatl gathered some seeds from the dry and withered cacao groves. Scattering chocolate seeds in his footsteps, he journeyed toward the east, bestowing once again his last precious gift, the beverage of the gods.

As a sacred beverage, chocolate was usually drunk only by the nobles and upper class. The average person might enjoy it only on special ceremonial occasions, such as birth, marriage and death. Chocolate was often ground and mixed with corn or nuts to facilitate transport from one place to another. Ground corn, flowers and honey were often added to make an aromatic beverage. In some regions mamey seeds, achiote or ground red chili added an unusual flavor.

Chocolate has had many uses. According to one of the Aztec codices, it was included as a part of the burial offerings that accompanied the departed as they travelled through the underworld and beyond. Cacao beans were also offered as a symbol of office when villagers accepted a government post. In the month of Muan, the Maya held a festival in honor of Ek Chuah, the god of cacao. A dog with chocolate colored spots was sacrificed and blue iguanas and copal were offered to the gods. Most importantly, chocolate was held in such high esteem that it was the primary form of currency in Mesoamerica. Even during pre-Conquest times, counterfeiting was not unknown, for unscrupulous merchants hollowed out the coveted beans and filled the empty shells with sand, avocado rind or wax. According to the Spanish chroniclers, a human slave could be purchased with 100 beans and a woman of the evening was worth 10, but a wife could be acquired for only 5 beans of cacao. Most of the cacao was imported from Tabasco, Chetumal and Honduras, although some of it was grown in areas where there was sufficient moisture and the water table was high.

There is much confusion and speculation regarding the origin of the word cacao. According to Eric S. Thompson, there were 13 Maya dialects that used the word cacao with some slight spelling variations throughout the Maya regions. The general Yucatec term for chocolate was *chacau haa*, meaning "hot water." Chocolate was cultivated in several tropical Maya areas, but little was grown throughout the Aztec empire. Thompson felt that the Aztec term *cacauatl* may have been borrowed from the Maya, rather than the other way around, as others have suggested. Cecilio Robelo theorized that chocolate came from the Nahuatl words *xoxo* (sour) and *atl* (water) because the elixir is rather bitter when drunk without sugar. Thomas Gage, a seventeenth century Mexican traveler, equated the sound of the chocolate beater as it swished round and round with the word *choco* and theorized that this sound gave chocolate its name.

Medicine: Chocolate (both the chocolate seeds and the pit) was prescribed for stomach pains and poisoning. It was widely used as a disinfectant for cuts and a balm for burns. In Nicaragua the natives believed that if one had consumed chocolate for breakfast, no snake would dare to bite during the day.

CILANTRO, Coriandrum sativum, Linnaeus:
This well-loved herb that looks somewhat like Italian parsley is sometimes called *Culantro* or *Culantro de Castilla* (Cuba). In Guatemala it is known as Saquil. Cilantro is often used in the salsas served in the cities, but is rarely found in the countryside.

CLOVE, CLAVO.

COATI or COATIMUNDI, PISOTE, CHIIC, Nasua narica yucatanica, Allen:
This little badger-like animal played an important part in Maya ceremonies, for it was closely associated with agriculture and the milpa. Gucumatz, the Maya creator god in the *Popul Vuh*, was also called *"Pisote."* According to Landa, "There is an animal which they call *chic*, wonderfully active, as large as a small dog, with a snout like a suckling pig. The Indian women raise them and they leave nothing which they do not root over and turn upside down and it is an incredible thing how wonderfully fond they are of playing with the Indian women and how they clean them from lice and they always go to them and will have nothing to do with a man in their lives. There are many of them and they always go in herds in a row, one after the other, with their snouts thrust in each other's tails, and they destroy to a great extent the field of maize into which they enter."

COCONUT, COCOTERO, Cocos nucifera, Linnaeus.

COFFEE, CAFÉ, Coffea arabica, Linnaeus.

CORN, MAIZ, IXIM, Zea Mays, Linnaeus:
The Maya creation legend in the *Popul Vuh*, describes how man was made from corn. Corn is the most important ingredient in any of the agricultural offerings to the deities and plays a crucial part in the daily diet of the village Maya. The average adult consumes at least two kilos of corn each day—more than four pounds. Every part of the plant is put to use. The husk is utilized as the wrappings for tamales and cigarettes. It also serves as a dish or pot scourer and is used to remove stains from laundry. Husks may serve as a filling for stuffing pillows or other soft objects and even provide a medicinal tea. The stigmas from the maize plant serve as a diuretic. *Bakal*, the cob, is used as fuel for

fires, bottle stoppers and toilet paper. Ground and mixed with honey dregs, the cob becomes forage for the animals. The leaves, green stalks and roots serve as fertilizer.

A few Maya still remember how to use their maize kernels to divine the future. This method of foretelling the future is called *xixte* and means "to separate the good from the bad." *Xixte* was at one time a principal method used by the *xmen* to determine the outcome of an illness. To ascertain a prognosis, a portion of grains is singled out from a container and arranged in piles of four. A favorable outcome for the problem at hand can be predicted if the piles of four are even in number and the remaining pile of kernels is also even. If both of the piles are uneven, the answer to the problem is unfavorable. When the piles are split, one even and one uneven, then the outcome of the event is difficult to ascertain. There is another method of using maize to predict the course of an illness. When corn kernels are dropped into a bowl of atole or *Saka*, floating kernels indicate a favorable prognosis. When corn sinks to the bottom of the bowl, the outcome of the situation appears grim.

Ix K'anle'ox, the goddess of corn and mother of all the gods, is associated with the color yellow and the cardinal direction, South. She has been given the Christian name of Santa María Magdalena.

COW, VACA.

CUCUMBER, PEPINO, Cucumis sativus, Linnaeus.

CUMIN, COMINO, Cuminum cyminum.

CURASSOW, CAMBUL, KANBUL, Crax globicera:
The curassow is a magnificently feathered bird that is said to be tastier than turkey.

CUSTARD APPLE (I), ANONA, OP, Annona reticulata, Linnaeus:
The Relación of Yucatan says, "There is another tree which the natives call *op* and the Spaniards *anona*, which is an island word. It has a fruit after the manner of the pineapple, and the rind has the same marks. The interior is white and delicate and of such good flavor that many call it blancmange. It has a quantity of black seeds, almost like those of the *chico-zapote*. A post-Conquest chronicle written by Nakuk Pech suggests that custard-apples were not eaten in Yucatan until after the arrival of the Spaniards, for the Maya called the intruders "annona-eaters." The fruit is consumed fresh or prepared in a blended fruit drink.

Medicine: The leaves were employed for snakebites, measles, scarletina and smallpox. The fruit was used for the treatment of stomach cramps and diarrhea.

CUSTARD APPLE (II), CHERIMOYA, POX, Annona cherimola, Mill.:

The *Motul Dictionary* describes the fruit as, "a certain large and spiny fruit, a species of annona." It looks somewhite like a green artichoke on the outside. The creamy white flesh within bears a few shiny black seeds. The fruit is sweet and aromatic.

DEER, CEH, Odocoileus totlecus, Saussure:

The Yucatan deer is a small white tailed variety that has become a symbol of "The Land of the Turkey and the Deer." The deer is associated with god M, the god of hunting and war. The month Zip was set aside for hunters to feast, celebrate and implore the deities for a successful hunt. It is no longer legal for restaurants to serve deer in Yucatan.

Medicine: Deer provided a remedy for respiratory problems, fainting, fever, toothache, and sore eyes. The Maya believed that if they shot a spike-horned deer while it was standing still, the tail of the deer would provide a talisman that protected its bearer from snakebite.

DOVE, PALOMA, MUCUY, Columbigallina refipennis, Bonaparte:

Evidently the ancient Maya not only hunted doves, but domesticated them also. Landa observed, "Some people raise doves as tame as ours and they multiply rapidly." Both the *tzutzuy* and *mucuy* are still raised in Maya homes.

DOVE, WHITE-FRONTED, PALOMA (I), TZUTZUY, Leptotila fulviventris, Lawrence:

DOVE, GROUND, PALOMA (II), MUCUY, Columbigallina refipennis, Bonaparte:

DUCK, PATO, KUTZ-HA:

The Maya use the word *kutz* to designate a type of small bird. The word *ha* means water—hence, water bird. It is stated in the *Relación de Yucatan*, "They also raise the native ducks of this land. They make use of their plumage in weaving their garments and eat them as well. It is good food." Landa enthused, "There are other very small ducks of great beauty which are called *maxix*. They are very tame and if they are raised in the house they do not run away ... They raise a certain kind of large white mallard ducks, which I think came to them from Peru for the plumage, and so often pluck their breasts, and they want that plumage for the embroidery of their garments .... There are mallard ducks which stay under water for a very long while fishing for food and are very bold and have a hook on their beak with which to fish."

EGGPLANT, BERENJENA, Solanum melongena, Linnaeus.

EPAZOTE, LUCUM-XIU, Chenopodium ambrosioides, Linnaeus:
This fragrant herb with its strong distinctive flavor is thought by many Mexican cooks to be essential for cooking beans.

Medicine: Epazote is native to tropical America, but is not mentioned in any Maya sourcebooks. Its name, literally translated, means worm-plant, indicating that the Maya were aware it was effacacious as a vermifuge.

FROG, RANA, UO.
The name *uo* is said to come from the frog's cry. Frogs also go by the general name of *much*. The *Motul Dictionary* describes their virtues with the notation that there are in Yucatan ... "certain frogs containing much fat and grease and {they are} good to eat." Uo is the second month of the Maya year. The frog may have been the totem of the Maya warrier, a custom that was shared with the Aztecs.

Medicine: The Maya used the gall from a frog to numb the gums so that a tooth could be pulled without pain. Frogs were also used for asthma, convulsions, nosebleeds and to prevent baldness.

GARLIC, AJO, KUKUT, Allium Sativum, Linnaeus.

GINGER, JENGIBRE, Zingiber officinale, Roscoe.

GOAT, BROCKET, YUK, Mazama pandora, Merriam and Odocoileus truei, Merriam:

According to the *Relación de Yucatan*, "There are wild goats which the Indians call *yuc*. They have only two horns like goats and are not as large as deer which have many branches on their antlers."

Medicine: Medicine men prescribed remedies from the *yuk* to help alleviate pain in the heart, colic and urinary problems.

GOPHER, TUZA, BA:

The *Relación de Yucatan* states, "There are other animals, which the Indians call *baa*, like a large rat. They are bred underground and live on roots. They catch them with snares at the outlets of their holes, and they are good food for the Indians." The Maya like to eat them in a *cham-cham*—an empanada.

Medicine: The *tuza* was employed to cure a skin eruption.

GUAVA, GUAYABO, PICHI, Psidium guajava, Linnaeus.

Landa stated that at least one species of guava was introduced by the Spaniards.

Medicine: The plant was used to treat asthma, coughs, knee pains, hemorrhoids, swollen abdomen and sore tongue.

GUAYA, UAYAM, Talisia olivaeformia (H.B.K.) Radlk.

A *guaya* tree can grow as high as 60 feet and is commonly found in the forest and villages. Landa wrote, "There is another very fresh and beautiful tree which looks just like filberts with the husk, under that husk they have a fruit like cherries and with a large stone. The Indians call them *uayam* and the Spaniards guayas." *Guayas* are sweet and look like a green hard-shelled grape with a large single pit inside.

HIERBABUENA, YERBABUENA, XAAK'IL'XIU, Mentha sativa, Linnaeus:

Hierbabuena is a member of the mint family. In different regions of Mexico other herbs go by the same name.

HONEY, MIEL, KAB:

Both wild and domesticated bees provide honey for the Maya. The bee god is named Kananholkan, Keeper of the Door to the Sky. This kindly deity repairs any broken wings or legs that have been injured when the hives are opened to extract the honey. Any bees that are killed during the honey harvest are buried with a bit of leaf to cover them and propitiate Kananholkan. Honey is an important offering to all of the Maya gods because it is a principal ingredient in their sacred beverage, Balché. The gathering of honey and tending of the hives is strictly governed by specific ceremonial rites.

IGUANA, HUH:

The Maya use the name *huh* as a general term for lizard. *Ah-Pach* refers to a crested iguana while *yax-icil* is the word for a green iguana. Held in high esteem by both the Maya and their celestial pantheon, these spiny lizards were often painted blue and sacrificed to the deities. Honored throughout pre-Hispanic Mexico, iguanas were also an important symbol for the Aztecs. Their day sign, Cuetzpalin, means lizard and corresponds to the Maya day sign K'an. K'an is the Cakchiquel Maya word for lizard.

Medicine: Iguanas were employed for sore eyes and pulling teeth. To pull a tooth without pain, one must burn an iguana with a yellow throat and use the ashes as a salve on a dog's tooth. If the dog's tooth comes out painlessly, then the same procedure may be tried on a man. If this does not prove to be successful, find an iguana with a green throat. If the ashes work on a dog's tooth, then they will also work on a man's dental problems.

JÍCAMA, CHICAM, Pachyrrhizus erosus, Linnaeus:

The ancient Maya ate the jícama raw with a sprinkling of salt, cooked into a conserve, or roasted in a *pib*. The jícama looks somewhat like a round potato with thick brown skin. Inside, the texture and color is also very much like a potato. The jícama is mild and just a touch sweet, a bit like fresh water chestnuts. They can be cooked or eaten raw. Derived from the Nahuatl, *xicamatl,* jícamas can often be found in the markets ready to eat, neatly cut into thin pieces and marinated in lime juice and ground red chili.

Medicine: The fruit is boiled in water to produce a wash for itching skin.

KOHLRABI, COLINABO, Brassica campestris var. napobrassica, de Candolle.

Kohlrabi is a root plant similar to the turnip. It can be eaten raw, but is most often found in soups and stews.

LENTILS, LENTEJAS, Lens esculenta, Moench.

LETTUCE, LECHUGA, Lactuca sativa, Linnaeus.

LIMA BEAN, LIMA, IB, Phaseolus lunatus, Linnaeus:

Lima beans are a dietary staple for the Maya. According to the *Chilam Balam of Chumayel,* lima beans were crushed and mixed with squash seeds and black beans to create the first *Bolon Tsacab*—and are thus associated with rain.

Medicine: Crushed limas were used for treating burns and skin rashes.

LIME, LIMON, Citrus aurantifolia (Christm.):

In Yucatan, limes or their juice are commonly used—lemons are not available.

LIMA AGRIA or LIMA, Citrus limmeta, var.:

This tiny little citrus fruit looks like a lime with a small bump on one end. It is used in beverages, adds flavor to a *salpicón* and stars in *Sopa de Lima.* Lime juice may be used as a substitute.

LOBSTER, LANGOSTA.

MAK'ULAN, XMAK'ULAN, Piper auritum, H.B.K.:

The shiny heart-shaped leaves of this piper plant are used in making tamales. The leaves impart a heavenly anise flavor to the masa. *Xmak'ulan* is a tropical plant that does not grow well when subjected to cool weather. The plant is called *Yerba Santa* or *Santa Maria* in Veracruz.

MAMEY, MAMEY COLORADO, CHACAL HAAZ, Callocarpum mammosa, (L.) Pierre, Lucuma mammosa, (L.) (Seler), Mammea americana, L. (Standley):

According to a Kekchi Maya legend, the mamey sapote was a sacred tree that began to sprout all of the fruits and vegetables in the world on its branches. This plant was at one time called *haz*, but when the Spaniards arrived in the New World and introduced the banana, the banana was given the name *haaz* and the *mamey* was renamed *chacal haaz*. The fruit looks something like a small brown football on the outside, but the inner fruit is a rich burnt orange. The mamey is a delight to cut into slices and eat fresh or it can be turned into colorful beverages and desserts. The *Relacion de Yucatan* stated that ... "There are other trees, very large, which are called *haz*. If you open the fruit, it is red inside. The fruit is an admirable sweet for eating; it has inside of it a large seed which is good for women to make them fair {blond}."

Medicine: The large pit from the fruit was used to make an oil that was used for skin problems, sore eyes, colds and indigestion.

MALANGA, Xanthosoma sagittifolium, Linnaeus, Schott.:

A member of the taro family, this vegetable tastes somewhat like a white potato. The flesh may be white or yellow, surrounded by a rough brown skin.

MELOCOTON or CALABAZA DE OLOR, Sicana odorifera, Naudin.:

The fruit of this plant is considered to be one of the most desired of all the calabazas. It may be eaten when green and tender or consumed later when fully ripe. *Melocoton* is especially appreciated when cooked as a sweet dessert.

MILK, LECHE.

MOJARRA, XAC, AH-XAC or POKOZ:
There are several names that seem to refer to a general term for the
mojarra. *Tzau* is a large fresh-water *mojarra*.

NANCEN, CHII, Malpighia glabra, Linnaeus:
The small red fruits from this shrub may be eaten fresh or cooked.
The fruit makes a delicious ice cream.

Medicine: The root of this shrub has been prescribed for dysentery.

NANCEN AGRIA, SAKPET, Byrsonima reassifolia (L.) DC.:
Landa wrote, "There is a tree which always grows in open ground
and never among other trees, but all by themselves, the bark of which
is very good for tanning skins and serves as sumach. It bears a palatable
little yellow fruit which the women consider a tidbit." These little fruits
don't have much flavor on their own, but are quite delightful when
pickled with vinegar, herbs and spices.

Medicine: The plant is said to aid coughs and asthma.

ONION, CEBOLLA, CUCUT, Allium cepa, Linnaeus:
In addition to the large-bulbed onion called *cebolla*, Yucatecans grow
cebollina, a large green onion that is often grilled or used to flavor stews.

ORANGE, NARANJA, CHINA, Citrus sinensis:
Although the Spanish word for a sweet orange is naranja, the Maya
call it *china*.

OREGANO, XAAK'CHE, Lippia graveolens, H.B.K.:
Mexican oregano is often referred to as *oregano del monte*. It is one of
the most important herbs for the Maya, who pick a handful of pungent
leaves from their kitchen garden to flavor their soups, stews and
recados.

PAPAYA, PUT, Carica papaya, Linnaeus:
Landa noted in his manuscript, "There is another tree, wonderfully
beautiful and fresh, and it bears a fruit like large eggs. The Indians pick

it green and ripen it in ashes and ripe it is wonderful and is sweet to eat and cloys like the yolks of eggs." *Put* means to bear a load on one's shoulders, a definition that describes how the little tree looks when it is overloaded with fruit. The *mamey papaya* has a deep orange flesh and exceptionally sweet flavor. Fruit of this gigantic variety can grow almost as large as a watermelon.

According to Venedicto Flores of Telchaquillo, the Maya plant their papaya seeds five days before or after the new moon. When the seedlings are large enough to transplant, the same lunar schedule is followed. Once the tree is ready to flower, two cuts are placed in the trunk of the tree, perpendicular to one another, to make a sign of the cross. This is said to "castrate the tree" and make the fruit grow large.

Medicine: Sufferers from skin rashes, sore eyes and hemorrhoids have often resorted to the many benefits bestowed by this versatile plant.

PARSLEY, PEREJIL, Apium petroselinum, Linnaeus.

PEANUT,CACAHUATE, Arachis Hypogaea, Linnaeus.

PECCARY or PIG, PECARI, KITAM, Pecari angulatus yucatanensis, Merriam.:
The peccary in general is sometimes called *keken-che*. The term *kitam* refers to a smaller variety of wild pig that is no longer plentiful in the forests. The domestic hog is usually referred to as *cochino*, but is also known as *keken*.

PEAS, CHICHAROS, Pisum sativum, Linnaeus.

PEPINO KAT, KAT, Parmentiera edulis, de Candolle:
A *kat* looks like a large pickle. It is also crunchy like a pickle, but is usually cooked with honey to make a dessert. Landa wrote, "There is a somewhat thorny small tree which bears a rather long fruit of the form of slender cucumbers. Its taste is somewhat similar to that of the thistle and is also eaten, sliced with salt, and the seeds are like those of the cucumber, very small and many in number and tender."

Medicine: The fruit was recommended for women's monthly problems, kidney problems, earache and "swollen scalp."

PHEASANT, COJOLITO, COX, Dactylortyx thoracicus, Sharpei and Penelope purpurascens, Wagl.:
Landa said, "There is another {bird} which they call *cox*, as large as the other {*Cambul*} with a furious step and waddle, and the males are all black as jet and they have very handsome crowns of curled feathers and the lids of their eyes yellow and very pretty."

PIGEON, IX-CUCUT-CIP, CUCUT CI, Columba flavirostris Wagler:
Landa wrote, "There are many birds of the field all good to eat for there are three kinds of very handsome little pigeons."

PITAHAYA, UO, UOOB, or UOB, Cereus undatus, Haw.:
The name for this unusual fruit means "frog" in Maya. A product of the night-blooming cereus, it looks somewhat like an artichoke. The inner flesh is creamy white and flecked with the tiniest of black seeds. Bishop Landa reported that the Spaniards were so fond of this strange sweet fruit that the Maya had a difficult time keeping the invaders supplied with the delicacy.

PLATANO, Musa Paradisiaca, Linnaeus:
The green *platano* is used as a vegetable in Yucatecan cooking. When a *platano* is ripe it may be used as a fruit and is often employed to make sweet rich desserts.

POMPANO, PALOMETA, KANTAAN.

POTATO, PAPA, Solanum tuberosum, Linnaeus.

PRICKLY PEAR, NOPAL, PAKAM, Opuntia dillenii, (Gawler) Haw.:
Landa describes this fruit as, "large as a good pear, very green and with thick skin, which they mellow by beating them all on a rock, and they are after this of very excellent taste."

PURSLANE, VERDOLAGA, Portulaca oleracea, Linnaeus.

QUAIL, BOLON-CHAC:
Landa commented, "There are wonderfully many quail and they are somewhat larger than ours and excellent to eat. They fly little and the

Indians catch them roosting in the trees with dogs and nooses which they throw around their necks, and it is very tasty game."

QUELITE, Chenopodium berlandieri, Moquin.:
   The leaves of this plant are used to flavor seafood and tamales.

QUIMBOMBO, Hibiscus esculentus, Linnaeus:
   The fruits of this plant are eaten in soups, stews and salads.

RADISH, RABANO, Raphanus saativus, Linnaeus.

Medicine: Radishes have been used to combat anemia and pulmonary problems.

RICE, ARROZ, Oryza sativa, Linnaeus.

ROBALO, CHIB-CAY:
   The *robalo* is a thin fish with two black lengthwise stripes.

SAK-TUK or TUK, Yucca elephantipes, Regel.:
   The flowers of this large plant are eaten raw or cooked.

SALT, SAL, CHAKBIL TA'AB:
   The ancient Maya traded salt from their rich coastal beds for many other products throughout Mexico and Central America. Salt is not only a vital table condiment, but is used in ceremonies that provide protection for the individual, his house, and his pueblo. Salt is also buried at the four corners of the village to keep the evil winds at bay.

SAPODILLA, CHICO SAPOTE, YA, Achras zapota, Linnaeus:
   Landa wrote, "There is another very leafy and beautiful tree which never drops its leaves and without blossoming produces a fruit of as much and more sweetness than the one I have spoken of above [*chacal haaz*—the mamey], small, very sweet and delicious to eat and very delicate, and some are better than others and so much better that they would be highly prized if we had them here."
   This is the tree that produces *chicle*. The Maya call this chewy latex, *cha*. The Aztecs were known to chew chicle in pre-Conquest times.

Archaeologists have not yet determined whether the ancient Maya used it for this purpose or not.

SAPOTE NEGRO, TAUCH, Diospyros ebenaster, Retz.:
The fruit of the black sapote looks like chocolate pudding in a green bowl. The outer covering is green, but the inner pulp is a deep brown. The soft sweet pulp is best eaten with a spoon. The Maya assigned a rather comedic name for this marvelous fruit. They called it *tauch*—monkey excrement.

SESAME SEEDS, AJONJOLI, SIKIL-PUS, Sesamum oriental, Linnaeus.

SHRIMP, CAMARONES, XEC-CAY

SNAIL, CARACOL, XOT, Melania levissima:

SOUR ORANGE, NARANJA AGRIA, NARANJA, Citrus aurantium, Linnaeus:
Juice from the sour orange is used as a marinade for meats, salads and vegetables. Its acidic flavor seems to complement almost everything. Vinegar, lime or lemon juice may be substituted if sour orange is not available. It is known in the villages as *naranja*, with the accent on the first syllable. Novelo states that this fruit also goes by the names *Pah-pak'al* and *Suts'-Pak'al*.

SOURSOP, GUANABANA, POL-BOX, Annona purpurea, Moc. & Sesse', — or TAKOB, Annona muricata, Linnaeus:
The *guanabana* is a member of the annona family. It makes a wonderful fruit beverage or may be picked and enjoyed fresh from the tree.

SPINACH, ESPINACA, Spinacea oleracea, Linnaeus.

SQUIRREL, ARDILLA, KUUK, KUKEB, Sciurus yucatanensis, Allen:

STAR APPLE, CAIMITO, CAYUMITO, Chrysophyllum cainito, Linnaeus:
The fruit is native to tropical America, but no name from the Maya sources has been identified. *Caimitos* are available in both purple and green varieties.

SUGAR, AZUCAR.

SWEET POTATO, CAMOTE, IS, Ipomoea batatas, Linnaeus:

Sweet potatoes are cooked in the ashes of a hearthfire, simmered in water, or roasted in an underground *pib*. According to Redfield and Villa, they come in four colors, *zac-iz* (white), *morado iz* (purple), *x-ya-ix*, (yellow) and *chacal-haaz* (red) — the same name as the mamey zapote.

SWEETSOP, SUGAR APPLE, SARAMUYU, DZALMUY, Annona squamosa, Linnaeus:

The 16th century traveler, Alfonso Ponce wrote, "*Zulumuy*, the rind of which is green, with certain points like those of a pineapple. The pulp is very white and very delicate, wholesome and tasty, and it is held in high esteem by everybody."

Medicine: The leaves were mixed with honey and used for convulsions and chills.

TABENTUN or XTABENTUN:

Xtabentun is the name for the honeyed anise liquor so famous in Yucatan. Honey for this much-esteemed beverage is derived from the delicate white flowers that grow on this tropical vine.

Medicine: This plant was praised by the Spaniards for its ability to open up the urinary passages, even when a kidney stone was present.

TARO, CUCUT MAKAL, Colocasia esculenta (L.) Schott:

The Maya eat the tender green leaves of the *cucut makal* and then feast upon the roots once they have matured. Taro is not a native plant, but the ancient Maya had a plant similar to it that went by the same name.

TOMATO, TOMATE, PPAC, Lycopersicum esculentum, Mill.:

The tomato is native to South America, but has been cultivated for centuries in Yucatan.

XKOL-I-PPAC:

The milpa tomato. It is tiny, somewhat tart and is said to produce better in the fields than in the home garden.

DZULUB-PPAC:

The small wild form of the milpa tomato.

TZUNUM-PPAC:
The hummingbird tomato. It resembles the cherry tomato, but is even smaller.

Medicine: The leaves of the tomato plant have been prescribed for skin disorders.

TOMATILLO, P'AK-KAN, Physalis, sp.:
The little green husked tomato is often cooked with chili in a sauce.

TURKEY, PAVO, CUTZ, Agriocharis ocellata, Cuvier and Meleagris mexicana:
Landa commented on the ocellated turkey, "There are many wild turkeys, which, though they do not have as beautiful feathers as those [peacocks] here in Spain, yet have very fine ones and are wonderfully beautiful and are as large as the cocks of the Indians and as good to eat."

The turkey represented rain to the Maya. During the years of *Kan, Muluc, Ix* and *Cauac* it was necessary to offer a turkey during the New Year celebrations.

TURMERIC, YU UILLA, Curcuma longa, Linnaeus.

TURNIP, NABO, Brassica napus, Linnaeus.

TURTLE, TORTUGA, AC:
Turtles and turtle eggs were at one time an important part of the Maya diet. The reverence shown for these well-loved reptiles is evident from their iconography. Turtles also had a role to play in astrology, for the *Motul Dictionary* tells of three stars, *Ac ek*, in the sign of Gemini that combine with other stars to form a turtle.

VANILLA, VAINILLA, ZIZBIC, Vanilla fragrans, (Salisb.) Ames. (Standl.):
Vanilla is the product of a delicate flowering vine that hugs the trees in certain areas of Mexico's tropical forests. According to ancient whispers that still reverberate through the jungle air, vanilla came into being through the deaths of two young star-crossed lovers.

Her name was Tzacopontziza, which translates from the Totonac as Morning Star. He was a handsome prince called Zkatan-oxga, the Young Deer. Because Morning Star was so lovely, her parents offered her services to the goddess, Tonacayohua, and promised that she would never belong to any man. One morning while gathering some doves to offer the goddess, Morning Star caught a glimpse of Young Deer. They were immediately enchanted with one another and could not bear to be apart. Disregarding her parents' sacred vow, Morning Star fled into the jungle with her dashing prince.

Tragedy struck before nightfall, as the young lovers were confronted by a horrid flaming monster. Forced into retreat, Morning Star and Young Deer tried desperately to escape, but they were no match for the priests sent by Tonacayohua. The messengers of the wicked goddess savagely attacked, cut off their heads, slit open their chests and extracted the still warm and pulsating hearts to give to Tonacayohua.

The murder scene became desolate, barren and dry, a haunted spot where nothing would grow. Then suddenly, miraculously, a lush green tree reached full-size within only a few days. Immediately, a fragile green vine began to entwine the tree, hugging it so closely that all who witnessed the spectacle knew that the coiling of the vine was like the caress of a woman. Without a doubt, Young Deer was transformed into a tree and Morning Star metamorphosed into a vine. Anyone demanding proof of this miracle need only gaze upon the delicate white flowers and elegant pods that emerge from these tendrils, as lovely as a Morning Star.

WATERCRESS, BERRO, Roripa nasturtium, Rusby.

WINEPALM, COCOYOL, TUK, Acrocomia Mexicana:
The *cocoyol* is a palm tree that bears clusters of nuts that have been compared to hazelnuts or almonds. The nuts may be roasted and eaten as is or cooked in honey for a dessert. The ancient Maya were said to have used them for making a breakfast atole with an almond flavor.

The *xmen* may employ the cocoyol to offer *Balché* during ceremonies when he asks the deities for protection. Sometimes a necklace is made of the seeds and used to ward off evil winds.

Medicine: The plant was used for kidney problems and diabetes.

YUCATAN BOB-WHITE, BECH, Eupsychortyx nigrogularis, Gould:
Highly prized by the Maya, the *bech* is both a meat and egg source. The little birds are often encountered in the milpa.

YUCATAN PLUM OR HOGPLUM, CIRUELA, ABAL, Spondias purpurea, L., Spondias Lutea, L., and Spondias mombin, L. (Standl.):

The Yucatan plum is found both wild and domesticated. The trees do not bear flowers. Instead, fruit develops on the tree before any leaves appear. The *ciruela* is available in a variety of colors, but most often found in purple, yellow and green. The green *ciruela* is used to flavor *Ontzikil*, but green olives may be substituted for a similar flavor.

Medicine: The leaves were used for sore gums and to painlessly extract teeth.

YUCCA, DZIN, Manihot esculenta, Crantz.:

Manioc or cassava was introduced to Central America from South America during pre-Conquest times. There are two kinds of manioc—the *yucca brava* has a poisonous juice unless it is cooked. *Manihot dulcis* does not suffer from the same problem. It is thought that manioc was brought to Yucatan by one of the influxes of Toltec invaders.

ZIRICOTE, SIRICOTE or CIRICOTE, KOPTE, Cordia dodecandra, DC.:

The *ziricote* is a little fruit about the size of a small plum and is either yellow or yellow-green in color. The flowers on the tree are a brilliant orange-red and have a trumpet shape. The fruit can be eaten raw or cooked in a light syrup. Beautifully patterned *ziricote* wood was used to build the lintels in Maya temples. The ending *"te"* is the word for tree in Chontal, Tzeltal, Tzotzil and Huastec Maya.

Bibliography

Andrews, E. Wyllys, IV. "Archeology and Prehistory in the Northern Lowlands: An Introduction." *Handbook of Middle American Indians. Volume 2: Archeology of Southern Mesoamerica.* G. R. Willey, ed. Austin: University of Texas Press, 1973.

Boserup, Ester. *The Conditions of Agricultural Growth: The Economics of Agrarian Change under Population Pressure.* New York: Aldine Publishing, 1979.

Carrilo, Antonio Bustillos. *El Sacbe de los Mayas, Los Caminos Blancos de los Mayas, Base De Su Vide Social y Religion.* Mexico: B. Costa-Amic, 1963.

Codex, Dresden. *Codex Dresdensis.* Austria: Akademische Druck-u. Verlagsanstalt, 1975.

Craine, Eugene R. and Reginald C. Reindorp, trans. and eds. *The Codex Perez and The Book of Chilam Balam of Mani.* Norman: U of Oklahoma Press, 1979.

Culbert, T. Patrick, ed. *The Classic Maya Collapse.* Albuquerque: U of New Mexico Press, 1977.

Duran, Fray Diego. *Book of the Gods and Rites of the Ancient Calendar.* Fernando Horcasitas and Doris Heyden, trans. and eds. Norman: U of Oklahoma Press, 1975.

Edmonson, Munro S., translator and annotator. *The Ancient Future of the Itza, The Book of Chilam Balam of Tiziman.* Austin: U of Texas Press, 1982.

Foster, George M. "Hippocrates' Latin American Legacy: 'Hot' and 'Cold' in Contemporary Folk Medicine." Reprint from *Colloquia in Anthropology*. R.K. Wetherington, ed. Volume II: 3-19. Dallas: Southern Methodist University and Fort Burgwin Research Center, 1978.

Gann, Thomas. "The Maya Indians of Southern Yucatan and Northern British Honduras." Washington, D.C.: Bureau of American Ethnology Bulletin 64, 1918.
—"The Chachac or Rain Ceremony, as Practiced by the Maya of Southern Yucatan and Northern British Honduras." International Congress of Americanists 19: 409-418. Washington, D.C.: 1915.

Marin, Alfredo Barrera, Alfredo Berrera Vazquez, and Rosa Maria Lopez Franco. *Nomenclatura Etnobotanica Maya, Una Interpretacion Taxonomica*. Mexico: Instituto Nacional de Antropologia y Historia, Centro Regional del Sureste, 1976.

Morley, Sylvanus G. *The Ancient Maya*. Stanford: Stanford U Press, 1976.

Motul Dictionary. *Dictionario de Motul, maya-espanol, atribuido a Fray Antonio de Ciudad Real y Arte de la lengua maya por Fray Juan Coronel*. J. Martinez Hernandez. Merida: Mexico, 1939.

Novelo, Narciso Souza., *El Maiz: La Milpa. Merida* Yucatan: Instituto Technico Agricola Henequenero, 1948.
—Plantas Alimentcias y Plantas de Condimento que Vivan en Yucatan. Merida: Instituto Technico Agricola Henequenero, 1950.

Recinos, A. trans. and ed. *Popol Vuh: The Sacred Book of the Ancient Quiche Maya*. Norman: U of Oklahoma Press, 1950.

Redfield, Robert and Alfonso Villa Rojas. *Chan Kom: A Maya Village*. Chicago: U of Chicago Press, 1964. --*The Folk Culture of the Yucatan*. Chicago: U of Chicago Press, 1970.

Reina, Rueben E. and Robert M. Hill, II. "Lowland Maya Subsistence: Notes from Ethnohistory and Ethnography." *American Antiquity* 45:74-79, 1980.

Roys, Ralph. "The Ritual of the Chiefs of Yucatan." *American Anthropologist* 25: 472-484, 1923.
—"The Ethnobotany of the Maya." New Orleans: Tulane University: Middle American Research Institute Publication Number 2, 1931.
—"Researches in Maya Life in the Sixteenth Century." Carnegie Institution Yearbook. Carnegie Institution of Washington, 1933-34.
—"Titles of Ebtun." Washington, D.C.: Carnegie Institution of Washington. Publication 505.
—trans. and ed. *The Book of Chilam Balam of Chumayel.* Norman: U of Oklahoma Press, 1973.
—"Lowland Maya Native Society at Spanish Contact." *Handbook of Middle American Indians.* Part II. Volume 3: 659-678. Gordon R. Willey, ed. Austin: U of Texas Press, 1973.

Smith, C. Earle, Jr. and Marguerita L. Cameron. "Ethnobotany in the Puuc, Yucatan." *Economic Botany* 31: 93-110, 1977.

Steggerda, Morris. "Maya Indians of Yucatan." Washington, D.C.: Carnegie Institution of Washington, Publication 531, 1941.

Thompson, J. Eric S. "The Meaning of the Maya Months." *Man* 25: 121-123, 1925.
—"Sixteenth and Seventeenth Century Reports on the Chol Mayas." *American Anthropologist* 3-: 584-604, 1938.
—"Notes on the use of Cacao in Middle America." Cambridge: C.IW. Notes 128, 1956.
—"Ethnology of the Mayas of Southern and Central British Honduras." Chicago: Field Museum of Natural History, Publication 274. *Anthropolical Series*, Volume XVII. Number 2. New York: Kraus Reprint Co., 1968.

Tozzler, Alfred H. "A Spanish manuscript letter on the Lacadones in the Archives of the Indies in Seville." London: 18th I.C.A. London: 1912:497-509.
—editor. *Landa's Relacion de las Cosas de Yucatan: A Translation.* Cambridge: Peabody Museum of American Archeology and Ethnology. New York: Kraus Reprint Co., 1978.

—"A Comparative Study of the Mayas and the Lacadones." *Archeological Institute of Americas, Report of the Fellow in American Archeology 1902-1905* New York: Macmillan, 1978.

Vasquez, Alfredo Barrera and Juan Ramon Bastarrachea Manzano, William Brito Sansores, Refugio Vermont Salas, David Dzul Gongora, and Domingo Dzul Poot. *Dictionario Maya Cordemex, Maya-Espanol/Espanol-Maya*. Mexico: Ediciones Cordemex, 1980.
   —Estudios Linguisticos. Obras Completas, Tomo I. Mexico: Fondo Editorial Yucatan, 1980.

Villa Rojas, Alfonso. "The Yaxuna-Coba Causeway." *Contributions to American Archeology*. Volume II, Number 9. Washington, D.C.: Carnegie Institution of Washington, 1934.
   —"The Maya of East Central Quintana Roo." Publication 559. Washington, Carnegie Institution of Washington, 1945.

Vogt, Evon. Z. *The Zinacantecos of Mexico: A Modern Maya Way of Life*. New York: Holt, Rinehart and Winston, 1970.

Index

International Cookbooks from Hippocrene . . .

WORLD'S BEST RECIPES

From Hippocrene's best-selling international cookbooks, comes this unique collection of culinary specialties from many lands. With over 150 recipes, this wonderful anthology includes both exotic delicacies and classic favorites from nearly 100 regions and countries. Sample such delights as Zambian Chicken Stew, Polish Apple Cake, Colombian Corn Tamales, and Persian Pomegranate Khoreshe.

256 pages • 5 ½ x 8 ½ • 0-7818-0599-6 • W • $9.95pb • (685)

THE ART OF ISRAELI COOKING

Chef Aldo Nahoum

All of the 250 recipes are kosher.

"[Includes] a host of new indigenous Israeli recipes with dishes that reflect the eclectic and colorful nature of Israeli cuisine."

—Jewish Week

125 pages • 5 ½ x 8 ½ • 0-7818-0096-X • W • $9.95pb • (252)

THE ART OF TURKISH COOKING

Nesret Eren

"Her recipes are utterly mouthwatering, and I cannot remember a time when a book so inspired me to take pot in hand."

—Nika Hazelton, *The New York Times Book Review*

308 pages • 5 ½ x 8 ½ • 0-7818-0201-6 • W • $12.95pb • (162)

EGYPTIAN COOKING

Samia Abdennour

Almost 400 recipes, all adapted for the North American kitchen, represent the best of authentic Egyptian family cooking.

199 pages • 5 ½ x 8 ½ • 0-7818-0643-7 • NA • $11.95pb • (727)

TASTE OF MALTA

Claudia C. Caruana

Includes 200 authentic Maltese recipes.

"Caruana presents several versions of Malta's signature dishes . . . [a] solid introduction to an intriguing cuisine."

—Publishers Weekly

305 pages • 5 ½ x 8 ½ • 0-7818-0524-4 • W • $24.95hc • 636

BEST OF REGIONAL AFRICAN COOKING
Harva Hachten

Here is a gourmet's tour of Aftica, from North African specialties like Chicken Tajin with Olives and Lemon to Zambian Groundnut Soup and Senegalese Couscous. With over 240 recipes that deliver the unique and dramatic flavors of each region: North, East, West, Central and South Africa, this is a comprehensive treasury of African cuisine.

274 pages • 5 ½ x 8 ½ • 0-7818-0598-8 • W • $11.95pb • (684)

TRADITIONAL SOUTH AFRICAN COOKERY
Hildegonda Duckitt

A collection of recipes culled from two previous books by the author, this volume provides ideas for tasty, British- and Dutch-inspired meals and insight into daily life of colonial Africa.

178 pages • 5 x 8 ½ • 0-7818-0490-6 • W • $10.95pb • (352)

ART OF SOUTH INDIAN COOKING
Alamelu Vairavan and Patricia Marquardt

Over 100 recipes for tempting appetizers, chutneys, rice dishes, vegetables and stews—flavored with onions, tomatoes, garlic, and delicate spices in varying combinations have been adapted for the Western kitchen.

202 pages • 5 ½ x 8 ½ • 0-7818-0525-2 • W • $22.50 • (635)

BEST OF GOAN COOKING
Gilda Mendonsa

This book is a rare and authentic collection of over 130 of the finest Goan recipes and 12 pages of full color illustrations. From Goa—a region in Western India once colonized by the Portuguese comes a cuisine in which the hot, sour and spicy flavors mingle in delicate perfection, a reflection of the combination of Arabian, Portuguese and Indian cultures that have inhabited the region.

106 pages • 7 x 9 ¼ • 12 pages color illustrations • 0-7818-0584-8 • NA • $8.95pb • (682)

THE BEST OF KASHMIRI COOKING
Neerja Mattoo

With nearly 90 recipes and 12 pages of color photographs, this cookbook is a wonderful introduction to Kashmiri dishes, considered the height of gourmet Indian cuisine.

131 pages • 5 ½ x 8 ½ • 12 pages color photographs • 0-7818-0612-7 • NA • $9.95pb • (724)

A SPANISH FAMILY COOKBOOK, REVISED EDITION
Juan and Susan Serrano

Over 250 recipes covering all aspects of the Spanish meal, from tapas (appetizers) through pasteles (cakes and pastries). Features a new wine section, including information on classic Spanish sherries and riojas.

244 pages • 5 x 8 ½ • 0-7818-0546-5 • W • $11.95pb • (642)

BEST OF GREEK CUISINE: COOKING WITH GEORGIA
Georgia Sarianides

Chef Georgia Sarianides offers a health-conscious approach to authentic Greek cookery with over 100 tempting low-fat, low-calorie recipes. Also includes helpful sections on Greek wines, using herbs and spices, and general food preparation tips.

176 pages • 5 ½ x 8 ½ • b/w line drawings • 0-7818-0545-7 • W • $19.95hc • (634)

GOOD FOOD FROM AUSTRALIA
Graeme and Betsy Newman

A generous sampling of over 150 Australian culinary favorites. "Steak, Chops, and Snags," "Casseroles and Curries," and "Outback Cooking" are among the intriguing sections included. In time for the 2000 Olympics in Sydney!

284 pages • 5 ½ x 8 ½ • b/w line illustrations • 0-7818-0491-4 • W • $24.95hc • (440)

COOKING THE CARIBBEAN WAY
Mary Slater

Here are 450 authentic Caribbean recipes adapted for the North American kitchen, including Bermuda Steamed Mussels, Port Royal Lamb Stew, and Mango Ice-cream.

256 pages • 5 ½ x 8 ½ • 0-7818-0638-0 • W • $11.95pb • (725)

MAYAN COOKING: RECIPES FROM THE SUN KINGDOMS OF MEXICO
Cherry Hamman

This unique cookbook contains not only 200 colorful and exotic recipes from the Mexican Yucatan, but also the author's fascinating observations on a vanishing way of life.

250 pages • 5 ½ x 8 ½ • 0-7818-0580-5 • W • $24.95hc • (680)

ART OF SOUTH AMERICAN COOKERY
Myra Waldo

This cookbook offers delicious recipes for the various courses of a typical South American meal. Dishes show the expected influence of Spanish and Portuguese cuisines, but are enhanced by the use of locally available ingredients.

266 pages • 5 x 8 ½ • b/w line drawings • 0-7818-0485-X • W • $11.95pb • (423)

THE ART OF BRAZILIAN COOKERY
Dolores Botafogo

Over three hundred savory and varied recipes fill this cookbook of authentic Brazilian cuisine, ranging from Churasco (barbecued steak) and Vatapa (Afro-Brazilian fish porridge from the Amazon) to sweets, and aromatic Brazilian coffees.

240 pages • 5 ½ x 8 ½ • 0-7818-0130-3 • W • $11.95pb • (250)

BAVARIAN COOKING
Olli Leeb

With over 300 recipes, this lovely collector's item cookbook covers every aspect of Bavarian cuisine from drinks, salads and breads to main courses and desserts. Includes a large fold-out map and cultural calendar along with 10 pages of color photographs.

"*Bavarian Cooking* is what a good regional cookbook should be—a guide for those who wish to know the heart and soul of a region's cooking, a book that anchors its recipes in the culture that produced them, and a cookbook that brings delight to the casual reader as well as to the serious cook."

—German Life

171 pages • 6 ½ x 8 ¼ • line illustrations and 10 pages color photographs • 0-7818-0561-9 • NA • $25.00 • (659)

CELTIC COOKBOOK: TRADITIONAL RECIPES FROM THE SIX CELTIC LANDS BRITTANY, CORNWALL, IRELAND, ISLE OF MAN, SCOTLAND AND WALES
Helen Smith-Twiddy

This collection of over 160 recipes from the Celtic world includes traditional, yet still popular dishes like *Rabbit Hoggan* and *Gwydd y Dolig* (Stuffed Goose in Red Wine).

200 pages•5 ½ x 8 ½ • 0-7818-0579-1 • NA • $22.50hc • (679)

ENGLISH ROYAL COOKBOOK: FAVORITE COURT RECIPES

Elizabeth Craig

Dine like a King or Queen with this unique collection of over 350 favorite recipes of the English royals, spanning 500 years of feasts! Try recipes like Duke of York Consommé and Crown Jewel Cake, or even a Princess Mary Cocktail. Charmingly illustrated throughout.

187 pages • 5 ½ x 8 ½ • illustrations • 0-7818-0583-X • W • $11.95pb • (723)

THE ART OF IRISH COOKING

Monica Sheridan

Nearly 200 recipes for traditional Irish fare.

166 pages • 5 ½ x 8 ½ • illustrated • 0-7818-0454-X • W • $12.95pb • (335)

ART OF DUTCH COOKING

C. Countess van Limburg Stirum

This attractive volume of 200 recipes offers a complete cross section of Dutch home cooking, adapted to American kitchens. A whole chapter is devoted to the Dutch Christmas, with recipes for unique cookies and candies that are a traditional part of the festivities.

192 pages • 5 ½ x 8 ½ • illustrations • 0-7818-0582-1 • W • $11.95pb • (683)

All prices subject to change. **To purchase Hippocrene Books** contact your local bookstore, call (718) 454-2366, or write to: HIPPOCRENE BOOKS, 171 Madison Avenue, New York, NY 10016. Please enclose check or money order, adding $5.00 shipping (UPS) for the first book and $.50 for each additional book.